Advance Praise for *A Carlin Home Companion*

"There are a lot of nights I still wish I could sit next to George and talk; this is the next best thing. Wonderful read."   —Jon Stewart

"Kelly Carlin writes with lucid humor and a breathtaking objectivity about her life and family. Her voice on the page is completely engaging. The parallels with my own life are uncanny, and I reveled in the solidarity."   —Rosanne Cash

"Drop all your expectations when you open this book. It is written in the DNA of a Carlin, honest, biting, savage, funny, sad, dark, and profound. Kelly Carlin takes us on a journey from growing up in the shadow of one of America's greatest comic icons into the light that it led her into. Hold on; like George Carlin, this book gives you a hell of a ride."   —Lewis Black

"As a fan, this book is essential. As a comic, this book is profound."
—Margaret Cho

"With *A Carlin Home Companion,* Kelly Carlin proves she can stay cool while standing next to the sun. As a Carlin-phile, I began reading hoping to peek behind the curtains of Earth's funniest man. I got more than a peek. Carlin opens the floodlights onto her childhood and the dysfunction in her house and in her mind. Her personal growth and awareness of self is inspiring. Kelly's stories are hilarious and so personal, at times it felt like I was reading her diary. For anyone that has ever not been sure who they are, this book is for you. There is a landing spot. Let Kelly Carlin be your beacon."   —Jay Mohr

"*A Carlin Home Companion* is one hell of a ride. With her unique perspective, Kelly Carlin shines a light on George Carlin, and gives great insight into a man who was a hero to many, but a father to one."   —Bill Maher

"The daughter of the great comedian speaks: funny and moving."
—Robert Klein

"George Carlin gave us all so much to be thankful for, not least of which is his daughter, Kelly. Her affection and admiration for her father jump off the page. And like her dad, her writing is funny, courageous, and wise; this book is a glowing testament to them both. An inspiring and beautiful read."
—Paul Reiser

"George Carlin spent his life dissecting the American psyche. Now his daughter, Kelly, continues the family tradition, wielding a scalpel of her own as she lays bare her life as a child, and an adult child, in the Carlin household. A brave and, naturally, hilarious book."
—Dana Gould

"In the hands of an accomplished writer, with a lifetime supply of research, this story would be a fascinating read. In Kelly's hands, we get SO much more. Ms. Carlin has shared her firsthand knowledge in a masterful, hilarious, and heartbreaking memoir of, and dedication to, one of the greatest comedic minds and performers in American history. Filled with wit, charm, and genuine, if not extraordinary prose. Bravo, Kelly!"
—Kevin Pollak

"Kelly Carlin has humanized her father, in a way that doesn't hold back and through her brilliant writing, brings him to life in a whole new way. In this book she shows she has her father's talent for writing, his awesome humanity, and a good dose of his twisted comedic mind."
—Lizz Winstead

"A heartwarming, hysterical read! Carlin the younger evokes a version of Carlin the senior we never had the pleasure of knowing: George Carlin the Dad! *A Carlin Home Companion* may be Kelly Carlin's story specifically, but it's also the story of the American family in general."
—Kevin Smith

A Carlin Home Companion

GROWING UP WITH GEORGE

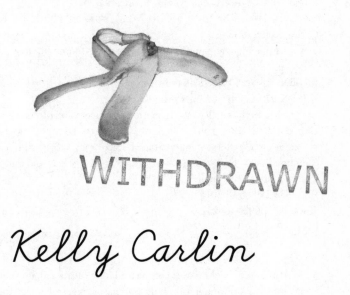

WITHDRAWN

Kelly Carlin

ST. MARTIN'S PRESS ♣ NEW YORK

A CARLIN HOME COMPANION. Copyright © 2015 by Kelly Carlin-McCall. All rights reserved. Printed in the United States of America. For information, address St. Martin's Press, 175 Fifth Avenue, New York, NY 10010.

www.stmartins.com

Designed by Steven Seighman

Library of Congress Cataloging-in-Publication Data

Carlin, Kelly, 1963–
  A Carlin home companion : growing up with George / Kelly Carlin.
      p. cm.
  ISBN 978-1-250-05825-6 (hardcover)
  ISBN 978-1-4668-6238-8 (e-book)
 1. Carlin, Kelly, 1963– 2. Television producers and directors—
United States—Biography.   3. Actresses—United States—Biography.
4. Radio broadcasters—United States—Biography.   5. Carlin, George.
6. Comedians—United States—Biography.   7. Fathers and daughters—
United States—Biography.   I. Title.
PN2287.C26855A3 2015
791.4502'33092—dc23
[B]

                                                    2015017795

St. Martin's Press books may be purchased for educational, business, or promotional use. For information on bulk purchases, please contact the Macmillan Corporate and Premium Sales Department at 1-800-221-7945, extension 5442, or write to specialmarkets@macmillan.com.

First Edition: September 2015

10   9   8   7   6   5   4   3   2   1

This book is dedicated to my husband Bob McCall.
You have given me the ground to stand on and the wings to fly.
Thank God you came along.

Contents

A Carlin Home Companion

CHAPTER ONE

The Moon and Venus Rise Together

CARLIN LEGEND HOLDS that all it took for me to come into the world was a little sperm, a little egg, a little weed, a little scotch, and something called the limbo.

"We'd been trying to get pregnant for months, but no luck," explained my mom to me, seven-year-old Kelly, as I sat on the bed watching my dad pack for the road.

Just moments earlier he'd said to me, "When I'm down in New Orleans, I'll get a postcard from the hotel you were conceived in and send it to you."

Confused by the word "conceived," I looked at my mom, and she quickly filled in the details. "We were down in New Orleans, must've been what, October of '62? We were at a club hanging out with some musicians we'd met, when someone announced a limbo contest. Well, it sounded like fun, and so I did it. Next thing I knew, I was pregnant."

Mom didn't mention the weed or scotch in her telling of my fateful beginning because she didn't need to. They were a given. Dad had been smoking weed and drinking beer since he was fourteen, and Mom started sneaking sips off her daddy's drinks at around the same age. And as far as the limbo goes, I'm still not clear about the mechanics of it all, but that's never mattered. It clearly worked. I am here.

For the two years leading up to the night of the limbo, my mom, Brenda, and my dad, George, had been constant companions, starving artists, and comrades-in-arms, chasing my dad's comedy dreams. They did hell gigs, packed and unpacked their suitcases hundreds of times, and traveled to almost every state in the country in their '57 Dodge Dart. My mom loved playing the role of on-the-road partner in crime to my dad's rebel artist on a mission. She was Dad's lover, party girl, and press agent all rolled into one—his full partner in life—and always his best audience. You could always hear her great laugh above the din of clinking glasses and mumbling patrons in every club they visited.

Because Dad was a complete unknown, on some nights she was the only person in the audience.

One night in Baltimore, no one was in the audience, not even Mom. Dad asked the club owner, "So exactly why am I going on?"

"Cuz if people come in, I want them to know we gots some entertainment," he was told.

I hear Dad killed that night.

During those lean years, Dad paid his dues but also got lucky. One night Lenny Bruce caught his act in Chicago, loved what he saw, and introduced him to his manager, Murray Becker. This was huge. My dad worshipped Lenny.

Taking every opportunity to soak up Lenny's presence, my mom and dad would often drive from New York to the Gate of Horn Club in Chicago, just to see him perform. One night while they were there, Lenny got arrested halfway through his set. This had become the norm. That night the cops did not like his use of the word "cocksucker." Looking to hassle the club, the cops began to ask everyone for their IDs. When they got to my dad, he defiantly told them, "I don't believe in 'identification,'" and the cops promptly threw him into the back of the paddy wagon with Lenny. When my dad proudly told Lenny what he'd done, Lenny looked at him and said, "What are you, a schmuck?"

My mom chased after their paddy wagon—on foot—all the way to the police station and bailed them both out of jail that night.

Growing up surrounded by stories like these, and living through many others myself, I've always felt as if my family's journey has unfolded like some kind of mythological legend. Our lives together have felt shaped by a force, threads of fate, or maybe even what my dad called the "Big Electron." Something was calling us forth, and interweaving exactly the right people, places, and things to form one amazing life together.

It's just always seemed so destined.

My dad should never, ever have come to be.

In 1936, a year before he was born, his parents, Mary and Patrick Carlin, had separated. Not for the first time, but for the fourth. Patrick, as my dad would say, "couldn't metabolize the ethyl alcohol," which meant he was a mean drunk. No longer able to take the verbal and physical abuse he doled out to her or their four-year-old son, also named Patrick (who the fuck hits a child across the face with a slipper?), Mary left him for what she wanted to believe was the last time.

But Mary could never stay away for too long. When Patrick wasn't drinking and raging, he was witty, handsome, and one of the top national salesmen of ad space for the biggest newspapers in the country. He had the Irish gift of gab and had even won a national Dale Carnegie speech contest. He was funny, smart, and charming—and irresistible. So irresistible that once again in the summer of 1936 Mary found herself in bed with him, at a motel in Rockaway Beach.

Six weeks later, at the age of forty, Mary realized she was pregnant.

She knew she didn't want to bring another child into this already complicated situation, so she decided the best thing to do was to get rid of it.

But that "Big Electron" had different plans. While Mary sat in the waiting room of "Dr. Sunshine," the Gramercy Park gynecologist who took care of such things for most ladies of import in New York City, she looked up at a picture of the Virgin Mary hanging on the wall and saw her own dead mother's face. A good Catholic, she knew a sign when she saw one. She promptly stood up and declared to Patrick, "I am keeping this child."

On May 12, 1937, George Denis Patrick Carlin was born. Eight weeks later, after months of trying to make the marriage work, Mary sneaked out the fire escape in the middle of the night with her two young boys, leaving Patrick Carlin and his rage for good. She'd seen the damage that her husband had already done to little Patrick, and she was not going to let sweet George be another victim.

This time it stuck. Even though Patrick tried to woo her back, she held strong. George never saw his dad again. In 1945 his father died of a massive heart attack at the age of fifty-seven. My dad was eight years old.

Without a man around to keep my dad out of trouble on the streets of the Upper West Side of Manhattan (or what he and his friends liked to call Irish Harlem), Mary took her job as both mother and father very seriously. She looked for ways to shape and control young George's mind and life. She succeeded in only one area—a love of language and words.

Mary encouraged my dad to look up words he didn't know in the dictionary, and then use them in conversation. One morning young George, wanting to show off a new word he had learned, excitedly asked his mother if she had "perused" the paper that morning. He anticipated her approval. Slowly she turned, sharpened her gaze onto him, and said, "I have not. Actually, I've only given it a cursory glance." George, chagrined, turned around and marched right back to the dictionary to learn the new word, "cursory."

This was Mary to a tee. Just when you thought you had the upper hand, she let you know who was really in charge.

Mary had big dreams for my dad. She wanted him to be an upstanding member of the Better Business Bureau someday—a man in a pin-striped suit who had a key to the executive washroom. But that was not his destiny.

When my dad was ten years old, he went to the movies, saw Danny Kaye on the big screen, and decided right there and then that he wanted to be just like him one day. And so he came up with his big "Danny Kaye plan": Step one—become a disc jockey; step two—become a stand-up; step three—become an actor.

By the time he was eleven, my dad was doing stand-up on the stoops on his block, imitating the priests, cops, and shopkeepers of the neighborhood. He also did his impressions of famous people on the radio, and even made up his own radio shows, dialogue and all. At Camp Notre Dame, where he went for three summers, he won the drama award for his routines every single year.

Mary saw the writing on the wall, and in 1951, for his fourteenth birthday, she bought him a reel-to-reel tape recorder so he could practice his voices, impressions, and routines. Who buys a reel-to-reel tape recorder in 1951? Mary Carlin. Her son might not become exactly who she wanted him to be, but her commitment to his excellence was fierce.

Growing up in the 1940s and '50s, my dad had plenty to inspire him: the verbal gymnastics of guys like Spike Jones and Danny Kaye, and the musical rhythms of guys like Dizzy Gillespie and Charlie Parker. He frequently hopped on the subway or onto the back of a truck heading downtown to Times Square to collect autographs of his heroes. These men of comedy and music were living his dream—expressing their souls and at the top of their game. He knew what he wanted, and he knew how he'd get there. His life was set. There was never a plan B.

By 1960, at age twenty-three, my dad was in the flow of his destiny. He was already at step two of his big "Danny Kaye plan"—becoming a stand-up. He was part of a fledgling comedy team—Burns and Carlin. Dad and Jack Burns had met in radio, hit it off, and soon went on the road as a comedy duo. They were quickly building momentum in their careers, doing smart, "modern" comedy—which meant that they weren't telling mother-in-law jokes but using material that commented on the times.

In August they booked a two-week gig at the Racquet Club—the Dayton, Ohio, version of a supper club. It wasn't the Playboy Club of Chicago, but it was a decent-enough gig back then. And in Dayton it was the *only* place to find quality entertainment, especially comedy. Most nights there was some shining new talent coming through—Phyllis Diller, Jonathan Winters, and even Lenny Bruce.

A week before their gig, the hostess of the club, Brenda Florence Hosbrook, looked at the promo picture of Burns and Carlin in the foyer, and said to her best friend, Elaine, "You can have the one on the top [Burns]. I'll take the one on the bottom [Carlin]. He's really cute."

Evidently my future mom also had her *own* "big" plan for her life. It was called the "Get the Fuck Out of Dayton plan."

Brenda had always felt like a stranger in her own life. She knew she didn't belong in small-town Dayton. She was like her dad, Art Hosbrook, who'd been a jazz singer in the thirties, "The Whispering Tenor." She was Daddy's little girl.

Alice, her mother, sensed that Brenda had Art's wild spirit in her, and kept her on a tight leash. In high school, while my mom wanted to be out wearing poodle skirts, singing along to pop music, and making out with boys under the bleachers, her mother had her wearing homemade clothes, practicing Debussy on the piano, and steering clear of all boys except for the approved-of boy next door, Ken. My mom, too afraid to rebel, remained the quintessential dutiful daughter. She made the National Honor Society, won piano competitions, and only let Ken go to second base. Her virtue was rewarded with a full scholarship to Ohio Wesleyan to study piano. She couldn't wait to escape and begin to live *her* life. But Alice would have none of that. "Women don't go to college," she said to my mom, and refused to let her go. Alice told her that she could get a job, but only until she married and started a family.

Seething with disappointment, my mom decided if she couldn't go to college, then at least she'd have sex. The story goes that my mom went to Ken and basically jumped his bones. She claimed she forced him to have sex with her. Of course I'm not sure how much convincing it takes to make a teenage boy "go all the way." Mom got her "revenge."

She also got pregnant.

Alice had always diligently marked my mom's periods on a calendar, so when it didn't show up, Alice knew immediately what Brenda had done. In the car ride home from the family doctor's office, where the bad news had been confirmed, Art quietly drove them as Alice informed my mother, "You've made your bed, now you must lie in it."

Brenda was forced to marry Ken. A few weeks after the wedding, while shopping with her mother in Rike's Department Store for furniture for their new apartment, my mom miscarried in the restroom. It was twins. After a miserable year of a sham marriage, she and Ken acknowledged that they weren't happy and amicably divorced.

As a divorcée at the age of twenty, my mom was deemed tarnished by Alice. In a flash my mom went from model student, musician, prized daughter to shameful, wanton whore.

Now, in 1960, Brenda was having the time of her life. Working at the Racquet Club she could let her hair down, drink and smoke as much as she wanted, and most important, rub shoulders with the type of people Alice would certainly never approve of—entertainers.

After his first show George couldn't help but notice Brenda

hanging out at the bar. Besides her musical and scholarly talents, Brenda was what they called a "knockout." When she walked into a room, she lit it up—fabulous cheekbones, an electric smile, blue eyes, and a laugh that made the whole world come alive.

After some chitchat, George asked Brenda, "So what does one do in Dayton, Ohio, after a show?"

"Well, you could find a diner and have some breakfast, or . . ." she replied.

And this is when Brenda Florence Hosbrook, Alice and Art Hosbrook's good-little-honor-roll-girl-turned-black-sheep-of-the-family took the leap of her life and looked the young, handsome, and funny George Carlin straight in the eye and said, "Or you could find a girl with a stereo hi-fi and go home with her."

George slowly but astutely asked, "Do *you* have a stereo hi-fi?"

Every night for the entire two-week run, George went home with Brenda, and they "listened" to her stereo hi-fi.

After the two weeks were up, Brenda told George, "I love you."

George told Brenda, "I'll call you."

It's not that he didn't like her, it's just that he had this big "Danny Kaye plan," and it had never included another person.

Months went by, but no phone calls or letters came. Then one day, out of the blue, George called her. The spark between them reignited immediately. He knew she was the real deal, and he had to see her again. They made plans for him to come down after his New Year's Eve gig in Chicago to spend a weekend with her.

The day came and went. The next day came and went. By the third day Brenda was officially heartbroken. He had once again disappeared without a trace. And then sometime during the lunch rush, when Brenda was seating guests, George entered and stood in the front. When she saw him she dropped all the menus and ran the entire length of the restaurant, straight into his arms. They left immediately. No one saw them for three days.

When they finally emerged from the "Sleep & Fuck Motel," they were engaged.

The next day George and Brenda sat across from Art and Alice at lunch, ready to break the news to them. But things were not going well. Alice just glared at George. Alice did not like entertainers. Because Art had been one, she knew entertainers too well. That's why, when they got married, she'd made him give up his music to get a real job so that they could raise a family.

Finally an opportunity arose when Art excused himself to go to the restroom, and George quickly followed him. As they stood side by side at the urinals in the restroom of Spencer's Steak House in Dayton, Ohio, George said to Art, "I'd like to marry your daughter."

Slightly startled, Art replied, "Oh, yeah? Okay."

It was official. Except for the engagement ring part. Due to a serious lack of funds, the ring had to wait. Eventually it came—in the mail. With my dad on the road, and no money for another trip back to Dayton, he couldn't hand-deliver it. But they didn't care about the formalities. They'd found each other.

And even though Alice admitted that she would never understand her daughter's choice, she made my mom's wedding dress and invited them to have their small, humble wedding ceremony in the living room of the house that Brenda grew up in on River Ridge Road.

On June 3, 1961, George and Brenda became husband and wife.

CHAPTER TWO

Westside Story

MY EARLIEST MEMORY is of my mom screaming while pulling her head out of the oven. No, she wasn't doing a Sylvia Plath and trying to off herself. She was just trying to ignite the pilot light when *boom*—the gas went up in a ball of flames, singeing her eyebrows, eyelashes, and a good portion of her bangs.

I, being barely three years old, began to cry. Mom began to cry, too. This was worrisome to me because normally she was a capable, adventurous, and most resilient human. I immediately wanted my daddy because I knew he could fix it. But he wasn't there. He was at work.

Mom, wiping her tears, picked up the phone and called him. She wanted my daddy, too. I don't remember the exact conversation, but I have no doubt it went something like this:

Mom: "Can't you just come home now?" (tears flowing again).

Dad: "Honey, you know I can't."

Mom (blowing her nose): "I know. It's just that—"

"You're okay, right?" Dad jumped in.

"Yeah. Yeah, I'm okay," Mom admitted.

"How's your hair?" Dad asked.

As she felt for her missing bangs, Mom said, "It's a mess."

"I bet you just invented a new hairstyle!" Dad said, hoping to cheer her up.

"I suppose," cracking a smile. "But I don't know what you'd call it," Mom said, her mood lightening a bit.

"How about 'Boom Bangs'?"

Mom exploded in laughter, "'Boom Bangs'! Yes."

Dad laughed with her, relieved that things seemed okay and that Mom had calmed down.

"How's Kel? Put her on," he asked.

My mom handed me the phone. "It's Daddy."

I hadn't quite recovered yet. "Daddy?"

"Hey, Kiddo. You my Stinkpot or my Baby Doll?" This was a familiar game my dad and I played with each other when he called.

"Baby Doll," I said insistently. I was never a stinkpot.

"Are you okay?" he asked.

I took some breaths between my sobs and saw that my mom had calmed down, too.

"I'm okay."

"Good. I love you, and I'll be home in a few hours. Now put Mommy back on the phone," he finished. I handed Mom the phone and heard her say, "Okay, I'll see you then. I love you too. Buh-bye."

Daddy could always make Mommy and me feel better.

But I was still worried. I'd never seen my mom look so alone, confused, and powerless. She looked frazzled. Of course, it could have been her singed bangs. They could make the Queen of England look frazzled. But it felt like more. Like some part of her could no longer cope.

After she hung up, I leaned against her and said, "It's okay, Mommy. It's okay," partly to make sure that she really *was* okay, and partly to let her know that even if Daddy wasn't there, I was. She noticed the distress on my face, quickly picked me up, and said, "Don't worry, Mommy's okay. I'm fine."

We went into the bathroom to assess the damage to her hair. She plopped me down on the counter, wiped her raccoon eyes (from crying), saw her crazy-looking bangs, and began to laugh. "Well, they *did* need a trim!" And with that laugh, something further relaxed inside me—I knew I was safe again. Mommy was okay.

But something inside me had been put on alert. My safe, idyllic world had a new wrinkle in it—sometimes Mommy needs Daddy, but Daddy isn't there, and this makes Mommy sad.

And that was when, somewhere in the shadows of my young psyche, a sliver of a thought was implanted in my unconscious—I must do everything in my power always to make sure that my daddy is happy so that my mommy stays happy, too. When they're happy, I'm happy.

Of course there was a very good reason my dad couldn't come home that day. Just months earlier, at the beginning of 1966, Hollywood had called, and the Carlins had answered. My dad was now the head writer and resident stand-up for *Kraft Summer Music Hall*, hosted by John Davidson, an ultracorny variety show that was a summer replacement for *Kraft Music Hall* with Andy Williams. Talk about processed cheese. But, hey, it was the 1960s, and Velveeta was all the rage. This job was the big break we'd been waiting for.

So, when the offer came in, Mom and Dad packed up what few items we owned and moved from an apartment on the West Side of Manhattan to an apartment on the Westside of Los Angeles.

The "Danny Kaye plan" was working out great for Dad. For Mom, not so much. Of course she was thrilled that he was finally getting the big break he deserved. There was no one else on the planet who believed in my dad's dreams and talent the way my mom did. She was just not too thrilled with this whole stay-at-home mom thing.

Who could blame her? She didn't know a single person in Los Angeles—we'd only moved there a month ago. She couldn't get a job—Dad wouldn't let her work because he didn't want me being a latchkey kid like he'd been growing up. But most important—right now she had no bangs. She was alone, bored, poorly coiffed, and hanging out with a three-year-old all day.

She missed the good old days. With Dad's career now being shaped by agents and managers, she resented being stuck at home expected to be Donna Reed, her only purpose being to cook up dinner, navigate the traffic of Los Angeles, and chase after her energetic, curious toddler. She was used to cooking up the next move for Dad's career, navigating the highways to gigs in their old Dodge Dart, and chasing after the Danny Kaye Dream. She loved me and being a mom, but she knew she was so much more. She'd never be contained in the traditional housewife role of the 1960s. She had too much spark and smarts in her for that.

This was not the life she'd signed up for. She'd survived too much the last three years for this to be her reward.

Back in the spring of 1963, between Mom's pregnant belly counting down to T-minus three months to my birth, and Dad's crazy schedule on the road, they both decided it would be best for her to leave New York, where they'd been living in my dad's old bedroom in Mary's apartment, and go home to Dayton to have Alice help her through the first precarious months of motherhood. Even though Mom and Alice would never see eye to eye on most things, they had managed to maintain a relationship, and even bonded on a new level with my impending arrival. My mom was actually looking forward to her stay in Dayton.

When she got off the plane, she was shocked. Her mother looked as if she'd aged ten years. It had been only two months since she'd last seen her. Mom had been home to help Alice through her recovery from a mastectomy. She knew the recovery was going slowly, but no one had prepared her for this, and, typical of her family, no one was talking about it, either. In order to find out what was going on, my mother had to demand the truth from the family doctor— Alice had only six to eight weeks to live.

My mom's world was shattered. Instead of coming home to Dayton to fall into the safety of her mother's arms, she now would watch her die. She felt so alone. Her mom pretended everything was fine, and her dad walked around in a daze. And my soon-to-be dad did his best to juggle time in Dayton with needing to be on the road to scrape together some dough.

Brenda and Alice did what they were good at—keeping busy. They spent their days decorating the nursery and sewing my baby clothes. And they spent their nights, sometimes until three or four in the morning, "trying to stretch out the time, trying to express all our feelings, asking questions that had never been asked before, and trying to seek answers to everything," my mom told me years later.

Despite Alice's stern and demanding nature, or maybe because of it, their bond was deep and strong. Brenda loved her mother, and now deeply feared a life without her. And yet it was inevitable. In April 1963, six weeks before my birth, Alice Hosbrook died of metastatic breast cancer.

Alice left, but thankfully didn't leave my mother empty-handed. There were many projects left unfinished—bootees to knit, decorations to make, and furniture to buy—to fill her time. This did little to dispel Mom's anxiety or grief, but it made the days until my birth go by quicker. But she found it difficult to function, and sleeping was almost impossible. Overwhelmed by it all, during the last month of her pregnancy she was prescribed tranquilizers to relax her and help her sleep.

Ah, the sixties.

I don't know if it was the tranquilizers or not, but it took me three tries to come into the world. After two false labors, which each time caused my dad to drop everything (I guess that would be the microphone?) and rush to the waiting room at Good Samaritan Hospital in Dayton, I finally arrived ten minutes shy of Father's Day on June 15, 1963.

Years later Dad commented on the event: "Daughter Kelly born. God Smiles."

I'm not sure which God he was talking about, but hey, at least he was smiling. As were my parents. They were thrilled with me.

Two weeks later, once I became travelworthy, Mom and Dad swaddled me up, and we all climbed into the old Dodge Dart and returned to New York. We landed in our very own apartment at 519 West 121st Street—the very same building where Mary still lived. The very same building my dad had lived in since he was seven.

The best news was that the apartment was all ours—all three hundred square feet of it. The second-best news was that Mary was now four floors away—close enough for babysitting but far enough to not meddle too much. The not-so-best news was that there was no kitchen. Mom had to cook on a hot plate. Luckily both she and Dad were fans of canned soup and scrambled eggs. Me? I stuck with breast milk.

For Dad's artistic development, New York was the place to be. At night he'd go down to Greenwich Village and hang out with the people who were changing the world. He was watching people like Joan Baez, Mort Sahl, and Bob Dylan step away from the mainstream culture and cut a new, fresh path where the truth, pain, and hope of the world could be expressed in new ways. By 1965 he was doing hootenannies at places like The Bitter End, Café Wha?, and the Café au Go Go. These weren't the straight audiences he'd find at the Playboy or Racquet Club. These were the young kids about to explode into the world and change it in the name of peace, love, and understanding. They were his people. On the outside my dad may have looked like the man his mother wanted him to be, with his clean-cut face and sharkskin suits, but inside he was a pot-smoking radical just itching to tell "the man" to go fuck himself.

But even though it was all very exciting, it couldn't pay the bills.

Even with his mainstream club gigs and the occasional TV spot, Dad barely made enough money for us to survive. Mary would help out by shoving a five into my mom's hand and telling her to go get some food. Luckily my mom was resourceful, and could stretch her money by making all my toys and clothes. But she had no budget for the extras in their life. One would need actual money to have a budget.

When Mom could scrape together some extra dough, she'd spend it on the one thing no young woman could live without—eye makeup. This was the midsixties, for Christ's sake! A woman couldn't fathom leaving the house without twenty-five pounds of that shit on her eyelids. And my mom, although not vain, did like to look good. So when one morning she woke up to find that I, her darling twenty-three-month-old daughter, had opened all the makeup that she'd just spent her last seven dollars on, and used it to paint a most magnificent mural (okay, it was a blob of blue and brown on the walls), she lost it.

She didn't yell. She didn't punish me. She just wept and wept.

She was trying so hard to make it all work. She felt she couldn't do anything right.

One early November evening my mother needed to warm my bottle, so she plugged in the hot plate. The entire city of New York went black.

Plug. Socket. Black. More tears.

With my dad on the road, still filled with grief over her mother, left alone with her thoughts and a rambunctious two-year-old, in a city she could not afford to live in, she truly thought for a few minutes that she and her little hot plate had caused the blackout of the entire borough of Manhattan.

Clearly she was not coping well.

In a letter to her best friend back in Dayton, Mom admitted that she was very depressed because "George will be traveling again through the holidays," leaving her alone in New York with only me and Mary, and very little money. But, she added, "I would never ask George to give up on his dreams. It's all he's got, and I really believe he can make it." This, two years after Dad had written a note to himself that had expressed his own take on it all: "In 1963, I made a total of $11,060. Between expenses, managers, and agents, this is a losing proposition."

But when Dad was home, things were great. He always made Mom laugh, and they explored Manhattan's nightlife together. They adopted "Somewhere" from *West Side Story* as "their song," and knew for sure that there was "a place for us."

And Dad always doted on me. When I was an infant he would spend hours staring at me in my crib, recording my bubble blowing and cooing. My grandma Mary insisted on buying me a proper baby pram—navy blue, big white tires, fancy filigree on the sides—and my dad walked me around his neighborhood, those very streets he had roamed and ruled as an adolescent, showing me off to anyone and everyone. As I got older Dad took me to the Central Park Zoo, where I could ride the elephants and see the monkeys and lions. We'd roam the city via subway or bus, and on almost every corner he had a story to tell about the history of his days living there—"That's where me and the gang used to drink and smoke weed," or, "That's where I stood for hours to get Louis Armstrong's autograph as he came out of the back of Birdland." I wish he'd been able to record all those moments at those places; I'd love to take the George Carlin tour of New York City again. New York with my dad would always be a special place for the two of us.

And thankfully, careerwise, things began to look up. There were more and more moments of real hope that his "Danny Kaye plan" was not just a Danny Kaye pipe dream. He began to get more spots on TV, and better club gigs.

I'm sure it felt like manna from heaven. And in some ways it was, because eventually it led us to the promised land—Beverly Hills.

CHAPTER THREE

The American Dream

IN A FLASH, a poof, a swirl of the magic wand, we, the Carlins, were officially living the American Dream.

After a year in a small apartment on Beverly Glen, where my mom had inadvertently invented her new hairstyle, "Boom Bangs," we moved into a three-bedroom house on Beverwil Drive, just inside the Beverly Hills border. And I mean *just* inside. Three doors to the south, and we would have been what they officially call "adjacent." Not that this was really important to Mom and Dad, but I'm sure it lifted their spirits. We were in Beverly . . . Hills. Swimming pools and movie stars!

The house itself was wonderful. It was a Spanish-style three-bedroom with a big modern kitchen, formal dining room, a laundry room, and a courtyard. Just off the courtyard, near the front of the house, my dad made an extra room into a home office—a place for his stuff. And in the backyard was a playhouse—a place for *my* stuff. It was perfect except for a huge cluster of ferns in the courtyard that I was convinced would eat me. To the adults they just looked like ferns. But in my four-year-old mind, they were the tentacles of a monster ready to come alive at any moment and snatch me up.

We were the typical American family. We had lots of pets that were all named by my dad: Squeezix the parakeet, Frick & Frack the hermit crabs, Bogie the Maltese terrier, and a black cat named Beanie, which came with the house. Mom seemed to be feeling better about being in Los Angeles now, and she eased into her new Beverly Hills–housewife lifestyle: She got her hair done weekly at a fancy salon; she relished decorating the house. She found wallpaper for the kitchen that said, "Ha Ha Ha, Ho Ho Ho, Hee Hee Hee," scattered in wild and wacky black-and-white sixties graphic writing—God, we were hip. And, being a proper 1960s Beverly Hills housewife, she immediately hired a black maid, Anner Rae, to do the housework.

Dad stepped seamlessly into his role as a 1960s clean-cut family provider/husband/father by rarely being home. He was on the road for weeks at a time doing gigs at big fancy clubs like the Copacabana and the Playboy to pay the bills. All this new money allowed him to buy Mom whatever she wanted for the house or herself. And although I wished he could always be home, it made the times he was around extra special for me. He taught me how to climb the tree in the front yard, how to ride my two-wheel bike along the sidewalk, and every day we'd go to Roxbury Park down the street, where he'd push me on the swings and buy me ice-cream sandwiches.

We were just so damn white picket fence.

Well, kind of.

"Now this bowl here is yours—'Kelly's Spice Cake,'" my dad said to me as I sat on the kitchen counter mixing the ingredients in the bowl he was pointing to. Then he pulled another bowl over, poured in another box of cake mix *and* a Baggie of weed. "And this one is 'Daddy's Spice Cake,'" he said as he put that bowl in my lap. I happily stirred in the extra "spice."

I loved spending time with my daddy. Especially in his office, where I'd spend hours and hours coloring and drawing pictures, while he wrote material, listened to music, and rolled joints. Rolling joints was a daily routine. I watched him clean the weed, roll the weed, and smoke the weed. By the time I was ten, I could also clean the weed and roll the weed. But it took until I reached the ripe old age of fourteen before I would smoke the weed.

Dad's office was filled with wild posters (an upside-down American flag, the Zig-Zag rolling papers, a few Bill Graham rock-and-roll posters), and crazy tchotchkes (a hand grenade, an ashtray in the shape of a hand giving the finger, an old toy car of an NYPD paddy wagon). The freshest rock and roll spun on the turntable—Dylan, The Stones, or The Beatles. I loved lying on the floor and looking at the pictures on the front covers of those records: the funny cake on a turntable of The Rolling Stones' *Let It Bleed*; the pen-and-ink drawing of *Revolver;* and then the strange one that was just white— *The White Album*. The very first song that ever registered on my young mind was from *The White Album*—"The Continuing Story of Bungalow Bill." Before that song, music was just sound in the background, but the day I heard the words, "All the children sing!" I was hooked. A children's song! I played the song over and over, skipping around the house singing at the top of my lungs, "Hey, Bungalow Bill/What did you kill, Bungalow Bill?"

When Dad was on the road it was hard on me, but on the phone before he'd sign off, he'd routinely ask, "Are you my Stinkpot or Baby Doll?" To make up for the long trips, he'd come home with lots of presents. He'd bring salt water taffy from Atlantic City, or a snow globe from Chicago, or a little stuffed animal from parts in between. When I got a little older he'd send me postcards from the road. My favorite thing was when he would buy a bunch of them and write only one word on each postcard so that I would have to put the sentence together myself. He was a big kid himself, which drove my mom nuts most of the time because she felt like she had to be both the mom and the dad in the house.

Because Dad was a picky eater like me, he made me peanut butter sandwiches whenever I didn't want to eat what my mom had cooked, much to her displeasure ("George, how will she ever learn to like new foods if she doesn't try them?" "Well, I never try new foods, and I'm just fine."). And sometimes, when Mom was out, he'd even make me pancakes for dinner.

My dad relished sharing things with me, this little person who knew nothing of the planet yet. He'd explain how things worked—cats purring or music coming out of the radio. And he knew the names of stars—he loved astronomy. He also taught me new words. No, not those words. I'd learn those words easily enough in a few years. But when I didn't know what a word meant, he'd write it and the definition down on a piece of paper for me. But the most special moments with my dad were what I would call "Daddy's big teaching moments." They came when the world was revealing itself in a new way and Dad knew that it was important for me to witness it and understand.

A perfect teaching moment showed up in 1969.

"Look, Kelly. This is really happening right now." Dad had woken me up in the middle of the night and plopped me down in front of the TV to watch the Apollo 11 moon landing. He, Mom, and I watched as the module sat on the chalky surface of the moon. He kept repeating, "This is really happening right now." Maybe he couldn't believe it himself.

Dad pointed at the TV. "This isn't like *Gilligan's Island*. This isn't a TV show. There are really men on the moon right now. This is the most amazing thing that has ever happened."

As he himself took in the enormity of it all, he wanted me to be a part of this species-size historical moment, too. He wanted me to understand that I was part of something bigger than myself. That we all were part of something wondrous.

And yes, he was probably high at the time.

With Dad on the road so much, and sometimes gone for special days like my birthday, my mom always found ways to make up for it. She was very clever and loved celebrating birthdays and holidays. For my fourth birthday she made it truly magical.

Like all kids growing up in the TV age, I loved watching TV. When I was almost three years old, my dad was on the variety show *The Jimmy Dean Show*. Mom was excited because I was finally old enough to watch Dad on TV with her. When the show began, she positioned me in front of the TV. The announcer proclaimed, "And here's George Carlin," the audience clapped, the intro music crescendoed, and Dad began to speak. I had no idea what was going on. Mom pointed to my dad on the TV and said, "Look, Kelly, it's Daddy. Daddy is on the TV." He started talking, but I wasn't clear on what was happening. Daddy? TV? All I knew was that my dad's voice was coming out of a box and that there was a really small man stuck inside it. I began to cry and scream, "I want Daddy!" I ran out of the room, hysterical.

Who wouldn't be, upon the realization that her father was stuck inside a box?

But now that I was four, I had gotten the hang of this TV thing. I no longer ran from the TV screaming when he was on, and I even got to stay up late to watch him when he was on at night. I still didn't understand exactly what the TV box was or exactly how my dad got in it, but I knew that was where he sometimes worked.

I loved to watch cartoons—Bugs Bunny, The Flintstones, The Jetsons—but my favorite show was *Hobo Kelly*, which wasn't a cartoon but a local children's show, and it was special. First of all the star was named Kelly. In all my four years on Planet Earth, I had never met another Kelly, and here was one living in the TV box, the very same TV box where my daddy worked.

But the real reason Hobo Kelly was the best was that every day she sent birthday presents to kids through the TV. She'd announce a name, "Billy Rogers in Encino, Happy Birthday!" And then the real magic began. Next she'd say, "Go look under your parents' bed!" Hobo Kelly sent a birthday present whooshing through the air. It would spin and fly on the screen.

When I got home from school one day, my mom handed me two Chips Ahoy cookies, and said, "Why don't you go and watch *Hobo*

Kelly?" I sat through the whole show, thinking nothing of it, and then at the end she said, "Kelly Carlin in Beverly Hills, Happy Birthday! Go look under your parents' bed!" And *Whoosh* the present spun and flew through the air. Once I realized that Hobo Kelly was really talking to *me*, I leaped up, flew up the stairs to my parents' bedroom, and practically threw myself under the bed.

And there it was—a perfectly wrapped present. Magic. Pure magic.

Hobo Kelly had sent me a present through the air! And not just any present but the perfect present—it was a set of Colorforms just like we had at school, and now I had my very own. My mom played her part perfectly, looking as shocked as I was as I ripped open the wrapping, "Look at that! Colorforms! Hobo Kelly knew exactly what you wanted!" I beamed and basked in the perfection of it all.

All during this time things were moving ahead with my dad's career. After the *Kraft Summer Music Hall* gig wrapped in the summer of 1966, Dad moved right into step three of the big "Danny Kaye plan"—becoming an actor. He played Marlo Thomas's agent, "George Lester," in an episode of *That Girl*. He quickly discovered what a pain in the ass acting was—he had to say other people's words while hitting marks for cameras, and then sit around for hours and hours until his brain atrophied from boredom, only to do it all again. He began to have serious doubts about this acting stuff.

Luckily he was also getting more TV spots. He was on the *Merv Griffin* and *Mike Douglas* shows, and in the summer of 1967, he landed another run on a summer-replacement show—*Away We Go*, with Buddy Greco and Buddy Rich. Most of the time he relied on his usual schtick, the bits that got him the jobs in the first place—the famous "Hippie-Dippie Weatherman" and "Indian Sergeant" routines. The TV hosts and producers loved those bits, and the gigs paid the bills, so he couldn't really complain. But he was getting bored with it all. He wasn't evolving as an artist, or getting to try out the new stuff he was writing. Even when he brought new stuff to the table, they'd say, "Just do that 'Hippie-Dippie' thing."

At least there was one saving grace—when he got to work with someone like Buddy Rich, the world-famous jazz drummer, there was plenty of good weed to go around.

With Mom and Dad doing their parts to create our American Dream, I did mine, too. My mom knew that spending too much time with only adults was not good for me. I needed friends and mental stimulation. So I was off to school—a Montessori school—at the age of four. Montessori was a school that allowed children to explore reading, writing, and 'rithmetic at their own pace. It let you find your own way into your own learning. Mom had prepared me well. Around the time I was two years old, she'd started teaching me my letters and numbers with beautiful flash cards she'd made by hand. I could dutifully recite the alphabet on request with only a slight misstep around the *w*. Regardless of what all the adults said, I *knew* that it must be pronounced "double-doo."

Though I was armed with a lunch box full of my favorite foods— a sandwich of Oscar Mayer bologna with Miracle Whip on Wonder Bread, Oreo cookies, and carrot sticks—my first day of school did not go as planned. As my mom backed out the door with all the other young mothers waving and smiling, thrilled to have a few hours of freedom in their day, I panicked. I realized I was not going with her.

I was positive that if my mom left, she might never return. My thoughts began to race along with my heart—*What if she set her hair on fire again? Then I would be left here forever with these strangers because Daddy was somewhere on an airplane. And I don't know where he is!*

I immediately leaped at my mom and clutched her leg. I held on for my very life. And then the tears came and came and came. I was inconsolable.

Finally the teacher, Miss Morgan, said to my mom, "I know it may be hard, but in the long run it's best if you just make a clean break and leave. She'll settle in eventually."

I heard this and thought, *Oh, yeah? We'll see about that!*

I did not "settle in."

Every morning as my mom tried to leave I cried and clung. Once she left, I transferred my clinging to Miss Morgan and followed her around the classroom. When she walked, I walked. When she sat, I sat—on her lap. I was cling wrap. She was a saint.

Eventually I realized that (*a*) my mom was going to keep dropping me off at this godforsaken place no matter what; (*b*) she was somehow managing to survive without me; and (*c*) she came back every afternoon to pick me up.

After two weeks I grudgingly settled in.

And *boy*, did I settle in. I quickly figured out what this place called school was all about. Sure there was playing "Red Light, Green Light" at recess, or finger painting in the afternoon, or even learning to peel a carrot (which I must admit was a bit of a revelation). But really, it was all about knowing the right answers. Seeing the happy look on Miss Morgan's face when I got a question right was pure bliss. Being first with my hand up and having the right answer, and making no mistakes in my reading and writing book, became imperatives for me. I felt the charge of having power over something.

Although I felt confident now about the things happening *inside* the classroom, I felt lost on the playground. It was like I was living slightly outside it all. "Wanna play jacks?" Lisa, a girl in plaid pants, asked me the first week at school.

"Sure. You go first," I said, not knowing what jacks were, but also not wanting to let that fact be known. *Did I miss the day where they explain all of this to you? Is there some manual I'm missing?* I never let on about my ignorance. I knew I'd be seen as stupid if I didn't pretend that I knew what was going on. So I faked it.

Because of Mom's hostess days at the Racquet Club, she loved to entertain, and now that she had a big house to do it in, she decided to throw a party—a surprise party for my dad's birthday. Parties and holidays gave her a purpose—eggs to devil, celery sticks to stuff with cream cheese, and decorations to hang. When coordinating an event or a project, my mother was in her full stride and glory.

I was especially excited about this party because not only had I never been involved in such a production, we were going to surprise my daddy. My mom gathered a few old friends (Elaine from the Racquet Club, along with her new husband, Bill Brennan, who had just moved to Los Angeles), a bunch of new friends from Dad's TV work, and our family (my dad's brother, Patrick, and his family, my aunt Marlene, and my cousins Dennis and Packy, who had lived in Los Angeles since the late fifties). Mom decorated the house with streamers and a huge sign that said, "Happy Birthday George!" and then we baked a cake.

Once the guests arrived, Mom gave me the most important job: to be the lookout who hid in the backyard to wait for my dad's car to come up the alley.

I did my duty, quietly hiding in my playhouse. When Dad pulled in to the garage, I rushed into the house to tell everyone to hide. Everyone immediately settled down and became quiet (it was quite the rush to see a room full of grown-ups settle down on my command). While Dad made his way through the kitchen, I thought I just might burst. Finally he bounded into the dining room, and we all shouted, "Surprise!"

Everyone began to sing "Happy Birthday," and Mom brought the cake out from the kitchen. Instead of saying "Happy Birthday," it said "Fuck You!" The whole room laughed, and Dad blew out the candles.

The party guests fawned over my dad and the funny cake. When their attention came toward me I hid my face in my dad's leg and clutched tightly. I felt as if I was supposed to know what all the fuss was about over the "Fuck You" cake. I, of course, did not know what all the fuss was about. But I could feel the crackle in the air that it had created. What I gathered from watching the adults was that it was daring, funny, and outrageous.

Years later I eventually realized what that "Fuck You!" was saying to all in that room—Let's celebrate that we are iconoclastic artist types living outside the norm. Look how daring we are! I know that's what my mom intended. But now, when I think back on that time, I wonder if some part of that "Fuck You!" wasn't an actual "Fuck you" from my mom to my dad.

My mom was still struggling. She hadn't really settled in to her new lifestyle. She felt useless, like an afterthought. She told my father once that she'd felt like a piece of furniture that everyone was walking around. Although most of our days on Beverwil Drive in Beverly Hills had been sunny and happy so far, as the year 1968 ripened, so did my mother's resentment and confusion about her place in the world.

Because Dad still didn't want her to have a full-time job, Mom attempted to find a place for her talents and passions once I was in school. She thought about getting her pilot's license, and it turned out that she was really good at flying. So good that the flying instructor told her she should become an instructor herself. Dad got nervous about the fact that one of Mom's other passions that she'd been pursuing lately was drinking. Dad told her she couldn't get her license.

She then volunteered at a local hospital as a Candy Striper cheering up patients and bringing them books from the library. She was good at that, too. Her warmth, natural curiosity about people, and sense of humor made her a favorite. But she started having panic attacks at work and then in the car, and she just couldn't manage anymore. She quit. Her doctor, Dr. Little (whom I nicknamed Dr. Doolittle) told her that she was probably having what they used to call an "identity crisis." It got so bad that at one point she couldn't even sign her name on her checks anymore. He prescribed her some Valium—"mother's little helper."

These Mother's Little Helpers—they did not help. They only made things worse.

One weekend, my mom and her friend Gail decided to have a

girls' weekend getaway in Palm Springs. Mom was pissed at Dad (they were arguing more and more about her being a piece of furniture and him getting to be a kid with me all the time) and wanted to blow off some steam. Mom and Gail went to the Riviera Resort—*the* hot spot in the desert, and a playground of the stars. The Riviera was known for the big bands that played there, and the celebrities who hung out—Tommy Dorsey, the Rat Pack, Desi Arnaz. Mom and Gail ate dinner and watched the show. By the time the show was over and the band had left the stage, Mom was riled up and drunk. She wobbled up to the bandstand and grabbed the microphone. A few hundred people looked up at her expectantly.

"Hey! Do you know who I am?" she asked them.

Hundreds of eyes stared back at her. Blinking.

"Don't you know who I am?" she asked again.

I'm pretty sure she really wanted them to answer the question. But she didn't wait for them to do so.

"Well, for your information, I am George Carlin's wife. The great comedian George Carlin's wife . . . and I want you to—"

The maître d' quickly grabbed the mike out of her hand and escorted her off the stage, where Gail, also drunk, led her away. The next morning, demoralized and mortified, Mom found the maître d' and apologized.

My mom felt alone in her pain, but she wasn't. Right by her side, Dad was also in the midst of an identity crisis. He no longer wondered if mainstream success was worth stifling the radical truth teller inside him. He now knew that it wasn't. And what a conundrum it was for him: Here was the dream he'd had since he was ten years old, unfolding before his eyes, and it wasn't what he'd thought it would be.

More and more he hated the variety and talk shows he was doing, because he knew that who he truly was wasn't present in his act. He felt like a performing monkey. The world was changing—MLK and RFK had been assassinated, Lenny Bruce was dead, men were walking on the moon, all his musician friends were speaking truth to power—and he was *still* doing the "Hippie-Dippie Weatherman" and "Indian Sergeant" routines. Even when he had an opportunity to do something different, like when he was booked on the *Smothers Brothers* show, he didn't know how to break out of the box, and he played it safe. He was trapped.

Middle America had fallen in love with George Carlin, just in time for him to have fallen out of love with them.

CHAPTER FOUR

The Three Musketeers

IN 1969 MY DAD DROPPED acid for the first time—and the second time—and most probably the twenty-ninth time. As he would say about it years later, "LSD is a values changer. . . . And I was able to see I was in the wrong place." He now saw very clearly that he was entertaining the wrong people. He was entertaining the parents of the people he actually wanted to be with.

When he went to do some shows at the Copacabana in New York City, things were what you might call . . . interesting. Some nights he did his act as usual, and then one night he just lay on the floor under the piano and described what he saw to the audience. Another night he brought the phone book out on stage and read from different sections. He was trying to get fired. They obliged.

Later that year he got hired to open for the Supremes in Las Vegas for twelve thousand dollars a week. The most money he had ever made in his life. It was enough money to reach his American Dream, which is what he'd *thought* he wanted. It was also enough money to put a deposit on a beautiful house in the San Fernando Valley, which is what my mom *definitely* wanted.

During the first show Dad did his new bit about the word "shit."

He said, "I don't say shit. Down the street Buddy Hackett says shit. Redd Foxx says shit. I don't say shit. I smoke a little of it, but I don't say it." Some members of the audience apparently took offense at his act, and the Frontier Hotel told Dad, "You say, 'Shit,' we say, 'Fuck you.'"

Dad got fired. Mom lost her dream house.

And I began to sleep on the floor.

My mom and dad began to argue more and more about money, and all the changes that were happening. They did their best to argue only when I slept or when I wasn't around. But being an only child, I knew exactly what was going on whether I wanted to or not. I felt the reality—things were tense between them. My dad said that he knew in his gut that their fighting had become a problem for me when I started mysteriously sleeping on the floor in the hallway in the middle of the night. This troubled him deeply. But all he could do was try to spend as much quality time with me as possible to offset any consequences of the war brewing in the house.

Late one night my dad was packing to go out on the road. I was sitting on the floor watching him, fascinated. Because he went on the road so much, my dad was a champion packer. And because he was slightly OCD, he would have stacks of his things all around the dining room—shirts in one pile, socks folded neatly in another, underwear stacked, toiletries laid out precisely. It was a production. Being with him during these ordinary domestic moments meant the world to me. It was a chance to soak up some special "daddyness" before he would be gone for two or three weeks. So there I was soaking him up, when my mom came in and said sharply, "Kelly, it's time for bed."

I looked up pleadingly. "Can't I stay up just a little longer, pretty please?"

Dad quickly chimed in, "C'mon, Bren. Let her stay up a little longer. It won't kill her. I'm going to be gone for three weeks."

Mom set her jaw, looked at my dad, and said loudly, "Fine, I'll just be the only Carlin in this entire household who never, ever, *ever* gets what she wants!"

I knew what was coming, so I got up and headed toward my bedroom, hoping my obedience would quell any arguing. But as I did so, my mom lost her balance, tried to right herself, but couldn't, and fell backward into Dad's half-packed suitcase. I held my breath, waiting for her to lose it. My dad tensed, too, even as he rushed over to see if she was okay. But instead of rage or tears, she began to laugh. It wasn't a fuck-you laugh, but a loose, silly, oh-my-God-look-what-I-did laugh. And with that, Dad laughed, too. They laughed together. It was a laugh that said, "We're in love and see all the good in the world and each other." It was the laugh of "Everything will be okay forever and ever." Confused but thrilled, I began to laugh, too. I felt a thank-God-everyone-is-still-happy moment deep inside my chest.

Dad helped her up and out of the suitcase, and Mom straightened out her nightgown. As she did this, I saw something that I'd never noticed before—she was wobbly and couldn't really stand. She couldn't really speak right, and there was a sleepy look in her eyes. This wasn't my everyday mom, but someone else who spoke, acted, and felt different. And although I didn't really know what to call it at the time, it was very clear—she was drunk.

And there it was again, like the day her hair caught on fire: a ripple of threat in my young and sensitive being. However, this time it wasn't a tremor on my human seismograph, it was more like an earthquake. I was now very worried—*What if Dad is gone on the road and Mom is acting like this? Will she know how to take care of me?* And even worse, I thought—*What if Daddy gets really mad that Mommy is like this and he leaves forever?*

My mother, the one I'd known my whole life, had disappeared before my very eyes.

But then Dad looked us both in the eye, put his arms around us, and said, "Come on, come on, group hug." We all gathered in a circle and hugged. He then said, "Just remember, we are the Three Musketeers, all for one and one for all."

That was the night the Carlins discovered the land of denial.

During the spring of 1970 my dad went into the hospital for a double hernia operation. He went in my daddy—a clean-cut man with groovy sideburns—and came home someone else—a man with a beard. A beard he would not shave for the rest of his life. I wasn't quite sure if this was really my daddy. This was very startling for me.

Mom was startled, too. Not so much by the beard, but by all the rest. Dad was ready to change everything. He was ready to walk away from the suits, the ties, and the audiences that didn't really understand him. This also meant walking away from the money that came with all that. To finally be able to fully express his truth, as many of his peers in music were doing, he was willing to risk everything. My mom was not as willing. All that she and Dad had worked for and sacrificed for the last nine years was at risk.

But even with her anxiety, which led to lots and lots of arguing for a few months, in the end she really did understand. She knew this change of direction for my dad was his "true north." It might not be full of safety and security, but it was full of authenticity. And she understood what it felt like not to live authentically—she'd been doing it since she was a teenage girl. Plus Mom had always loved the "David vs. Goliath" fight, the us-against-them lifestyle. It's what made her feel alive when she first met my dad.

Yes, she had wanted the house in the Valley with the pool; yes, she loved having a successful husband; but she had also felt brushed aside the last five years because of that success. Something had died inside her. With Dad igniting a new vision for his life and work, something sparked in her, and she looked him square in the eye and said, "Let's go!"

Giving up on the white-bread version of the American Dream meant we were now going to live our own version of it. In the late fall of

1970, we moved out of Beverly Hills and into a three-bedroom apartment on Pacific Avenue near the Venice Canals. We were now living among "our" people—the freaks, bikers, and hippies of Venice Beach. It was a tough neighborhood, so the first week we lived there my dad taught me how to walk down the street like a New Yorker. "So, you know," he explained in a thick New York accent, "no one will fuck with you." He took this teeny wisp of a seven-year-old out onto the sidewalk in front of our building and showed me how to do this New York–style walking—head up, eyes front, walking like I had a place to go.

A few months after we moved in, I was awakened by a very large bang—like a truck had hit our apartment building. Before I knew it the whole place started to shake. I leaped out of bed and ran as fast as I could to my parents' room. The whole world kept shaking. I jumped into their bed, and Dad hovered above Mom and me so that if the roof caved in, he'd take the brunt of the damage. I don't know what was more traumatizing that morning—the 6.6 magnitude earthquake or the fact that as Dad protected us, I could see his balls.

When Dad wasn't on the road, he was in his office listening to albums, smoking weed (he was also growing a huge pot plant in there), and working on new material: It was something he now did with real fervor since he now had a new audience for it—college kids all across America. But unlike only a few years earlier, I no longer spent endless hours with him. I now hung around with my friends, a couple of girls I had befriended in the neighborhood. We ruled the back alleyway as only girls on pink-and-turquoise Schwinn Sting-Ray bikes could.

After school my best friend, Cheryl, and I could be found playing handball against the open walls of the apartment building's carport, and in the summer we were on the beach. These were the days when all you had to do was tell your mom where you were going and when you'd be home. Sometimes that would mean eight to ten hours of free-range playing. We roamed the canals—which back then had few houses and were mostly open space—built forts, sucked on honeysuckle, and sailed Popsicle-stick boats in the canals. I committed my first crime—I shoplifted an Abba-Zaba candy bar and a candle from Alan's Market. My life of crime was short, though. I felt too guilty to ever do it again. We also roamed the beaches all the way from the marina to the lifeguard station up near Venice Boulevard, ruling the swing sets, building sand castles, and gorging on candy. We were never hassled, bothered, nor molested. It must have been my New York walk.

When Mom was home, she was usually partying with her friends. My friend Cheryl's mom had become my mom's best friend, and they often went gallivanting out in the neighborhood together. I began to notice that my mom was drunk or high during the day more frequently, and her moods were all over the place—some days she was euphoric and others a bitch. She was now popping a rainbow of pills. I tried to predict what might set her off. Was it my room being messy? Or maybe it was my coming home a few minutes late? I couldn't figure it out. I didn't know how to act around her anymore, and so I began to pull away from her. I talked to her less, confided in her almost never, and generally avoided her. I became afraid of her and relied on my dad to be my only emotional foundation.

When she and Dad fought, which was more often and much louder than it used to be, I began to take my dad's side. I felt he was the more logical one, and so I would back him up. But this only made the atmosphere in the household worse. More and more often I found solace by disappearing into my bedroom, where I'd sink into a quiet and dark mood, or I'd flee out the door to find someone or something to distract myself.

When it was time for dinner, Mom was sometimes nowhere to be found, and I'd have to go look for her. One of her regular spots was a local bar called Hinanos. I'd lean just inside the doorway and yell, "Brenda Carlin! Are you here, Brenda Carlin?" When she was there, and not too deep into her Cutty Sarks, she'd come home to get dinner ready. But if she wasn't there, or if I saw that she was already drunk, I'd go home alone and make my new favorite thing—a Swanson's TV Dinner. Fried chicken or Salisbury steak were my favorites. (Though I must admit I could have done without the corn infiltrating my chocolate brownie, thank you very much.)

On those nights when Dad was in town and Mom had cooked a meal, the three of us would set up our TV trays in front of the big console and watch some shows together. Those were my favorite nights, because it felt like everything was right with our world. Mom and Dad loved the crime shows like *Mission: Impossible, Columbo,* and *Mannix.* But we were also fans of the animal shows like *The Wonderful World of Disney* and *Wild Kingdom,* because Dad would do the voices of all the animals. He'd pick a different voice for each animal and do funny dialogue, making Mom and me laugh hysterically.

Not only were we in a new neighborhood, but I was now going to a new school—Santa Monica Montessori. With my new school came a school-bus service, which my parents loved. They no longer needed to wake up early, or be sober enough to drive at eight in the morning! I, on the other hand, hated it. Since they didn't have to wake up to drive, they'd often sleep in, leaving me to wake myself up, eat breakfast, and get ready for the day. Increasingly I'd wake up to the bus honking in the alleyway. A dagger of anxiety would stab me in the stomach when I'd realize I was late again. Sometimes Millie, the bus driver, would wait the ten minutes while I scrambled into my clothes and grabbed a Pop-Tart for breakfast. But most of the time I'd wave her on and then have to wake my parents to take me to school. Mom or Dad would groggily stumble about, throw on some clothes, and drive me up to Santa Monica.

One morning I woke up for school and found both of my parents already awake, dressed, and in the kitchen. This confused me deeply.

"What's going on?" I asked.

What had happened was that my mom, who was now volunteering at the LA Free Clinic, had gone for a drink after work with a few coworkers, and on the way home she'd gotten pulled over by the cops. When they searched her purse, they found a bunch of loose pills.

She told them, "They're my medicine. I have a prescription at home. If you take me there, I'll prove it to you."

And so they did. It was 2:00 A.M. and my dad by this point was frantic and worried. He'd been up waiting, and in the meantime had rolled a nice joint to smoke. Just as he lit it, there was a knock at the door. "Thank God you're—" Instead of finding my mom at the door, he found two of LA's finest standing next to my mom in handcuffs. They quickly took my dad into custody, too, searched the apartment, and found the six-foot-tall pot plant growing in his office.

The cops shuffled my parents off to the local lockup, where they quickly got bail. I had somehow managed to sleep through the whole thing until waking for school. I guess it was all that training I got sleeping in clubs as a baby. (I probably would have slept through the Stones at Altamont.)

My mom wasn't the only one creating havoc in the family with her intake of "chemicals." One afternoon she came into my room and said, "Kelly, Daddy's taken something, and he's not feeling well, and I need you to help me." We walked into their bedroom and found my dad standing in his boxer shorts, holding a framed picture of his old head shot—the clean-cut face—smiling at us. The frame was shattered, and Dad's hand was bleeding.

"Daddy, are you okay?" I asked. My dad took the picture and threw it against the wall, and then he collapsed in a pile of tears and rage. Mom quickly sat on him. I then jumped on him, too. He rambled on unintelligibly about his mother, himself, the world. He was shouting at things that weren't in the room and making no sense to me. Mom soothed him. "You're going to be okay, George. You're going to be okay."

I was terrified that he'd lost his mind. I shook with fear. My father was gone. As tears streamed down my face, I bravely followed my mom's lead and tried to soothe him, "It's okay, Daddy. You're going to be just fine."

We sat on him for a torturous forty-five minutes until he finally cried himself to sleep.

Dad had gotten hold of some bad acid. It seemed that becoming a counterculture god to the youth of America was not as easy as it looked.

At least that's what it felt like Dad had become—a counterculture god. By mid-1972 Dad's second album, *FM & AM* (a mix of old material—the *AM* side—and new material—the *FM* side), had come out and gone gold. With that feat, everything had changed, again.

To the world, just a few years earlier he'd been the clean-cut guy who made a nice living "working clean," as evidenced by his "Indian Sergeant" routine (done in the voice of an Irish guy from the old neighborhood): "Now, a lot of youse guys have been asking me about promotions. . . . Well, the results of the tests have come in and youse doin' beautifully. 'Burning Settlers' Homes,' everybody passed. 'Imitating a Coyote,' everybody passed. 'Sneaking Quietly Through the Woods,' everybody passed, except Limping Ox. However, Limping Ox is being fitted with a pair of corrective moccasins." Now Dad was the long-haired hippie-freak in blue jeans making a great living "working blue," as seen in his bit titled "Shoot": "I got fired last year in Vegas for saying shit—in a town where the big game is called craps. That's some kind of a double standard. I'm sure there was some Texan standing out in the casino yelling, 'Oh, SHIT! I CRAPPED!' And they fly those guys in free. Fired me . . . shit."

He now headlined on almost every college campus in America. Not only had he found success, but he'd found it by stepping into his true nature, where he could speak truth to power and question everything. He had finally stepped over the line to the "other side." And during those heady times in America, that line was firmly drawn and sides were vehemently chosen: the hippies vs. the establishment, the freaks vs. the straights; the heads vs. the blockheads.

In the summer of 1972 Mom and I went on the road with Dad. The road was always a fun adventure. Some of my earliest memories from the road are of waking up in a hotel room, both my parents dead to the world, and spending the next few hours coloring, watching cartoons with the volume all the way down, and staring out the window at the city below. Finally, when I was starving, I'd nudge my parents awake. Dad would run down to a local diner or store (or, as he got more successful, order room service) and buy a bunch of those miniboxes of Rice Krispies and a quart of milk. He'd then carefully take out his pocketknife, cut open those teeny boxes, and magically transform them into an instant bowl. Abracadabra— breakfast was served! And although I never heard it, I am absolutely sure that it was on one of those mornings that Dad heard that famous "Snap, crackle, fuck you."

Our first stop that summer was Kent State. My dad took me to the memorial for the four college kids who had been shot by the National Guard a few years before. He explained that they'd been protesting the war, standing up for what they believed in, and that the government silenced them by shooting them. This was one of those "Daddy's big teaching moments." He wanted me to understand the importance of people standing up for what they believed in, especially those who were willing to stand up to their government to make their point. He explained how the government had always silenced those who did not have a voice to begin with— blacks and Native Americans especially—and how young, white American girls and boys were now in that category, too. I felt there was no safe place for anyone.

Being a nine-year-old only child, and one who felt an increasing need to be more mature than my years, I acted as calm, cool, and collected as I could. I tried to show my dad that I understood the lesson of civics and morality that he was trying to teach me. But it was just a calm veneer, because all I could think was, *If the government was shooting these people for standing up for what they believed, would they shoot me or even my dad?* It was a terrifying thought that now echoed in the back of my mind.

The next stop on our summer of '72 tour was Summerfest in Milwaukee. Summerfest was basically an ocean of beer surrounding an island of sausage disguising itself as a music festival. You know, what they call "good clean American fun." And when you think "good clean American fun," don't you also immediately think George Carlin?

Dad opened for Arlo Guthrie, and struggled to do his new material while connecting with the enormous audience of over ten thousand people. He began to do his new routine, the "Seven Words You Can Never Say on Television," which he'd just recorded on his third album, *Class Clown.* The album wouldn't be released for another few months, so I'm pretty sure the promoter didn't know exactly what he had signed up for when he booked my dad. The routine was both hilarious and an intellectual examination of the usage of language in our culture. However, it consisted of words, according to Dad, "that'll infect your soul, curve your spine, and keep the country from winning the war. Shit, piss, fuck, cunt, cocksucker, motherfucker, and tits." Yeah, those words.

Because Summerfest was an outdoor venue, the main stage act could be heard throughout the fairgrounds—meaning it could be heard by lots of mommies and daddies and little kiddies. So there was my dad onstage, killing. Most of the audience was loving it, while Mom and I stood in the wings, also enjoying the show. That's when the promoter rushed up to my mom and said, "The cops are here. They're complaining about the language, and they're going to arrest George the minute he walks offstage."

I guess when my dad said that he'd like to "fuck everyone in the audience," the nice Midwestern policemen took some offense.

Knowing that he was carrying drugs in his pocket—both grass and coke—my mom thought fast, grabbed a glass of water, and walked out onto the stage. Dad, confused, took the water, and Mom whispered, "Exit stage left. The cops are here."

Dad wrapped it up, exited stage left, and we all quickly hustled into the dressing room and locked the door. I anxiously watched as Mom removed a rather large Baggie of coke from her purse and stashed it in a bass drum, and Dad took out the joint and small vial of coke from his pockets and handed them to the promoter. The promoter was trying to keep things calm, when suddenly, *Bang!*— it sounded as if a gun had gone off. I leaped into my mom's arms and began crying hysterically. As she tried to calm me down, nothing else happened. Someone said, "It was probably just a balloon." Someone had popped a fucking balloon! Mom, Dad, and the promoter all laughed a nervous laugh, but I was now unhinged. Terror streaked through my body. I couldn't breathe. I felt like I was going to die. And that's when the door opened, my dad walked out, and within a few seconds policemen cuffed him. I screamed, "Daddy!" I was sure that I would never ever see him again. My mom held me back as I cried.

I don't know how long it took, but she finally calmed me down enough so that she could leave to get my dad out of jail.

Luckily my mom knew exactly what to do because of Lenny Bruce's arrest in Chicago in 1961—You get a civil rights lawyer. I went home with the promoter to his house and family, where I spent the rest of the weekend distracting myself by swimming with his kids in something that as a Southern California girl I had never seen before—an aboveground pool. I almost didn't know what to do with it.

After one of the most harrowing weekends of our family life, Mom paid something like $250 to get Dad out of jail, and we were ready for his next gig: Carnegie Hall, New York City.

We stayed at the Plaza Hotel. Well, actually, we lived at the Plaza Hotel for almost a whole month. Are you familiar with the character Eloise? Now imagine Eloise in a tie-dyed T-shirt, sneakers, and a denim jacket with a patch that said, "Make Love, Not War." That was me. I read all the Eloise books, roamed the back stairs and halls, and got to know most of the staff by name. Every day I ordered a hot fudge sundae and charged it to the room, and every night I went to the basement theater, the Plaza 9 Music Hall, and watched the musical *Curley McDimple*. This was *my* Danny Kaye moment. I sat in the dark, watched a young girl, Robbi Morgan, sing and dance her way across the stage as a Shirley Temple–like character, and I decided right there and then that I wanted to be just like her someday. Having watched the real Shirley Temple on TV my whole life, I had certainly fantasized about being her. But it was just TV, and in black-and-white, which made it feel so remote, so I never really saw it as something I could do in my life. But here I was now, sitting in the hush of a theater, watching a real girl only a few years older than me in a play about a Shirley Temple character. It felt very real. I eventually met the cast, and my mom told them that I had memorized all the words to all the songs. I began to hang out with Robbi before and after the shows, and one weekend I even got to go across the bridge to New Jersey to her house, where her mom and dad taught me how to do the time step. At the end of our stay at the Plaza, the producers let me audition for what could have been the West Coast premiere of the show. I had no singing or dancing experience, so I felt like a bit of a fake, and yet there I was up on that stage singing my heart out. Unfortunately there never was a West Coast premiere.

Then the big night finally came: Carnegie Hall. Outside on the posters my dad's name shone for all of Midtown Manhattan to see— "Carnegie Hall Presents George Carlin"—a huge coup for my dad, who grew up a latchkey kid not sixty blocks away. His mother, Mary, his aunt Aggie, their friends, and of course lots of Dad's friends from the neighborhood were all out there in the audience to cheer him on. Mom, Dad, and I were all hunkered down in the dressing room. Dad checked his notes and paced like he always did. Mom was immersed in a deep and intense conversation with a person she had met only ten minutes earlier—fueled no doubt by whatever chemical mixture she was doing that week. And I, after roaming the halls to find the vending machines, sat in the corner reading *Archie* comics and eating Fritos. Suddenly we got the knock: "Two minutes, George."

Escorted by the promoter, Mom, Dad, and I left the quiet of the room to make our way through the bowels of the building. As we walked past people, they said things to us like, "Go get 'em, George," and "Knock 'em dead." I did not know these people, and they did not know me. But they knew my dad. Everybody knew my dad. As we came up from the basement, we started to hear feet stamping and the chant, "George, George, George!" There were over a thousand voices saying my father's name over and over again, and when he stepped out onto the stage, they erupted into a roar. Every hair on my body stood straight up. I felt energy all around me, and a joy ached inside my chest. I felt extremely alive. And although I understood they weren't cheering for me, I still felt connected to it all. It was very intoxicating, and I knew that all I had to do was stay right next to my dad, and this buzz would be free.

When we got home, things got interesting.

CHAPTER FIVE

She's Leaving Home

BECAUSE *FM & AM*, and *Class Clown*, made us a ton of money, we now lived in a huge modern house on Tellem Drive, atop a hill in the Pacific Palisades. Dad said it was the perfect street for him because "That's what I do. I tell 'em." But mostly it was not so perfect because the neighborhood was a bastion of the Republican Party. We were surrounded by lots of Governor Ronald Reagan's best friends: next door a National Security Council bigwig, and across the street a Rand Corporation executive. The only way we could have picked a whiter, squarer part of Los Angeles to move to is if we'd lived in a piece of Wonder Bread. This was the autumn of 1972—the Nixon vs. McGovern campaign was in full swing, and I'm pretty sure we were the only house on the block voting for Mc-Govern.

One early evening I stood with my dad on the driveway, looking across the street at a cocktail party the Rand Corporation executive was having. Like most cocktail parties, it consisted of couples dressed up in suits and cute dresses talking animatedly and tinkling fancy cocktails. However, unlike most cocktail parties, this one came with its own sideline commentator. As Dad and I stood there taking in the scene, he turned to me and said in a very loud voice, "Hey, Kel, look at all the assholes over there." Conversation stopped, glasses no longer tinkled, and heads spun our way; fun times for a ten-year-old.

Dad was now saying stuff out loud often to people's faces, which made me want to disappear. Part of the reason for this was that his very presence provoked reactions. Dad's hair was now halfway down his back, and this would raise the hackles of the "straights." Sometimes they gave him a look that said, "Cut your hair, hippie!" Sometimes they'd actually say it out loud to his face. Either reaction triggered my dad to spout a few of his famous "Seven Dirty Words," usually with a few additional choice words tacked on for good measure.

Once when we were on a cross-country flight on a 747 coming home from a trip back east, Dad disappeared into the bathroom for a long time. After about ten minutes a big guy with a big Texan accent banged on the door and told my dad to hurry it up. Dad was taking his time in there, rolling and then smoking a joint, and I'm sure doing a few lines, too. After about twenty minutes the big Texan was starting to get really loud, threatening my dad. When my dad finally came out, the Texan sneered at him and called him a freak. My dad told him to stick a dildo up his ass. The Texan lunged at my dad, and a few stewardesses had to get between them. About ten minutes before we landed, one of the stewardesses came over to tell us that the Texan had complained to the pilot and also mentioned that he smelled marijuana. The cops would be at the gate to meet us. My stomach clenched with terror. I didn't want to see a repeat of Milwaukee, or worse. Then the stewardess said that she and the other girls on board were huge fans, and that if we wanted to, they would sneak us off to safety. After we landed we lingered on board and then sneaked out the back stairwell with the stewardesses, and into their van. It was as if we were secret agents making a getaway! We went straight to the Airport Marina hotel on Lincoln Boulevard with them and hid out. We ordered room service, and I watched cartoons. Finally, after about four hours, one of them called to say that the coast was clear and we could go home.

Although I was young, I knew that Dad's volatile behavior probably wasn't the best strategy for succeeding in life. But my dad couldn't help himself. His general attitude toward authority (which had gotten him kicked out of every institution he had ever been a member of—middle school, high school, the air force), combined with the quality and quantity of cocaine he was now regularly ingesting, resulted in mounds of unfiltered rage.

Doing ridiculous amounts of cocaine must be some kind of prerequisite to becoming a counterculture god. My current theory goes like this: Fame brings lots of people into your life, and with these people comes genuine admiration, and with genuine admiration come gifts, and during the early seventies, most gifts came in the form of drugs. Therefore, if not all, then most of the people who came into our lives at some point handed my dad a little packet of white powder. Although I was meant not to, I usually saw the exchange, but never acknowledged it. I mean, what could I possibly say as I waved at folks leaving our house? Thanks for coming by. Oh no, it's fine. I like it when you bring all those drugs into the house. My life is way more fun when Mom and Dad stay up for days and nights, and end up arguing right outside my door at 3:00 A.M. I mean, what else could I possibly be doing? Sleeping? No, no, really.

The upside of Dad's cocaine use (strangely, there *was* an upside, even for me) was that he'd be up at all hours doing all kinds of stuff, and I could hang out with him. One night I found him in the living room on the floor surrounded by piles of nails, screws, washers, bolts, paper clips, and rubber bands. He was sorting them. He had a little cabinet with about fifteen little drawers in it, and he'd created a system that involved the size, color, and use of each object. He was in his joy. Sorting his stuff was such a joy for him that it ended up becoming the source for one of his most famous routines: "A Place for My Stuff": "That's all I want, that's all you need in life, is a little place for your stuff . . . That's all your house is—a place for your stuff." My dad believed all was right in the world when, and only when, there was a list, a pile, a folder, or a Ziploc bag to contain the chaos of his life.

Even his ideas needed to be contained. Everywhere in our house, for as long as I can remember, there were pads and pens in every room so that when an idea popped into his head, it had a place to go. He would then collect all those notes, organize them into themes, place them in folders, and then build his bits from there. This is how he did fourteen HBO specials of groundbreaking comedy over a forty-year span—he wrote his shit down. Anyway, that late night when I saw him hovering over the piles of nails, screws, washers, bolts, paper clips, and rubber bands, I happily plopped down, learned his system, and got to the task at hand.

Other times in the middle of the night, I'd find him immersed in music. Like my parents, I was a bit of a night owl. I'm not sure why. It might have just been my nature, or it might have been nurture—having spent my first few years on the road. But during this time I suspect that it was because some part of me was always subconsciously on alert for any problems that might arise between my parents. When I couldn't sleep, I'd stand by my door to listen to see if my mom was awake. If I didn't hear her I'd sneak into the living room, and if I was lucky, there'd be my dad bopping his head to an unknown beat that only he could hear through his headphones. I'd stand and watch him until finally he'd notice me and say, "Kel, Kel, you gotta hear this." He'd then place the headphones on my ears. I never knew what to expect. Would it be the groundbreaking sound of the albums *Tubular Bells* or *Switched-on Bach* or the bluegrass soul of Doug Kershaw? Or maybe even Harry Nilsson singing, "You're breakin' my heart/you're tearing it apart/So fuck you"? I'm guessing that not many other ten-year-olds in my neighborhood were being turned on to Harry Nilsson by their parents.

I always listened intently, trying to understand what exactly it was Dad loved about each piece of music he shared with me. I so wanted to be in his head, to understand his world. When Paul Simon's

"Kodachrome" came out, my dad played it over and over again on the big stereo in the living room at full volume. He'd say, "Kel, listen to the harmonies," and then he'd sing with the record, "They give us the greeeeeeeens of summers./Makes you think all the world's/A sunny day, oh yeah." The joy in his face coupled with the purity of those notes created an explosion of love in my heart. To this day I cannot hear that song without thinking of him and those moments. To this day I love the harmonies because of him. Those moments in the middle of the night were like little life rafts in our life of increasing chaos. A safe haven of daddyness.

Although Dad had always shared his music with me, it was during this time that I discovered my own musical tastes. It started when I picked a few albums from his collection and played them for myself. When Dad noticed this, he gave me my own turntable for my room. Dad was an early adopter of technology, and I benefited his entire life from this by being first in line to get all of his technological hand-me-downs. The first album I took into my room was *Sgt. Pepper's Lonely Hearts Club Band.* I played it over and over until I had memorized every word of every song. The song "She's Leaving Home" had a particularly powerful impact on me. Somewhere on the edge of my thinking, I wondered what my parents would do if I'd suddenly disappeared from their life. I didn't want to leave them, just the chaos. It was the first time I ever entertained the thought that I could choose to do something different and separate from them in my life. If I were like the girl in the song who chose to leave, would they understand that my anxiety and loneliness from their drug use and fighting had pushed me out the door? But those thoughts and feelings were way too scary to actually have, so I pushed them somewhere into the basement of my mind. I knew I'd never leave. We were the Three Musketeers.

As music became my sanctuary, I looked outside of my dad's collection for even more music. Every week Dad got *Billboard* magazine, diligently marking where his albums were on the Top 100 Charts, and keeping the pages in a folder. But before he tore the pages out I looked to see what the top songs were, and then got him to take me down to the little record store in the Palisades Village to buy some 45s. Some of my first purchases were "Love Train" by The O'Jays, "Spiders & Snakes" by Jim Stafford, and "Rock On" by David Essex. I know. I know: "Spiders & Snakes," really? What can I say? No doubt my eclectic taste came straight from my dad.

For the first year in the house on the hill, Mom seemed to be happy, which really meant she had more good days than bad. I think it was because she had a project to sink her teeth into—decorating the house. The house was one of those just-built modern homes, and it was all glass. The view was stunning. We were able to see all the way from Santa Monica Bay to downtown Los Angeles. It was an open-concept design that Mom filled with gorgeous modern touches like glass coffee tables and lights that swooped over the couch like drooping orchids. But there was also a fair share of quirky items, too. In the hall powder room, when you sat on the toilet you looked at the dashboard of an old Edsel, steering wheel and all. And in the area that had the dining room table and baby grand piano (a new addition), there was a full-size British phone booth sitting against the wall. Next to that was an old barber's chair with a life-sized carved wooden mannequin that looked like a Native American, and in the corner was a naked male store mannequin. Mom's humor, playfulness, and adventurous spirit were on display everywhere. She was such a joyful being in her essence, which made her dark moods and drinking that much harder to live through. When she was happy, she was a delight. When she was not, she was a nightmare.

As time progressed, so did Mom's drinking. Her behavior got more and more erratic, and Dad and I did our best to manage it. We had secret conversations in which we'd talk about what we might do about it. We usually concluded that there wasn't a whole lot we could do except try to slow her down. We became like the East German secret police, watching her every move, questioning her every motive. This, of course, pissed her off and made her feel we were ganging up on her. We were, but we weren't. We were just trying to get our heads and arms around this force that had taken over her life, our lives—addiction.

Dad, of course, worried about her and my safety when he was on the road, and so he hired a guy, Fred, to help around the house. Fred drove me to where I needed to go and kept an eye on Mom. Although it was Fred's job to watch her, it did little to relieve my hypervigilance. My mind was already so ingrained with ways to manage, change, or work around Mom's increasing dysfunction that I couldn't just turn it off. I didn't know how to fire myself from the position of chief Brenda wrangler. And it wasn't just in the house; I had to try and monitor her while we were out, too. Mom had begun to practice a new form of driving. It wasn't exactly off-road driving; it was more like off-street driving. More than a few times, as we'd make our way up the winding road to our house late at night after dinner at Bill and Elaine's house in Malibu, she'd drive the car up and onto our neighbor's lawn. After she'd done this about half a dozen times, I began to fake being asleep at Bill and Elaine's so that I wouldn't have to get in the car with her. I hoped that she would stay, too, and sleep it off. That rarely happened. She'd usually just leave me there and find her way home on her own.

Fearing she'd really hurt herself or someone else, I began to hide her car keys to prevent her from leaving the house in the first place. That worked the first few times, but then she caught on, and would threaten me if I didn't give them to her. Then I came up with the next strategy: I hid her alcohol from her. One day when she was out, I emptied the shelves of the wet bar, hid the bottles in my closet, and then left the house to go out and play. When she came home and found the shelves empty, she went ape-shit and searched the house. When I came home, she marched me straight to my closet, pointed at the twenty or so bottles of alcohol on the floor, and asked, "Kelly, what the hell is going on here?"

"Um, I don't know," I answered.

"Answer me! What the hell is going on here? Are you some kind of alcoholic?"

Oh, denial, how you make me laugh!

There was laughter. Especially when the TV was on. It seemed that nothing could go wrong with the TV on. I'd crawl into Mom and Dad's bed, get right between them, and we'd watch all the great comedies of the day: *The Mary Tyler Moore Show* (Dad loved Ted Knight's Ted Baxter character), *Laugh-In* (I loved Lily Tomlin's Edith Ann, and did one hell of an imitation of her), and *The Bob Newhart Show* (we all waited for the Mr. Carlin character to show up). But our hands-down favorite was *The Carol Burnett Show*. Carol Burnett was my Danny Kaye. I was around ten or eleven years old when I started to think, Hey, maybe I could do that someday, like my dad had done when he formed his "Big Danny Kaye plan." My thoughts were much more nebulous than his had been, though. I never formed a plan. When I watched Carol (or Lily or Lucy) there was always a rush of energy that made me feel connected to others, and more importantly, connected to something bigger than myself. I wanted to make people feel connected, too. *That* is what made me want to be just like Carol. That, and making my dad laugh.

Although Carol Burnett was my hero, ironically, it was doing an imitation of another cast member that is my earliest memory of really making my dad laugh. Vicki Lawrence's Mama character from "The Family" sketch had a line that went something like, "I don't want to play no god damn Parcheesi!" I mastered this line and could make my dad melt into a pool of laughter whenever I recited it. Making my dad laugh was a conduit straight to nirvana. Hell, just seeing my dad laugh was pure bliss. Maybe that's why *The Carol Burnett Show* was so special to me—every time Tim Conway tried to get Harvey Korman to break in a sketch, my dad laughed so hard he cried. No moment is more perfect than watching the man who makes the world laugh laugh himself.

When we moved to the Palisades, I quickly made friends with my next-door neighbor, Amanda, and her friend Tom. Amanda was the daughter of the guy who worked for the National Security Council. She was a few years older than me, had short blond hair, a perky, flirty personality, and was wicked smart. Although her father worked for the Nixon administration, and her family looked like a "normal" family on the outside, it was just as strange as mine. When I met her, one of her brothers had just returned home from some dustup in Washington, DC. Her father had pulled some strings to get him out of a scrape with the law, or maybe it was the mafia; either way, he was now hiding out on the West Coast. The first thing he did to repay his father was to spell out "Fuck Nixon" on his chest with masking tape and fall asleep in the sun. Once his sunburn set in, he took Amanda and me down the hill for ice cream at Baskin-Robbins in the village. Before he got out of the car, he took his shirt off. He and my dad got along very well.

Yet another brother was also a nice guy, but he had no heels. I was told that a few years before, he'd had a brain operation in which they'd put him in ice, and during the procedure he'd ground down his heels to nothing. I was fine with the big scar on his head; it was his lack of heels that always gave me the willies. To round off the family, Amanda's mom had some kind of degenerative neck problem, which limited her mobility, and so she got to stay in bed all day wearing a neck brace and watching TV. I thought she was the luckiest person in the world.

Amanda's dad, thankfully, was rarely home. He scared me. Not only did he work for the government, but one day we sneaked into his office and found some books that contained horrific photos of dead soldiers who had been torn apart by shrapnel. I may have been able to say the "Seven Dirty Words" in my house, but my dad had always sheltered me from violent films and images. The pictures in those books shattered my innocence. But her dad wasn't all bad—when he came home from his "business trips" abroad, he would bring us beautiful gifts. Most of them came from a faraway place called Iran. Looking back on it now, I realize that he must have been hanging out with the shah and propping up the regime. When the tension in my house got to be too much for me, I'd go over to Amanda's. They may have been a strange family, but at least there wasn't a whole lot of yelling and screaming in their house. One person's weirdness is another person's refuge, I guess.

Tom, my other best friend, lived down the hill, and was really cute. He had sun-bleached hair down to his shoulders, freckles, glasses, and a great smile. I had a crush on him, but didn't know how to have a crush on him because I was a tomboy. Or maybe I was a tomboy because I didn't know how to have a crush on him? Either way, any glimmer I felt of wanting him to kiss me I shoved far away, deep inside my psyche. Focusing on tricking out our skateboards, collecting Wacky Packages (funny stickers that made fun of consumer brands, they came with bubble gum), or playing with our Corgi Toys (high-end British die-cast toy cars) was way easier. The best time I ever had with Tom was the weekend my dad taped *New Year's Rockin' Eve* on the *Queen Mary* in the fall of 1973 (it had been retired to Long Beach in 1967). Tom came with us on the ship for the whole weekend. I thought I'd died and gone to heaven. Not because I got Tom all to myself or because we had the run of the entire *Queen Mary*, or even because we were hanging out with Dick Clark, Billy Preston, and the Pointer Sisters, nope. It was because there was an onboard toy store devoted to selling Corgi cars from the UK. Talk about your sexual sublimation. As Freud used to say, "When is a cigar not a cigar?" When it's a Corgi car.

As I approached my twelfth birthday, my body made the inevitable changes—hair in places I'd never seen it, painful little mounds on my chest, and emotions that felt more like demonic possession than something human. Although Amanda was only two years older than me, her body was way ahead of mine. She was fourteen going on thirty. She already had boobs and hips. While I actively hid my budding sexuality under layers of oversize T-shirts, Levi cords, and Wallabee shoes, Amanda's was front and center. When we were around boys, she just knew how to work it, which made me feel even more invisible than I already felt in my "boyish" body.

Amanda fully embraced her budding womanhood, and did what she could to show me the way. She showed me how to shave my legs, put on eye shadow, and how to use the waterspout in the bathtub for more than just filling it up with water. But still, it wasn't an easy transition for me. And my mom didn't make it any easier. When she saw that I had shaved my legs, she flew into a rage.

"You're too young to shave your legs! Now you're stuck having to do it for the rest of your life! Why didn't you come to me?!"

I broke down in tears, even more ashamed of my body now. I stormed into my room to cry and sulk. But really I was just so mad at her for being mad at me. I wanted to say to her, Sorry, Mom— next time I start puberty, I'll make sure to check your calendar to see if there's an opening somewhere between you and Dad raging and you passing out on the couch.

After that encounter I kept any and all questions, curiosities, and anxieties I had about sex, boys, or my body to myself. The closest our family ever came to "the talk" was when I accidentally walked into my parents' bedroom and saw my dad walk out of the bathroom with an erection. Horror! That sight alone scared me off sex for another four years.

One of my biggest joys during those days was when Amanda and I choreographed skateboard ballets. Living on a steep hill made normal skateboarding rather treacherous. Luckily Amanda had a long and flat driveway—the perfect skateboard-ballet venue. One of our best was a lyrical modern piece we did to the Rolling Stones' "Angie." While we crisscrossed the driveway, we streamed colorful scarves behind us. But the crowd favorite (the "crowd" being our parents) was the one we did to the Beatles' "Maxwell's Silver Hammer," a rather silly romp. Although I loved doing them, I knew there was no future in skateboard ballet, so we turned to variety shows instead. Our tour de force, in the summer of 1974, was a three-ring circus/variety show starring Amanda, Tom, me, and my abundant stuffed-animal collection. We were clowns, acrobats, and had animal acts, too. Gunderilla, my blue-velvet-jumpsuit-wearing stuffed gorilla, stole the show. But of course he did! Who wouldn't, in a blue velvet jumpsuit?

In the summer of 1973 the Carlins hit the road again. Something magical always happened when we went on the road together—all the friction, fighting, and frustration would just melt away. After my dad did a few gigs in New England, we rented a camper van and toured the area. Mom made us stop at every antique store in search of turn-of-the-century medicine bottles, and Dad loved to stop at historical monuments. After a week or so, we ended up in Vershire, Vermont, to visit Uncle Pat and Aunt Marlene. They now lived and worked at a private school/summer camp that catered to rich kids who just wanted to "turn on, tune in, and drop out," but whose parents wouldn't let them. Everyone had long hair, wore tie-dyed shirts, and didn't care for authority. This was a perfect place for my uncle and aunt, since they themselves had definitely turned on, tuned in, and dropped out, and never much cared for authority to begin with. Aunt Marlene ran the kitchen, and Uncle Pat provided "security." The Derek and the Dominos' song "Layla" reverberated throughout the main building. It must have been the only album that the campers had, because I don't remember any other song playing that entire summer. My cousin Dennis and I roamed the forest, learned to play mumblety-peg from the older campers, and bought Mountain Dews and Oh Henry! candy bars at the gas station down the road—the only place to buy anything for miles and miles.

My mom and dad headed out for more gigs, leaving me there for the rest of the summer. By the time they came back, I'd learned to ride a horse, play soccer, and helped write the end-of-summer play. But, my most vivid memory of that summer was seeing all the adults huddled around a little black-and-white TV eagerly watching a bunch of politicians yammer on and on about who-knows-what. Little did I know it was the Watergate hearings, and our parents' dreams were coming true—President Nixon would soon be disgraced and forced out of the White House. The summer of 1973 was rather perfect for all of us.

Another trip we made around that time was a bit less than perfect. Or maybe it was completely perfect. Dad had a bunch of dates in the lower Midwest, so we were flying from gig to gig in small single-engine planes. One day we were flying from Charleston, West Virginia, to somewhere in Pennsylvania. Mom sat in the copilot's seat, as she always did, because she told the pilot that she'd had some flying experience (she loved talking to the pilots, and they always let her fly the plane). Forty-five minutes into the flight, the plane started to get thrown around like it was made of balsa wood. We were skirting the edge of a huge thunderstorm. The pilot was doing his best to get around it, but the storm was faster than we were. The plane pitched and rolled violently, and I clutched my dad. He held me tight.

"We're okay," my mom said as the pilot physically strained to keep the plane level. In a cheerful voice, Dad added, "It's just like a roller coaster. Up. Down. Right. Left. It can be fun if you let it." I was not sold. I began to cry.

The pilot shouted, "Dammit, the radio's gone out!" He turned to my mom. "Take the controls." Mom grabbed onto the controls as they moved about as if they had a mind of their own. The pilot worked on the radio. Mom battled to keep the plane steady. I hid my head in my dad's chest. I was sure we were going to die.

As the ferocious storm tossed us about, Dad held me tightly. "Everything's going to be okay. We're going to be perfectly fine," he kept whispering in my ear. I think he was talking to himself as much as he was to me. After what felt like two and a half eternities, but was more like ten minutes, the pilot finally yelled, "Got it!" He'd fixed the radio. He grabbed his controls, and Mom and he flew through the rest of the storm. Finally a patch of blue sky emerged in the distance, and we flew toward it.

For the next week my mom could barely move her arms. She'd pulled every muscle in her upper body keeping that plane aloft. She saved our lives that day.

Now it was our turn to return the favor.

CHAPTER SIX

This Is the End

BY THE SUMMER of 1974, life in our house on Tellem Drive was like living in a hurricane. There were long periods of buffeting chaos punctuated by respites of calm and normalcy, as if the eye of the storm were passing overhead. Still, I always knew that the calm was temporary, and I'd better prepare for what came next.

Living with this level of uncertainty forced me to create a kind of expertise. Over the years I'd become adept at being able to tell what my parents had been smoking, drinking, and snorting just by looking at them: bloodshot eyes and cottonmouth—pot; pupils pinned and grinding jaw—coke; dark circles under the eyes and slurring speech—booze. When I'd walk in the door coming home after school, or in from playing, I would immediately assess the temperature of the space. Is it quiet? Do I need a knife to cut the tension in the air? Has Dad slept yet? Is Mom coming down, or just getting going? I was like the "addict whisperer."

It really would have been much easier on me if my mom and dad had just had some kind of color-coded flags to raise on the front lawn so I could be warned before I walked in. A green flag might have signified that they were awake, talking to each other, and sober (well, sober-ish—I'm not sure either of them was ever fully sober during this period). A yellow flag might have meant that they were both asleep, which meant I could relax but should be on the alert for when they woke up (who knew what might have happened before they passed out?). A red flag would have been a warning to enter with great caution. Most likely I'd find my dad rearranging his vinyl album collection again (this time by genre, with alphabetical subheadings), which definitely meant that he was high on coke, had been up for quite a while (maybe days), and that Mom was most likely high, too. This would be a tinderbox ready to go up at any moment. Add to this mix the high probability that Mom was also drunk, and the flag waving outside the house should have been an upside-down picture of the Carlins, signifying, "Enter at your own risk—screaming, yelling, and object-throwing imminent."

When Dad wasn't home, leaving Mom and me alone, I had additional criteria to assess the situation: Was Mom awake and cooking dinner? Excellent! Sigh of relief. Was she in her pajamas at 3:00 P.M. and having coffee and a cigarette? Good—but the rest of the day could go either way. Best to be on my toes. Was she in her pajamas at 3:00 P.M. having a scotch and a cigarette? Not so good. When my mom was day-drinking, the house was a minefield. I walked around precariously, avoiding too much in-depth conversation with her, fearing that any contact might create a spark that could ignite a shit storm. "How was school?" she'd ask.

"Fine. I'm going over to Amanda's. Be back later," I'd answer, already out the door, escaping unscathed.

If she was in one of her wine-soaked dark moods, everything was an affront, or a sign of disrespect, or an excuse to bring back to full flame last night's argument or irritation. Little things like leaving my shoes in the living room, or having a messy bedroom, or a certain look on my face might be the trigger. It wasn't consistent or rational. It would inevitably lead to some resentment or bitterness about my dad. Because he and I were partners against her drinking, we both became the enemy.

And it wasn't so much what she said; it was *how* she said it. There was a sharpness in her tone that would cut right through me, making my soul feel like there was no love left inside her. An acidic bitterness laced each word, further deepening the pain of it. I lived in fear of the moments when it would come spewing toward me. When she was in her darkness, which was most of the time in those days, there was no sign of the loving, joyful mother who had loved me unconditionally my first seven years on the planet.

My mission became to find any glimmer of love within her to prove to myself that the love I had seen and felt before was real. I wanted to pull that love back from the abyss. Whenever I saw a sliver of brightness in her eyes, or the hint of softness in her smile— proof that she was in any way approachable—I would do what I could to lure it out even more. I'd make her a drawing or a card to cheer her up. I'd show her my latest dance routine. I'd ask her if she was hungry and bring her some food from the kitchen. I'd even pour her a drink, if that would keep her mood elevated for a few more minutes. But inevitably the chemicals would accumulate in her bloodstream, and she would turn back into the other version of herself, which was unreachable. Dad and I referred to this version of my mom as "Nazi Brenda." It was like a stone wall would build up around her, and I could no longer feel her heart. My stomach would toss and turn, and I would become rigid with anxiety, holding my breath, waiting for the other shoe to drop.

That summer I escaped the turmoil of the house by following Amanda down the hill to audition for a production of *Oliver* at St. Matthew's Day Camp. Although I auditioned to be in Fagin's gang with Amanda, I ended up in the general chorus. I didn't care. I was going to be on a real stage with real people singing real songs! I'd had a little performing experience from piano and ballet recitals at school, but nothing like this.

Fortunately my mom and dad weren't pushy stage parents. Although Mom had lost the chance at her scholarship to Wesleyan to study piano, she never pushed me to fulfill some life she never got to live. She certainly wanted me to be successful, and often pushed me toward things that were outside my comfort zone (which was admittedly quite narrow). But because we were at odds more often than not, I usually resisted on principle anything she suggested. What I really wanted was for my dad to push me instead. He'd say things like, "You can be anything you want. Just do what you want." Which was great on the surface, but coming from the guy who was a god to me, I wanted more. I wanted him to encourage me, see my talent and my gifts, and then take me under his wing and help me fly toward the stars. But since he had felt so much pressure from his own mother trying to mold him into what she wanted him to be, he was determined to let me find my own way.

And that summer I did. For six blissful weeks of rehearsal, I sang and danced my way through "Food, Glorious Food," "Oliver," "Consider Yourself," and "Who Will Buy?" It was a life raft for me. I spent six hours a day either in rehearsal or watching others rehearse. One of the guys from our block, Thomas Newman, was our musical director. He would later follow in the footsteps of his father, Lionel Newman, and become an Academy Award–winning film composer. It was pure bliss. After all the rehearsing, around the end of the summer, we did two shows in the auditorium of Santa Monica High School.

For the opening number, I was in the front row of orphans, spooning my way through a bowl of gruel, singing, "Food, glorious food. Hot sausage and mustard!" My mom was in the audience, sober and genuinely thrilled for me. My dad wasn't in the audience. He was on the road and couldn't make my big debut. I was heartbroken. I so wanted him to see me up there onstage and be proud of me. The only thing that almost made up for it was when a dozen roses and a telegram arrived from him before the show. I was the only person backstage who got either. I felt like a diva.

When the summer was over, it was back to school, and back to the hurricane in the house. More and more my parents were jumping down each other's throats, and I jumped in after them. It often went something like this: Dad would send out the first salvo, usually about Mom's drinking, which then led Mom to bring up Dad's cocaine use. Dad would brush that aside, leaving Mom to bring up the popular topic of the women he must be sleeping with on the road (which was probably true), which always led to who Mom might be sleeping with while she stayed home. Inevitably this led to Mom saying that she wasn't sleeping with anyone or doing anything because there was nothing for her to do, which brought back the tried-and-true topic of how she had nothing to do and nowhere to go, which is probably why she drank so much.

And around and around it would go until I entered the fray. I tried to protect my dad from my mom's alcohol-fueled irrationality by defending his behavior, and I'd protect my mom from my dad's cocaine-laden volatility, and at times violence, by trying to calm him down. When that didn't work, I called their therapist, Al Weinstein. He'd try to scare some reason into both of them. He'd remind them that they were not only damaging themselves with all the drugs and chaos, but that they were damaging me, too. On a good night it would work, and after they hung up the phone with Al, Dad would say, "Come here, you two. Remember, we are the Three Musketeers." And the three of us would hug.

But some nights nothing would reach them, and I'd have to do what I could to shut them up. One night they raged in the hallway, right outside my door.

"I don't fucking have it. You can frisk me if you want!" Mom growled at Dad.

"I know you took it. Where else could it have gone?" Dad asked while he held open a book and riffled through its pages looking for his cocaine stash. Lately he'd been stashing it in books in the bookcase, but it wasn't where he remembered it. I lay in bed and could hear every word through my door.

"Well, it wouldn't be the first time you forgot where you fucking stashed it," Mom answered as she opened another book, hoping it would fall out.

"If you stayed away from my stash, I wouldn't have to hide it," Dad offered.

"Stay out of *your* stash? You're the one who's always taking mine and doing it all."

"Well, I do pay for it."

"Don't fucking start that again." Mom leaped at Dad. Dad grabbed her wrist. She cried out, "You're hurting me!"

I ran and opened the door before it got any worse. "Stop it! Just *stop* it!" I shrieked.

Dad let go of Mom. I said, "Don't hurt her. I'll help you find your fucking—"

"Watch your mouth, young lady—" Mom started.

"Really, Brenda?" my dad said to her.

I interjected, "Can we just please look for the stuff?"

I began to look through the bookcase that was filled with more than six hundred books. I methodically took out a book, shook it, and then moved on to the next one. Dad and Mom followed suit. After about five minutes, Dad held up a small Baggie of coke and exclaimed, "*Be Here Now*! Ram Dass. How could I forget that one?" Finally I could get some sleep, while they got some more "awake."

This endless cycle of arguing and then reconciliation was taking its toll on all of us, and my dad knew it. He didn't know how much more any of us could take. This is when he decided that something needed to change for the Carlins. No, we were not going to family therapy. No, they weren't giving up drinking or drugging. No. Instead we were going on a Hawaiian vacation.

For Easter week of 1975, we went to Maui. It was our very first trip there, and I was very excited. We stayed at the Napili Kai, a fancy resort on the west coast of the island. It had a beautiful, calm bay to swim in, a cute little hut to rent snorkeling gear from, and every night a grand hula show opened with a gorgeous young Hawaiian man blowing on a conch shell. It was a very nice resort, but I couldn't really take it all in because I was stuck in our bungalow, once again refereeing the latest matchup of Carlin vs. Carlin.

It started the second day. We had spent the entire day in a bar in Lahaina so my dad could score some coke and weed. Now, a few days later, Dad had gotten too little sleep, and Mom had gotten too much Mateus rosé, and they were in full-flung insanity. The coke was running low, Mom wanted more, and Dad wouldn't share. They fought, threatened divorce, and argued about every trespass they'd ever committed against each other in their fourteen years together. Then Mom picked up a kitchen knife, and Dad did, too. I screamed and hurled myself between them.

"Stop! Stop! Please, please just stop this—I can't take this anymore." I collapsed in tears on the ground, spent from the endless chaos. "You're making me crazy. CRAZY. I can't be crazy anymore. I can't, I can't."

I must have *looked* crazy, because they dropped the knives, the spell of rage between them broken. Dad rushed to me and hugged me. He turned to my mom in tears. "We can't keep doing this. Look what we're doing. We have to do something different."

Everyone calmed down, and I hatched a plan. I wrote out a UN-style peace treaty that stated, "I, George Carlin/Brenda Carlin, will no longer buy or snort cocaine, drink alcohol, or argue with each other for the rest of the vacation. The undersigned agrees to these conditions so that we can all have a perfect Hawaiian vacation." I even drew those little lines with their names underneath, and they both signed it. All for one, one for all. The Three Musketeers were back. There was a calm, a glimpse of peace. Our Hawaiian vacation could finally begin.

About twenty minutes later Dad went to the bathroom. When Mom went to open the door, it was locked. Mom banged on it and accused Dad of bogarting the blow. He told her, "Don't be ridiculous," but he didn't open the door. Mom then proceeded straight down to the hotel bar and ordered herself another bottle of Mateus rosé. I spent the rest of the vacation as far away from them as I could. I befriended the girl who ran the snorkeling-gear hut, and pretended to her and all whom I met that at least *I* was having the perfect Hawaiian vacation.

Around eleven in the morning the day after we got home from Hawaii, my dad rushed into my room and woke me with the words, "Kelly, I have something important to tell you." Now, these words scared the shit out of me because I was sure he was going to tell me that he was finally leaving my mom. I knew in my heart that it was the only thing that might finally make my mom get some help for her drinking, and so I was ready for it. I sat up in bed and braced myself for the blow of the news, when he said, "Kelly, the sun has exploded and we have eight, no—seven and a half minutes to live."

"What?" I asked, trying to take in this new information.

I knew my father had been doing a lot of cocaine, and God knows what other assorted chemicals in Hawaii, so I thought he was probably just freaking out or something. But he was my dad, and no matter how fucked up he was, he was still my dad, and so I got out of bed and went to have a look.

My parents had very thick curtains in their bedroom to block out the midday sun, so we slowly parted them and made our way through the curtains to the backyard. When we got outside, the sun was blinding. You couldn't even open your eyes. It was too painful even to squint them open. We were like some mole family suddenly thrown into the midday sun. I thought—*My God, I can't see! My God, what if he's right? My God, are we going to die?* I didn't really think so. At least I hoped not. What I was hoping was that there was a very reasonable explanation. I offered up a few: "Maybe it's the smog? Or maybe it's just that LA sun is different from Hawaii sun?"

And then my mother chimed in, "Maybe it's the fact that you

haven't slept for more than four fucking hours in the last three weeks?" She did have a point.

Contrary to how it may have seemed at the moment, my dad was a very rational man. He decided that he needed to check and see if this phenomenon was happening anywhere else on the planet. As he paced in the bedroom, he explained, "We could call Doc in New York, but New York is three hours later, which might mean that the effects of the sun exploding wouldn't be so prominent on the East Coast. No, we need someone on this coast! I'm calling Joe."

So Dad called his old friend Joe Belardino in Sacramento. I sat on the edge of my parents' bed tensely listening as Dad hurriedly explained to Joe what was going on. "Joe, it's George. . . . I need you to do me a favor. . . . Well, I need you to go outside and check and see if the sun is okay. . . . Yeah, I think it may have exploded. . . . Yeah, yeah, I know. . . . Um, do you think you could go now? I don't think we have much time."

With a look of hope on his face, Dad covered the mouthpiece and said, "He's checking."

Now, here was the moment of truth for me: Either the news was bad, and the sun had definitely exploded, but my dad was a genius for being able to calculate something that involved the speed of light! Or the news was good, and the sun hadn't exploded, but my dad had completely lost his mind to drugs, confirming, once again, that the only sane and rational person in this household was an eleven-year-old girl who wanted doughnuts for dinner.

And just like all the other weird shit that made up my daily life, I could not talk about this with anyone, anywhere—especially at school. When I returned to school after the Hawaii trip, the day after the sun had not exploded, my teacher asked, "So, Kelly, how was your Easter vacation?"

Mustering a look of complete neutrality I said, "It was . . . good. Fine. It was fine."

Things were anything but fine, but at least at school I could pretend they were. School was my safe haven. No one there knew anything about my home life, and I didn't know what kind of trouble my parents would have gotten into if my teachers had known. But I would have never ever told anyone—we were the Three Musketeers—one for all, all for one. Besides, my home life was normal to me. I never thought to talk about it with other people or kids. I didn't want my parents to think that I couldn't handle it. From the time I was five years old, my dad and my parents' friends had called me an "old soul." "She's wise beyond her years," they'd say. I had a reputation to uphold.

I'm not sure if I loved school more because it was my safe haven, or because it made me feel special. Mrs. Dresser, the principal, would often take me out of class to meet prospective students and their parents. She'd introduce me as one of the smartest kids in school. I never saw her pull anyone else out of class, so I concluded that I wasn't *one* of the smartest, but *the* smartest kid in school. This didn't make me feel superior to my classmates per se. I mean, I never had the thought, Oh, I'm smarter than they are—but it did make me feel different in a good way.

I liked most of the subjects at school, but I loved math. Unlike my home life, where the answers to problems were out of my grasp, math had problems that I could always solve. My math teacher, Ms. Wildman (whom I ate lunch with most days of the week), said that she would have to read up on algebra just to stay ahead of me. I was starved for solutions, and math fed me. For seven hours a day I didn't think about my mom's drinking or my dad's unhappiness, I just reveled in being able to solve for X.

All my teachers were great, and even my bus driver, Kathe, was cool—she'd blare the rock-and-roll station on the radio and stop at Marquez Liquors, the liquor store at the bottom of my hill, so we could buy snacks (Funyuns and Wacky Packages were my two staples) on our way home. But climbing on the school bus at the end of the day was not all fun. As we headed up Lachman Lane toward my house, I'd get really quiet. By the time we took the right onto my street, the pit of my stomach would sink like a rock. As I got off the bus, I'd look at our front door and start to wonder: Are they asleep? Are they fighting? Are they alive?

At the beginning of 1975, sometime during the cold of the New York winter, my grandma, Mary, had come out for a three-week vacation. Three weeks turned into three months, and three months turned into six. She and Mom had become drinking buddies. Mary, the master manipulator, fed my mom's bitterness by whispering into her ear all the ways that my father had disappointed her as a mother (never mind that she bragged about him to every person she encountered), and how, therefore, he must be a horrible husband, too. She'd do this as she was pouring my mom another glass of wine. Avoiding my mother and her moods was challenging enough for me. Avoiding my grandmother and her twisted sense of entitlement was another matter. One day Amanda and I decided to boil a few ears of corn to eat. My mother always reminded me to ask my grandma if she needed anything, so I asked her if she wanted to join us for our snack. Per her usual routine, she gave her, "Oh, no. I'll be fine. I don't need a thing" answer, so Amanda and I carried on making our own snack. A few hours later, after I'd been playing outside, I came home to find my mother sitting with my grandma and fuming. "I can't believe how selfish you are!"

Confused, I replied, "What? What are you talking about?"

"Your grandmother told me that you and Amanda made some corn and didn't even ask her if she wanted anything."

I was stunned, perplexed, and stunningly perplexed. What the fuck was she talking about? I defended myself immediately. "Yes we did! I asked her if she wanted anything, and she said she was okay."

My grandmother sat there with this disappointed look on her face, like she was saying, You poor child. You should be ashamed of yourself. My mom said, "Apologize."

"But I didn't do anything wrong! She's lying."

"Don't call your grandmother a liar."

Had these people lost their mind? Clearly, yes. I tearfully apologized, feeling more rage than I'd ever felt in my life.

Not long after that, for Mother's Day, Dad and I took my mom and Mary to Will Rogers State Park for a picnic. The house was now clearly divided: Brenda and Mary vs. George and Kelly. After about an hour it became clear to my dad that the two of them were going to be drinking their way through the picnic, so he said to me, "Let's take a walk." Because things had gotten so weird at home, my dad had been trying to find ways to make my life more normal. One day, he came home with a baseball bat, ball, and glove so he and I could have some quality time together playing. It was so cute. He was trying to learn how to be some idea of a "good dad." I might have been a tomboy, but I had no wish to play baseball. But the fact that he made the effort to buy them and carve out time for us together still warms my heart. So I was more than happy to take my dad up on the offer to walk around Will Rogers, and find something fun to do. As we walked up the hill away from the polo grounds, I saw the horse barns and practice rings. A woman, the trainer, was teaching a riding class of about five or six girls. As we got closer, I felt a blossom of excitement in my chest. It reminded me of Vermont. We watched the lesson for a while, and then Dad said, "You want to do that? Take a lesson?" It was like he read my mind. But unsure about almost everything in the world that day, I only shrugged my shoulders and said, "I think so."

He went on, "I think it would be great for you. You loved those horses in Vermont. What do you think? Should we give it a try?" I smiled and nodded my head yes. Before I knew it, Dad got the attention of the trainer, Jill, and asked her about lessons. We set an appointment for me to be there the next Saturday for a beginner's lesson.

The entire summer, I spent practically every waking moment at that barn learning how to post the trot properly, clean hooves, braid manes, and forget about the hurricane at home.

By the end of the summer of 1975, the damage to the Carlins was palpable. My mother barely ate, or bathed, or bothered to get out of bed. I was now calling down the hill to Marquez Liquors to order cases of wine for her. With Dad on the road a lot, there was no one to come between my mother screaming from her bed for me to bring her another glass of wine, and my dutifully bringing it to her. I knew it was killing her, but what choice did I have?

Things had been escalating for months. One night she hallucinated that the entire LAPD SWAT team had surrounded our house. She'd heard a noise, looked out the peephole in the front door, and saw blue-and-red lights everywhere. She thought that cops in cars and helicopters were everywhere. Luckily I was not there that night. Another night, when I came home from a friend's house, the therapist Al Weinstein was there. My mother had returned from a visit to a psychic on the Santa Monica Pier, and had come home and begun writhing and speaking in tongues. Al said she'd probably been hypnotized, but who really knows?

On yet another night, after I had hidden the keys to the car, my mom found them after I went to sleep, and drove my dad's brand-new BMW 3.0 down to her favorite watering hole, the San Ysidro Inn. When she got into the car to come home, instead of driving straight out of the driveway, she reversed the car straight through their lobby. The cops were called, and she got her second DUI. Strangely, the police officer who had arrested her did not show up for the court date, and the charges were dropped. Thank you, expensive Beverly Hills lawyer man.

By mid-August, Mom was down to eighty-seven pounds. She crawled to make it to the bathroom, and took in nothing more than water and wine. Her hands shook so badly that she could barely drink a drop. She had already been hospitalized once in the last year for malnutrition, but now the doctor gave her three weeks to live. Dad and I begged and begged her to go to rehab.

After a week she finally agreed to go, but she truly believed she would die there. She felt there was no hope. This was before Betty Ford. This was when rehab was the mental ward. Literally. At St. John's Hospital in Santa Monica, their Chemical Dependency Center was in its infancy, and its patients were housed in the psych ward.

On August 17, 1975, my mom left our house thinking she was about to die. The doctors and counselors at St. John's thought she just might do that, too. They didn't know what to do with someone who had a triple addiction to cocaine, alcohol, and Valium. They put her on antiseizure drugs hoping that the detox wouldn't kill her. I knew none of this. I was just relieved to know that finally something might change.

CHAPTER SEVEN

Sober-ish

FOR CHRISTMAS OF 1975, my alive, sober, and doing-pretty-damn-well mother insisted on getting the three of us out of town. In the past, Christmas Day with the Carlins was always abundant and joy filled. Mom bought way too many presents, and they were exactly what you wanted. Mom was Mother Christmas.

But this Christmas, because she was just getting her bearings in her newly sober life, she needed a break. Besides that, I'm not sure she wanted to replicate the Christmas from the year before. It went well enough on the actual day, but it didn't end well. Technically it almost didn't end at all. It wasn't until the week after Valentine's Day that my mother finally managed to take the tree and trimmings down. And thank God. Not only was the tree a major fire hazard, but I didn't know what to say to Amanda and Tom after mid-January had passed and the stockings were still hung with care.

So off to Hawaii we went. More specifically, the Kahala Hilton on Oahu—the place where "Hollywood" went for their Christmas paradise in the 1970s. And it *was* paradise. There were dolphins swimming in the inner lake of the hotel, poolside waitresses willing to bring my mom and me virgin strawberry daiquiris all day long, and most important, no drug-induced insanity for miles around. I was very, very happy that I was finally getting my perfect Hawaiian vacation.

At the Kahala Hilton we saw no cocaine, no alcohol, and no knives being brandished. Instead we got Steve Lawrence, Eydie Gormé, and Sammy Davis, Jr. Unbeknownst to us when we booked our room there, Steve and Eydie and Sammy were doing a New Year's Eve show in the ballroom, and because we were who we were and they were who they were, we got to sit with them at their table for dinner that night. I remember it well: Eydie Gormé looking glamorous in her light-blue chiffon dress; Steve Lawrence persuading me, the pickiest eater in the world, to eat something that looked like onion rings. It was octopus. Yuck! But the octopus was quickly made up for by the show, which was a perfect seventies-trying-to-be-hip-but-oh-so-schmaltzy Steve and Eydie, with the highlight of the night being Sammy Davis, Jr., singing "The Candy Man."

After the show we all stood around schmoozing. I hung out with my dad and Sammy Davis, Jr. They talked about all that had been going on in their lives, and my dad mentioned my mom's recent sobriety and both their battles with cocaine. Sammy chimed in about his own troubles with it, and how he was trying to move on from its insanity, too. Although I was only twelve years old, I stood there listening, nodding, and relating to what they said. I certainly knew the all-too-harsh reality of cocaine's promise of paradise.

Being there with my dad and Sammy that night after the show was the first time that I felt like I belonged. For most of my life, when I was backstage I felt invisible. Normally when Mom, Dad, and I walked into a room, all eyes moved to my father. Then people with faces beaming and hands outstretched would move toward him, telling him something they loved about him (usually a line from his show, which they would try to say just like him, and which always made me cringe) or, they handed him a gift: My favorite was a tie-dyed T-shirt with a drawing of what I assumed was my father's likeness, but because it looked more like a combination of Jesus and

Charles Manson, I was never truly sure. My mother and I would then be introduced, and people would politely spend a nanosecond of time with us, but then we'd quickly be forgotten. It was as if we had just disappeared. Well, not always. Sometimes Mom got attention because she was seen as a potential conduit to Dad, and even if the person couldn't be "George's new best friend," it was almost as good to say that they were "Brenda's new best friend."

But for me it was different. In order for me to feel seen, I'd have to work it. We'd be backstage in some college town, and Dad would be surrounded by well-wishers, and I, feeling small and ignored, would come up to them and just wait. Then some person might glance at me, unsure of who this child was, and I'd think, *You don't know who I am, do you?* Then I'd touch my father, or ask him a question, as if to say to the doubter of my status, "I'm with him." The other person would smile at me with comprehension in their eyes, and I would then feel safe and seen, and think, *Yes, now you understand. Now you know who I am,* believing that my status, my connection to the crackling luminosity surrounding my father, had been affirmed in their eyes. Not understanding yet that in reality, I was only trying to affirm my own status in my own eyes.

As my mom, dad, and I emerged out of the dark age of their chemical-fueled chaos, we weren't quite sure who we would become in the future, but at least now we knew we had one. It felt like our new life had arrived in a *Poof!* It was as if an evil spell had been broken. It was like we'd lived in a fairy tale and the wicked witch of addiction had traumatized our small village with her spooky evil force, and then, *Poof!* she was gone. We slowly walked away from our past with our hearts feeling a combination of confusion and relief; the new calm and peace alien to us, and strangely, almost as difficult as the old way. I was just unsure if I should trust it.

My mom had no doubt. She didn't just survive rehab; she conquered it. She was now an Alcoholics Anonymous rock star—

attending meetings (what seemed like twelve hours a day, seven days a week) and pulling drunks out of skid row and onto their feet. Her sponsor, Tristram Colcutt III, an ex-pill-junkie who had been a renowned neurosurgeon, taught her rigorous honesty, how to have fun while sober, and the importance of service. She was alive, happy, and glowing. She once again had a purpose. She had a life.

My dad? Well, he was sober-ish. He continued to party on the road, but quit doing drugs at home. Mom didn't expect him to follow her to rehab, but she was adamant about what was and was not allowed in the house—weed was fine (it wasn't her drug of choice)—cocaine was not. He was good with that. He certainly knew enough to not come home coked up to the gills in front of someone who had just scraped and clawed her way out of the clutches of death. Plus, he'd have done almost anything to make sure that Mom stayed sober. In fact, he did. Before she came home from rehab she had only one ultimatum: Mary had to leave. Dad, only too happy to oblige, rushed back to the house, packed Mary's bags, and within a few hours escorted her onto a plane back to New York. Queen Mary's reign of terror was over.

Dad, as always, was busy with his career. During the fall of 1975, he was on the road promoting his two newest albums, *Toledo Window Box* and *An Evening with Wally Londo, Featuring Bill Slazso*. He also hosted the first episode of some experimental NBC show called *Saturday Night Live*. Knowing that he didn't want to be in any of the comedy sketches that filled the show, he asked if he could do two monologues instead. He did a bit about airports (which is eerily prescient about airport security today), and a bit about religion. Although they cut out the more controversial parts, it was incendiary enough for New York Cardinal Terence Cooke's office to call the station and demand that they pull the plug on him.

And me? What was I doing now that Mom was sober? Well, suddenly, at age twelve, I was no longer the only adult in the household. All the many skills I had mastered over the years—denial, caretaking, and crisis management—were no longer necessary. I had been downsized. No longer did I have to referee drug-inflamed arguments at 3:00 A.M. No longer did I have to hide my mother's car keys. No longer was I responsible for my parents' happiness and safety. It was all finally over.

And I had no idea what the fuck to do with myself.

When my dad hit adolescence, he had been a rebellious, street-smart kid who had his "Danny Kaye plan." When my mom hit adolescence, she had been a conforming, book-smart kid with her "I'm going to get the fuck out of Dayton someday" plan. When I hit adolescence, I was a perfect combination of them both: I was a conforming and rebellious, book-smart and street-smart kid.

But I had no plan.

I did have a "sort of" plan, though: Westlake School for Girls. After years at my freewheeling Santa Monica Montessori School, and a free-for-all household, I felt an intense need to balance the scales with nightly homework, school uniforms, and final exams. I was twelve years old and in my last year at Montessori. I knew I had to go somewhere, and I knew it wasn't going to be public school.

The thought of public school terrified me. I knew what happened out in the harsh, real world. I'd seen it on TV. One night I caught the TV movie *Born Innocent* with Linda Blair, and after watching her being raped with a broom handle, I assumed that this is what happened in all public institutions. Therefore I decided no public schools in my future. Of course, with hindsight, I'm sure my decision had nothing to do with actual broom-handle raping, but something way more terrifying to me—not being special.

Westlake School for Girls was an elite college prep school nestled in the bosom of the hills of Bel-Air, filled with young women obsessed with Louis Vuitton purses. I was forced to learn new words like "Halston," "Gucci," and "Fiorucci." The first few months, I walked the halls in fear that these young women would discover that I didn't know anything about their precious world. Suddenly the most important thing determining whether or not I was worth knowing was what label I had on my shoes. Even though my dad was famous and made pretty good money, we were not like these people. My father's fame had come from pressing hard up against the status quo to see if it would break. These people *were* the status quo, and I wanted nothing to do with them. I discovered I was a snob about snobs.

Luckily, as with all institutions, there's always a small group of people who are bristling against its values. I found those people quickly. Creatively I immediately bonded with a girl who was very funny and smart—Carrie Hamilton. When I found out who her mother was—Carol Burnett—I nearly died. But to me she didn't need her mother's status to have status. Carrie was fearless and really knew who she was, and I wanted some of that. She and I sat around the lunch tables for hours and plotted our future: our very own variety show—the *Carlin/Hamilton Hour*. We came up with characters, sketch ideas, but mostly we just made each other laugh. And I *so* needed to laugh. I needed to drink up the freedom and joy of not having a care in the world while distracting myself from the discomfort of adolescence. But even Carrie wasn't enough to soothe my screaming hormones, unexpressed rage, and free-floating anxiety. That took something a bit stronger. I found my people for that, too.

One day, my friend Piper and I were soaking up some rays after lunch. Knowing we had twenty minutes before the bell rang, I said, "I am so dying for a ciggy. The seniors are so lucky. They can leave campus anytime they want."

Piper replied, "I've got keys to my friend Beth's car."

I thought about it for a minute. "We can't leave campus. If we're caught—"

"We don't have to leave. All you have to do is get in her car, turn the air-conditioning on, and take a few puffs."

I had already started to sneak a few cigarettes at the barn where I rode horses, but that was easy. No one who cared was around. Smoking at school felt insane. Westlake had piles of arcane rules that mostly entailed limiting the exposure of our legs: Socks—blue or white only; hems—no shorter than six inches above the knees; tights—not allowed. If you were caught "out of uniform" you'd get a mark; enough marks and it would affect your GPA.

I thought that if they had so many rules about what I had to wear on my legs, I couldn't even imagine the medieval punishment they'd concoct for smoking. But there I was, on a cool winter day with the keys in my left hand and a ciggy hidden in my right, walking toward the white Datsun 240Z, about to smoke this cigarette no matter what.

Just a few months before, I'd been the kid hiding my mom's alcohol, writing nasty messages on her cigarettes, and muttering to myself that I would never ever be like "them." But as I got in the car I felt the terror of getting caught being eclipsed by the thrill of breaking the rules. As I turned on the air-conditioning, I felt the exhilaration that comes with claiming the powerful space where the grown-ups and their rules were no longer present. As I lit the cigarette I felt a shift in my internal world—the old Kelly was no longer welcome, and the new one said, Here I am.

Within a year I was stealing roaches from my dad's stash and smoking weed every day. Piper and I would find ways to sneak down the Nature Trail (an area of overgrown trees and bushes on campus) during a free period to take hits off a joint. Getting buzzed took the edge off the crushing academic pressure and the cliquish and insidious superficiality of Westlake School for Girls.

To make matters worse, my dad was making my life at Westlake even more miserable. He could never manage to get me to school in time for the beginning of first period.

"Oh, look who has decided to join us again!" my British History teacher, Mr. Smith, would remark when I walked in late, six minutes after the bell. His snide comments hurt because I really liked him. And I really wanted him to like me. But even though my father wrote him many notes that my tardiness was not my fault, my grade was lowered. It was the only C I ever received, and I blamed my dad.

This was new for me. I'd never felt angry at my dad before.

By the winter of ninth grade I just wanted out. My parents knew this, and we'd already started looking at new schools. When I told my parents that there was a class trip to Yosemite Valley in February, I was sure I wouldn't have to go. They never made me do things I didn't want to do. Well, Mom might have made me do a *few* things I didn't want to do, but Dad certainly didn't. And I didn't want to go to Yosemite. Being with strangers away from my parents terrified me in general. I still had horrible separation anxiety, and rarely even slept over at a friend's house. I'd end up calling late at night to get my mom to come and take me home. Even though my mom was now sober, my anxiety had not lessened but increased. And I had something new to worry about—my dad's heart.

At the beginning of ninth grade, my mom unexpectedly picked me up midday. "Your dad's in the hospital," she said, answering the confused look on my face. I began to tear up.

She touched my hand. "He's fine. They just want to do some tests on his heart." But I could tell she was really worried when she said, "He just needs to rest a few weeks." No one ever said the words "heart attack," but that was what it was. They thought it was related to his cocaine abuse. Even though he had curtailed his usage somewhat, he was still abusing it. This event set him on a path of eventually quitting completely. And he did recover. He was lucky it was a minor incident.

Now, a few months later, after I mentioned the Yosemite trip to my parents, my mom said predictably, "It'll be good for you. You might learn something about yourself." I didn't fight her because I knew that in the end I would not be going. I knew that in the eleventh hour, my dad would come to my rescue like he always did. The night before the trip, when my mom still wouldn't budge, I began to cry. I knew that if I cried, Dad would rush in and save the day. Mom saw my tears as a ploy.

"You're fourteen years old. These tears are no longer going to work. You will be fine. You'll probably have a good time once you get there," she said.

"I just don't want to go," I managed to get out between gulps and sobs. "I just don't want to go." Not having any better reason than that in my corner, I went another three or four rounds with Mom. Finally my dad came in.

"Take a few breaths," he said. Thankful that he was there, I did. "You know, Kiddo, I think it would be good for you to get away from us. To find out who you are away from here. I think your mom is right, and you should go."

What? This sentence was more shocking than the one he spoke to me the day he thought the sun had exploded. "I think you should go"? Dad was agreeing with Mom? I wailed, gnashed my teeth, and, I'm pretty sure, threw my body on the ground in some kind of act of insanity, hoping they'd think that I'd come unhinged and needed serious psychiatric help; anything not to get on that bus.

But in the end none of it worked. At 6:00 A.M. the next morning, I clenched my rage-filled tears back as I was forced to get on a bus with my fellow classmates to be taken hundreds of miles away from my home in the middle of the winter into the damn forsaken wilderness called Yosemite Valley.

After crying my eyes out for the entire six-hour bus ride through the foggy, hideous San Joaquin Valley, we arrived in Yosemite Valley to discover the ultimate insult—our cabins had no bathrooms. To pee in the middle of the night, we had to go out in the cold, wintry air and find the public bathrooms. After they warned us that there might be bears in the area, I secretly hoped I would be eaten by one so that my mother would have to live with the guilt for the rest of her life. Why I didn't want my dad to feel this guilt, I do not know.

The first morning we met our guide, Felix. I was quite sure he was a madman. He had a scraggly beard and hair, wild brown eyes, and wore a beret à la Che Guevara. He spoke excitedly about eating bugs for survival, and I feared he'd make this group of stuck-up, privileged daughters of Hollywood do just that as some sort of victory for the proletariat! I was positive he'd torture us in innumerable ways all week long. I wanted to pull him aside to say, Hey, I'm not really like these girls. Look, my dad is George Carlin. Get it? I am not like these girls. I'm part of the counterculture. I even once helped my dad through a really bad acid trip. Don't you understand? I'm special.

But that day I didn't say any of that. Thankfully Felix didn't make us eat any bugs. He did, however, make us hike sixteen miles on that first day.

The second day, Felix took us on a hike alongside the Merced River. After a few miles we stopped to eat, and one of our teachers asked us to write in our journals after lunch. Ugh. I hated journal writing. It always felt like the world was looking over my shoulder as I wrote.

In order to do my dutiful writing, I decided to cross the Merced River via a very large fallen tree. I'd seen several of my classmates do this, and it seemed like fun. Then the trip suddenly became even more painful than it already was—I fell straight into the icy grasp of the Merced. After breaking a thin layer of ice and plunging about three feet down, I somehow shot my body straight up and out of the water. And I do believe that I actually walked on water to get back to shore. I would have pointed out this miracle to the others, but the realization that I was going to have to strip naked in the woods to change into my thin rain pants quashed any urge to draw attention to my sudden Christ-like powers.

Day two: still not happy.

On day three we hiked to an area that had evidence of the native people who used to occupy this land—the Ahwahneechee. It was the first thing in this whole trip that actually sounded interesting to me, until I was told that the evidence of the Ahwahneechee were paintings in caves. I don't like caves. I don't like caves because they take so much effort to interact with—you need artificial light, you need a strap and rope to hold you so that you don't plummet to your death, and essentially you need the belief that climbing down into the belly of the earth is a good idea. My theory is that because of all the effort it takes, God doesn't really want us bothering with them. And even though I had just walked on water, I was not one to argue with God. Therefore I decided this was a good time to redeem my "special" privilege—I told my teachers and Felix that I did not like small spaces. The minute I did this a few more girls, and even a teacher, also chimed in about their discomfort with caves, and so a small group of us were relieved of having to go. I was feeling good now. That is, until another guide, Peggy, said in an overly cheerful voice, "Hey, I've got a great idea! I'll stay with you guys and teach you some Indian songs."

Damn. Why can't these people just leave me the fuck alone?

Peggy led us to a spot that overlooked the whole valley. It was the most magnificent view on earth. In one glance I saw Half Dome, El Capitan, three different waterfalls, and the bluest sky I'd ever seen. We sat in a small circle, and she told us about the Ahwahneechee customs and rituals. Then she began to sing: "Wicha tie tie, Heemoo aye, Ahwahneechee, Ahwahneechee, no aye. Water spirits springing singing round my head, makes me feel glad that I'm not dead."

I couldn't help but think about my brush with the Merced River the day before—"makes me feel glad that I'm not dead."

She asked us to sing along. We did so—reluctantly. Like most adolescents we were caught somewhere between falling into the moment, and having complete disdain for it. But before I knew it, I was looking out at the splendor of the valley below and singing with the others in a round, "Wicha tie tie, Wicha tie tie, Heemoo aye, Heemoo aye." But not wanting to spoil the illusion of my misery, I made extra sure I looked like I wasn't enjoying it.

On the last night we all went to a community center to do some square dancing. One would think that this group of angst-ridden rich girls would not have taken too kindly to this. But something had happened. I don't know if it was the fresh air or the magnificent display of nature, or the fact that we had been away from our neurotic West LA lifestyle for five days, but we jumped into it with abandon.

We enthusiastically learned the moves, clapped our hands, and giggled our way through the whole evening.

Instead of taking the bus back to the cabins, a few of us decided to walk. The air was very cold and crisp, with nothing around us but empty trees, the moon, and the stars—millions of stars. At first we walked in silence—what group of fourteen-year-old girls can do that? And then quietly I began to sing, "Wicha tie tie, Heemoo aye, Ahwahneechee, Ahwahneechee, no aye." After a few times the others got the words and joined in. Soon our voices were one with the stars, and the air, and the moon rising over El Capitan. I felt myself stretched wide open. I was bigger than my thoughts. I was more than my body. Everything was perfectly placed. I felt a part of something, connected, not alone anymore. *Wow!* Why hadn't someone told me that all this had always been here for me? I felt a hope, a glimmer of light, a plan of some kind, and thought, *If there was a plan for all of this, then maybe there was a plan for me, too?*

CHAPTER EIGHT

Häagen-Dazs and Sinsemilla

"QUAALUDES!" CHRIS N. SCREAMED as he threw what looked like a handful of pills into the middle of the classroom floor. As they landed, everyone jumped out of their seats, snatching them off the ground. Art, the math teacher, chuckled. "Okay everyone, let's get back to the problem on the board." He'd seen right away that they were just candy hearts for Valentine's Day. I sat at the back of the class, grinning and observing. I was checking out a new school, Crossroads School for the Arts and Sciences, to see if it was where I wanted to go for high school. I'd had a strong inkling that this was the school for me. After that display, I had no doubt.

I'd been hanging out with kids from Crossroads for a few years now. My new best friend, Vickie, whom I'd met riding horses, went there. Vickie and I, from day two of meeting, had become inseparable. The first day we met, I did not like her. We were both in a riding class when she turned around and sneered. "Don't get too close to my horse. He kicks."

Bitch.

But as Vickie and I hung out that summer of 1975 at the little barn at Will Rogers State Park, I realized she was anything but a bitch. She saw the world much as I did, through a goofy but some-times wickedly funny lens. We laughed a lot. Laughter and horses were the medicine that got me through my mom's initial recovery and my years at Westlake. Now, three years later, Vickie and I were practically living at each other's houses, and that's how I became good friends with her brother, Peter, who was also a Crossroadian.

When I first met Peter, I didn't like him. He picked on Vickie, whined incessantly to his parents for money, and was obsessed with status symbols. I thought the girls at Westlake were snobs, but I had never seen a guy so consumed by his Fila shirts and coiffed hair. But that was soon ignored. One thing led to another, and be-fore I knew it, we were pooling our money weekly to score weed, and then smoking it in the bushes at Rustic Canyon Park across the street from his parents' house. Although he was my age he was over six feet tall, so he always felt a bit like an older brother natu-rally looking out for me and protecting me. He had a wicked sense of humor, and I quickly folded myself into his group of friends and found my new home.

Crossroads was also an elite college-prep school. But unlike Westlake, it was not nestled in the bosom of Bel-Air. No. Crossroads straddled a dirty alleyway in Santa Monica. The school occupied three buildings among other industrial businesses. One of which was an auto body shop. We could hear the clanging and whizzing of tools all day long. It wasn't so bad. The guys who worked there would at least let us bum smokes from them. Yes, it was 1978, and with a note from our parents, we at Crossroads were allowed to smoke cigarettes on campus. Of course that's not all we smoked. Any free period I had, I would hop into a car with Kirk, or Peter, or Lisa, or Andy, or Chris, or any other stoner, and go and smoke a joint. Being stoned at school was the norm. Amazingly, it did little to impede my academics. I got As in all of my classes, including AP Chemistry and Physics. It turned out that taking a bong hit was the perfect preparation for my trigonometry and geometry homework. But the one class it didn't help with was English. It was already difficult enough for me to express myself, and being high did not facilitate articulation. Except for one day.

That day a friend and I decided to take magic mushrooms in the middle of the school day. I rarely did something this crazy. I did have limits. So I didn't eat a lot, just a few bites. Then we went to English class. When forty-five minutes had gone by and they hadn't come on, I figured that they were bad or stale. I left class to go to the bathroom. As I walked down the hall everything was fine, but when I sat down in the stall, the walls began to move as if they were breathing. As the walls slowly inhaled and exhaled, I knew I was fucked. I couldn't ditch class—I really needed to keep up my GPA (this was eleventh grade, and college applications were looming). So I went back into class, trying to maintain my composure.

I quietly sat down on the floor in the corner (this was a very casual school, where you could sit at a desk, or on a couch, or on the floor) hoping to just ride out the last fifteen minutes of class. We were studying *The Great Gatsby* at the time, and I hadn't read the chapters for that day's discussion. Katherine, our teacher, asked the class, "In this first section, what does the moon symbolize to Gatsby?" I had no idea, and clearly no one else did either—there were just blank stares and quiet from everyone. It was late afternoon, and no one, not even the sober kids, wanted to be there. I knew I certainly couldn't answer because suddenly there was a roiling sea of orange shag carpeting crashing up against Katherine's ankles (I'm pretty sure that the whole purpose of ugly 1970s shag carpeting was just for the amusement of people on psychedelics). As the orange bobbed up and down, I became lost in the idea that the whole surface of the earth was really this liquid—nothing was really solid. I wasn't solid. Katherine wasn't solid, nor was F. Scott Fitzgerald.

I snapped out of my reverie when I heard my name. "Kelly? What do you think the moon symbolized to Gatsby?" My eyes slowly made their way up from Katherine's ankles wading in the liquid shag carpet to her now-blue reptilian face. I took a beat and said, "The illumination of his love for Daisy?" Katherine looked at me, studied my face, and I knew she could tell that I was about three feet to the left of my own body. A rush of anxiety came over me. *This is it,* I thought. *I'm finally going to be busted for getting high at school,* when a smile came across her face and she said, "Very good, Kelly," and turned around and wrote it on the blackboard. Phew.

Even though I'd found my "crowd" at Crossroads, I got along with almost everyone. Because I was in all the AP science classes, I felt at home with nerds who were now doing something called "programming a computer." One time they programmed the computer to display the shape of a sexy woman. The woman was made up entirely of the text, "Kelly is a Sexual Goddess," written hundreds of times. I was flattered and mortified.

Because I was creative, I also loved hanging out with the kids in the Drama Department. I still longed to be on a stage, to be Carol Burnett someday, but with all my partying with friends and the training of my seven horses, six days a week, at the barn in Malibu that my parents had just bought as a business investment, I was too busy to pursue acting or comedy. I was moving up the ranks of the equestrian show circuit, raking in ribbons up and down the state of California, thus too busy for the rigors of the Drama Department. I felt that many of those kids knew what they wanted and where they were going. I don't know if that's true, but some did end up directing films (Michael Bay) and writing on big sitcoms (*Friends*) in the eighties and nineties. Some seemed to have had a clear plan for their lives (much like my dad's "Danny Kaye plan"), and they were on their way to fulfilling it. I, too, had finally stumbled upon a plan of sorts: Step one—wake up, step two—place bong in mouth, step three—repeat as often as necessary.

I filled the void of my teenage unease with everything and anything I could get my hands on, which was really good timing on my part since, at that same time, my dad was filling a very large bucket of guilt with yeses. When my dad was leaving for *The Tonight Show* one afternoon, I shouted out, "Dad, for my sixteenth birthday can I have a Jeep with a four-inch lift kit and those cool KC lights?"

"Yes, of course," he replied. "But don't forget—be safe."

While talking to him on the phone when he was on the road somewhere in the Midwest I asked, "Dad, can I have another horse? This one is for Junior Jumpers, and it can jump six feet!"

"Yes, of course," he said, and then added, "But, don't forget—have fun."

On my way out to school one winter morning in the eleventh grade, I casually said, "Dad, can I have a hundred bucks to go buy some weed?"

"Yes, of course," he answered. "But don't forget—when you get home leave me a few joints in my office."

I had the coolest dad ever. It was the only way he knew how to be a dad. He didn't know any other way. How could he? He'd never had a father of his own; and he was, at his core, a rebellious teenager himself. Plus he carried an enormous guilt for those dark years on Tellem Drive. He wanted to erase the pain by giving me anything and everything. He just wasn't wired to be the hard-nosed dad.

While my high school escapades were going full speed, my dad's career was losing traction. After his minor heart attack in 1978, he began to feel a bit lost. When he spoke about this time in his life he said, "Given the chance to bend back around toward the middle, I took it." After his meteoric rise with *Class Clown* and culture-shifting "Seven Dirty Words," he was back doing TV shows like the *Tony Orlando and Dawn Show* to pay the bills. With a barn full of horses, a driveway full of German cars, and an expensive new house, there was a lot of pressure to maintain the lifestyle.

About six months after my mom got out of rehab, we moved a few miles east of our old place into a ranch-style home on Old Oak Road in an area called Brentwood. It was a bit out of Dad's price range, but Mom cried, and so we moved in. She told me that she'd never done anything like that before, but that's how good this place was: It was worth crying for. And Dad knew how important it was for us to move on from the house on the hill where all our dark days had occurred. I remember after the movers had moved all the furniture out of the house on Tellem Drive, my dad took me up there to say good-bye. He thought it was important to make a conscious ritual out of it. I walked through every room giving each a teary farewell, knowing I'd never have to endure that kind of pain and terror again. We said good-bye to it all.

But by 1979, with the success of *Saturday Night Live, Monty Python*, and Steve Martin, my dad was no longer the shiny new thing on the comedy scene. He'd become an institution, part of the establishment, something even other comedians could make fun of. *SCTV* did a parody of him, with Rick Moranis imitating him going on and on about beets: "Beets. Beets. Beets. Beats me." Dad was no longer cutting edge. He'd spent so much time contemplating his navel, he'd fallen in and gotten stuck there. In 1979 Steve Martin was selling out arenas; my dad was barely filling seven-hundred-seaters.

The only exciting thing that came about during this time for Dad's career was a small, upstart cable channel called HBO. They weren't in very many homes, but they were looking to make a mark in the industry, and one way they did that was by inviting my dad to do unfiltered, uncensored comedy specials. He did his first one at USC in 1977. The way I know that it wasn't considered a big deal is the fact that I don't remember it ever being discussed.

It wasn't until the next year, 1978, when he was asked to do another one, that I became aware of this HBO, and that was only because my mom insisted on making me part of the production team. Mom produced, I was the Xerox/coffee girl, and Dad did his thing. Mom took me under her wing and taught me how to be in the workplace. It did a lot to heal things between us. It was like the good old days when we were on the road, supporting Dad's dream and living in the glow of his success. The Three Musketeers were back! We went to Phoenix and shot it in the round at the Celebrity Theater. It was all very exciting. But we had no idea if HBO would even be around the next year. And Dad didn't do another HBO special, or another album for that matter, for another three years. He was definitely lost.

My mom, on the other hand, was definitely found. She was the busy AA queen. She had a whole new group of sober friends. When she wasn't out and about at meetings, she was frequenting the Hollywood Park racetrack. She loved to gamble and now she had a racetrack nickname that she proudly put on a vanity plate for her light-blue Mercedes 450 SL—"Ohio Red." When my dad and I had picked up the car for Mom's birthday the year before, I had asked, "Is this a rich person's car?" Dad had answered, "You could say that."

Thankfully Mom's gambling was not like her drinking. She actually knew how to gamble in moderation. But gambling was just for fun. Really, my mom was ready to sink her teeth into something meaty and meaningful. With her sobriety now firmly established, and me off doing my own teenager thing, Dad could no longer hold her back. She enrolled in UCLA's Certificate in Drugs and Alcohol Counseling program. She was a natural therapist already. She was always the one to lend an ear to a troubled soul, or even try to rescue them. She'd been that way even when she was using.

My mom didn't bring home stray dogs; she brought home stray people.

One Fourth of July we were at the beach watching the fireworks, and a guy was sleeping on a blanket twenty feet from us. After about an hour Mom realized he hadn't moved. She got a few big guys to get him up and walking, and brought him home with us. She then called the paramedics when she realized he had probably overdosed. A few months later he knocked on our door thanking her for saving his life that day. Now that she was sober and so grateful for her own life, she was ready to save the world. She volunteered at the VA helping vets stay sober with her warmth, humor, and her own sobriety story.

Which makes my parents' letting me and my friends get high at our house sound insane. But I was living in a house where only a few years earlier my father had been convinced that the sun had exploded. I was used to this special homespun Carlin logic. My parents both figured that if I was at home getting high, at least I was *safe* at home getting high. And this worked out well for me, since this era was the trifecta of stoner life: the original cast of *SNL*, a proliferation of Northern Humboldt County sinsemilla, and the introduction to America of Häagen-Dazs.

In my junior year the headmaster of Crossroads, Paul Cummins, brought my father and me in to "have a talk." I was terrified. I was a good girl, and certainly didn't want to be in trouble, or for my headmaster to be mad at me. I sat with my dad in Paul's office, staring at my feet, when Paul began, "George, it has come to our attention that Kelly and her friends are smoking pot on the weekends, and we have heard that some of this is happening at your house."

Dad countered, "Well, Brenda's and my rule is that as long as she stays on the property, and they're not getting into cars, we are okay with it. In fact, she and I often share our weed." He liked Paul, but certainly didn't want to be told how to conduct his life.

"I see," Paul cautiously replied.

"What is her grade point average?" my dad asked. Paul looked to find my transcripts. He looked up at my dad: "3.85."

"Well, it doesn't seem to be affecting her academics," Dad said, looking at Paul directly.

"No, it doesn't appear to be," Paul replied.

"Anything else?"

"No, I guess not."

We all got up to leave. I wasn't quite sure what had just happened, but I was relieved that I wasn't suspended, or worse. As we walked out, Paul said, "And thank you again for doing our annual fundraiser. We're really looking forward to it."

"Of course. My pleasure."

Being teens with all the privileges of being adults (money and cars) without any of the responsibilities (jobs or paying the bills), my extended tribe and I were fearless in our pursuits of pleasure.

Fridays were spent collecting money to buy our drugs (weed, coke, and ludes mostly) so we could spend our weekends speeding up and down Sunset Boulevard in the cars our parents had bought us, going to parties, clubs, or houses where parents weren't home. So much for being safe at home. We charged our expensive meals at Mr. Chow's or the Bistro to our parents' credit cards, and we girls got older men to buy us drinks at places like On the Rox or Dan Tana's. Hollywood was filled with clubs that barely glanced at your fake ID, especially if you were a girl. My introduction to Hollywood was Gazzarri's. It was a club that had hit big in the sixties with bands like The Doors and Buffalo Springfield. It was filled with go-go dance cages and no fresh air. Our friend Cheryl knew the lead singer in a band called Seagull. Every time they played there, we'd go to see them and their opener, the band Venice. Wearing my Dittos jeans (I had them in at least ten colors) and a sassy little stretch top, I'd dance until I couldn't stand anymore. Gazzarri's was a sweatbox. Leaning up against the wall, you could actually feel the condensation. If we weren't dancing there, we'd head to West Hollywood to inhale amyl nitrate and dance all night to Donna Summer at the gay disco the Odyssey, or maybe over to the Starwood Club to see new-wave bands like The Motels or The Knack.

Music was a huge part of my life. I believe that Tom Petty, Elvis Costello, and Pink Floyd kept me alive during those years. I would smoke a bowl, put my headphones on, and fall asleep to "Wish You Were Here." Pink Floyd reminded me to "Shine On You Crazy Diamond." Because I had access to a record label through my dad, I went to lots of concerts. Our parents would all pitch in for a limo, and a group of six to eight of us would pile in, ingest mounds of drugs and alcohol, and be whisked off to see bands like Boston, Styx, Fog Hat, Santana, The Police, Rod Stewart, and the Eagles.

We went to see the band Yes once. About six months afterwards I mentioned to a friend that I would really love to see them someday. He told me we already had. I guess the Quaalude I'd taken that night had wiped my memory of the whole evening.

During the day, when we got bored, my guy friends would commandeer my Jeep and we'd terrorize Brentwood and Bel-Air by running over mailboxes and doing doughnuts on people's lawns. I knew it was wrong, and I always felt guilty, but I didn't want to look like a wuss or give the cool boys any excuse not to hang out with me. I always went along for the ride. I must admit there was something thrilling about pissing off people and getting away with it. Maybe I was a rebel after all. It felt like we ruled the world—we were rich, popular, having fun, and going to live forever.

CHAPTER NINE

Sex, Drugs, . . .

IN THE ELEVENTH GRADE I'd hit a bit of a snag. I was sixteen. I had an ulcer. I was sleeping all day. I was falling apart. I needed help but I didn't know how to ask for it. I needed to tell my parents what was going on, but I had no idea how to do that. Plus I didn't really want to face up to it myself. I guess that's what all the drugs and partying were all about. My mom knew something was up, and she was covering for me at school a lot. She was being the kind of mom she and I both thought we wanted—the cool mom. This is how cool she was: One weekend when she went out of town, my friend Vickie and I stole some Quaaludes from her stash of sleeping pills. She came home early and found us all luded out, and all she asked was, "So, you girls having fun?" We were. But what I really needed her to ask was, Kelly, are you sure you're okay? You've seemed a bit lost lately. I needed her to stop being the cool mom and start being the mom.

My snag came in the form of a boy—a boy I'll call Terry. Terry was a wild boy. I first met him just after he'd broken his collarbone by jumping—or should I say throwing his body—over ten chairs lined up in a row in the school auditorium. He was a walking and talking episode of *Jackass* twenty-five years before it was even a glimmer in Johnny Knoxville's eye. I was never sure what Terry might do. He wasn't stupid, he just had this reckless, unbridled spirit that made being around him thrilling. That, and he had the most gorgeous blue eyes. I was a sucker for blue eyes. Still am. And he was funny. Wicked, wicked funny. I was also a sucker for funny. I still am. But mostly he had a magical charisma. He would walk into a room, and the air would crackle. All the girls felt it, and every one of them had a crush on him.

I was doomed. The gravitational pull I felt toward him could not be countered. I could barely think in his presence.

The first few years I knew him, I never let on that I liked him. In December 1978, Vickie and Peter's parents, Jud and Carole, took all four of us teens to Aspen for a ski trip. We drove there in a big camper that Jud borrowed from my dad. You read that right— borrowed from my dad. He'd bought this camper (it was a big beige GMC thing Dad called "the Big Turd") with the ambitious intention of the Carlins actually going camping someday. Yeah, right.

It mostly sat in our driveway, just like a big turd, going nowhere.

As Vickie, Peter, Terry, and I sprawled out on the back bed of "the Big Turd" through Nevada and Utah, we listened to the only two eight-track tapes we could find at the truck stop in Barstow—Steve Martin's *Let's Get Small* and *Best of Bread*. Heady shit for a fifteen-year-old girl. Between the combination of Steve Martin's revelatory comedy, Bread's perfect articulation of the longing of every cell in my hormonal body, and the proximity of Terry, I was done for. I fell head first and headlong in love. But I didn't dare share this information with Vickie or Peter, and certainly not with Terry. I didn't even display a word or a gesture or a hint. I didn't know how. I may have been already experimenting with drugs by the age of fifteen, but I was not experimenting with boys. I'd never even kissed a guy. Somehow I had avoided spinning a bottle, playing "doctor," or whatever other childhood games kids find to explore the opposite sex.

My one and only chance to kiss a boy came and went on the last day at the Montessori school when I was twelve years old. I'd had a huge crush for the whole school year on a boy named Todd. He was blond, blue-eyed, and a surfer. All the girls knew I had a crush on him because I had revealed it during one of our many games of fortune-telling (with one of those origami folded thingies). But I was too terrified to do anything about it. As we were all saying our tearful final good-byes, someone yelled out in front of Todd, "Todd, you should kiss Kelly." I panicked and ran into the girls' bathroom and hid. He came in looking for me, and I would not come out of the stall. I'm not sure what I thought would happen if I kissed him. So here I was now, three years later, wanting to be Terry's girlfriend more than anything, and pretending I had no interest in him.

By avoiding my chaotic hormones for most of my adolescence, I had become like a white-knuckled binge dieter resisting the ever-powerful allure of the dozen chocolate doughnuts for as long as possible, but then succumbing and eating the whole damn box in one fell swoop. One night, in the late spring of 1979, in the attic of Peter and Vickie's house, I went from never having kissed a boy to fumbling my way through *all* the bases with Terry. It was a drunk and stoned blur of lips, hands, skin, ouch, and finally sleep. As it goes for most of us, it was both anti- and nonclimactic.

But it ignited a storm in me. Every cell in my body had awakened, and it wanted more. I wanted to possess Terry. I wanted to run away with him and let the world fade. Yes, I wanted to fuck his brains out night and day, but really, I just wanted him to love me. I wanted his attention and his being to revolve around me, and only me. I was sure that the moment after we "did it," we would now be boyfriend and girlfriend—holding hands in public, making out at parties, calling each other pet names like couples do.

None of that happened. He clearly had other ideas. There was no hand-holding. No PDA. No cute pet names. We kept fucking, but that was it.

I had no idea if we were a couple or not. All the people we hung out with had no idea either. Peter and Vickie figured it out because the first few months Terry and I were together, we were having sex in every available room in their house—the attic's twin beds behind the TV room, where I lost my virginity; the basementlike downstairs with a bed ensconced in a niche—the perfect place to fall asleep hoping that Terry would find his way down to me, which he did on many a night. And pretty much any other available flat surface. The secrecy of it all was maddening and heartbreaking, and the most exciting thing ever. Maddening because it was so illogical—Terry and I were already attached at the hip as friends, so why not just show our affection in public? Heartbreaking because I already felt less than most girls, and his refusal to announce his affection for me in public just underlined my unworthiness. Exciting because I was Terry's secret lover—at parties there were glances from him, surreptitious brushings up against each other, and quick make-out sessions in bathrooms. It was electrifying. The not knowing and the suspense kept me off-kilter. I never really knew where I stood with Terry. I was in love. I was insane.

I wasn't the only crazy one. Terry was one of those tricky types. There were moments when he would flash me a glimpse of the real, soft, damaged human that he was underneath. I could clearly see the lonely and wounded parts of him that just needed to be loved, and I would run toward them, hoping to protect and heal him. Hoping that in return, he would do the same for me. But then he'd lash out at me, as if I were evil, diseased. The first time it happened we were hanging out in my bedroom, listening to music, taking bong hits—an average day—when his voice got sharp and low, and I watched his pupils suddenly dilate. He grabbed my wrist and twisted it, and said, "You—you—you drive me fucking crazy." I can't remember what I said or did to make him do that, and I'm not sure it really mattered. His reaction was such a non sequitur that I didn't know if it had anything to do with me. It's not like we were arguing or that there was even some tension between us. I thought at first he must be kidding, and let it slide, but more and more of these moments started popping up out of nowhere.

It was during this time that Terry was in a car accident with one of his closest friends, Steve. They were going to a party up Laurel Canyon when a drunk driver T-boned them, flipping Steve's Jeep and killing him instantly. We were all confused and traumatized by losing someone our age. For many of us it was our first encounter with death. I can't even imagine what it must have been like for Terry. He survived the crash with only a broken arm, but something inside him had broken, too, and his lashing out at me escalated. It felt as if my attachment to him fed his rage, and he regularly struck out at me verbally—"You disgusting whore!"—and physically—a death grip around my arm or a bite on my face. Confused, I'd walk around with bruises on my body and my soul, and I'd try to use logic to understand the cause: *I must have provoked him by wanting him too much; I must have said or done the wrong thing; if I just don't do that thing again, he'll come back and stay forever.* I could never figure it out exactly. While most girls my age were worrying about what to wear to the prom, I was worrying about whether *what* I was wearing to the prom would cover my bruises. I didn't tell a soul about this behavior of his. I had to tame him. I had to heal him. And I knew that if I could, I'd finally be worth something.

Then all the pain and rage that I could not or would not feel and express toward Terry, my family's chaotic past, and even myself wound itself tight around me, and I couldn't see straight. I began acting out. I stopped taking my birth control pills. Within a month I was pregnant. I told Terry. He was upset and, I think, scared. I told my mom. She was lovely about it, and I was glad I could turn to her. She took me to take care of it. But she didn't do what I really needed her to do, which was to help me get away from my abusive relationship. Of course how *could* she? She didn't know anything about it. I couldn't tell her, and so I carried on as if nothing was wrong, and nine months later, I got pregnant again. My mom took care of me again.

This time Terry wasn't scared; he was infuriated. I came home to a note on my bed reading, "You stupid fucking cunt. This is all your fault." And it was. I'd played Russian roulette with my birth control pills and lost. I was hoping someone would stop me. I had no idea how. I wouldn't walk away from Terry. I thought if I did my whole life would collapse. It was like the Three Musketeers—all for one, one for all. But instead of my parents being my protectors, it was my friends, and they were too young to protect anyone but themselves.

For most of those days in the eleventh grade, I couldn't tell if I was coming or going. Who am I—the great rebel leader's daughter or the Brentwood disco queen? What is important—finally owning my rage and sorrow or taking another hit off the pipe? Who loves me—my parents who are watching as I sink deeper into fear, or my friends who are the very weight pulling me down? I walked around in a constant state of confusion. There was no sense of self, and what little there was was all in service of keeping this monster, this boy, at bay so that I could have just five more minutes of validating love from him.

I know my mom wanted to do more to rein in my life—give me a curfew, control whom I saw, get me off drugs—but she was determined not to lose me the way her mother had lost her, by pushing her around like a pawn. And my dad was busy, busy, busy, and distracted, distracted, distracted. Not only were the heart attack and his career on his mind, he also had a new challenge—an enormous tax problem. Between his resistance to opening the letters from his accountant, a really bad investment in a movie that never got made, and the fact that—*Surprise!*—as far as the government was concerned, the horse ranch in Malibu was not actually a business investment, my parents owed more than a million dollars to the U.S. government.

Dad and I would pass each other in the hallway and he'd ask, "Are you all right?" not really wanting a real answer. And I'd say, "Fine," not really wanting to give one. It's not that we didn't care; we just didn't know how to do it any differently. Plus the last thing

I wanted to do as a hormonally out-of-control teenager was talk to my dad. Mom hadn't told him about anything that had happened.

And then I got pregnant a third time. This time I even kept it from my mom. I felt like a whore, a loser, an insane person. I knew I had to take care of it myself and figure out my next move. I briefly considered suicide. But in the end I confided in my horse trainer, Jill, who was like a surrogate mother to me. Because she was so worried about me, she immediately told my mother. And that's when the ugly truth about all the abuse came pouring out of me. I couldn't pretend anymore. I didn't care if I never saw Terry again; I just wanted the pain to stop. My mom told my dad about everything. It was over.

A few days later Terry showed up at our house. I'm not sure why he came—to apologize, to charm me again, to tell me I was a whore? My dad saw him outside the gate at the end of our long driveway. He went inside his office and grabbed his baseball bat. As my dad marched down the driveway toward Terry, he said, "You come near my daughter again, I'll bash your fucking skull in."

It was the proudest day of my life—my father had finally fathered me.

. . . and Rock and Roll

"HEY, YOU'RE A REALLY GOOD dancer. Wanna go out on a date?" Mark asked me. We'd been dancing for a few songs now. "Boogie Nights" had just ended, and we were now in the middle of "Rock Lobster."

"Uh, sure. That'd be great," I answered as I made my way slowly to the ground as Fred Schneider, the lead singer of the B-52s sang, "Down . . . down . . . down."

At the beginning of my senior year, I met a new boy. His name was Mark Lennon. I met him at my friend Cheryl's 1960s-themed birthday party. I'd shown up wearing a pink vinyl miniskirt, white go-go boots, and my favorite T-shirt, which said, "Earth is not my planet." When Mark asked me to dance, I almost died. Not only was he one of the best dancers I'd ever seen, he was also a singer in the band Venice, the very band that I'd been dancing to at Gazzarri's since I was fifteen. And he had long blond hair and blue eyes. I was in heaven.

After we danced to a million songs together, we walked around the party holding hands, kissed at the end of the night, and before I knew it, we were dating. One of the first dates we had was to go up to Ojai to a Lennon family reunion. As we drove up the coast in my Jeep, we listened to the Doobie Brothers' *Minute by Minute* album. Mark knew all the words and sang perfect harmony to all of them. My heart exploded with joy.

When we arrived in Ojai, I thought I had just entered the twilight zone. There were almost a hundred people there. Mark was the youngest of thirteen kids in his family alone. And they all had blond hair and blue eyes. He was part of the famous Lennon family—as in the Lennon Sisters from *The Lawrence Welk Show*. I had no idea how to keep track of all these Lennons before me. But it didn't matter because I'd never met a more lovely and normal family. Everyone sang, danced, and was cheerfully fun. Being an only child, I felt like an alien, but it was also manna for my soul.

At Mark's gigs with Venice he'd sing love songs, all the girls in the crowd would swoon, and then he'd come offstage and walk right over to me, grab my hand, and kiss me. We were a couple, and everyone knew it. He loved and adored me, and I loved and adored him. He was considerate, sweet, and funny. He didn't have a mean bone in his body. I had moved on from Terry.

Even though he was in a rock band, Mark was the most sheltered teenager I had ever met. It must have been the Catholic upbringing and the "Lawrence Welk" in his family. When I met him he was seventeen and didn't drive, smoke cigarettes, or get high. Within six months of knowing me he was smoking cigarettes and weed and had tried magic mushrooms, but he still wasn't driving. Three months after that, we split up. I don't think it was the not driving that split us up. It was that being with him was too easy. There was no drama. Just like he didn't know how to drive, I didn't know how to do normal. I was addicted to chaos. I knew it was over when I found myself making a late-night booty call to Terry. I felt like a total schmuck, and I didn't want to hurt Mark. I knew it was wrong on every level. And so I immediately broke up with Mark. We both cried. I hated hurting him. We genuinely cared for each other, and to this day he and I are still friends.

We still kill it on the dance floor.

In July 1981, I was eighteen and had just graduated from Crossroads. Unlike most of my peers, who were spending their summer preparing for their futures, I spent mine trying to undo my past. I was still extricating myself emotionally and physically from Terry. I would resist him for a while, then fall back into bed with him. The abuse was over, but I was still obsessed with him. But after two years of this back and forth, the part of me that had believed that he was my soul mate now just wanted its soul back. I knew it was time to be done with it all forever. Moving forward, I was going to take care of myself, be more mature, and hang with a fresh group of friends, so I decided one night to hang out with Griffin O'Neal and Leif Garrett.

Griffin, Tatum's brother and Ryan's son, and Leif, the *Tiger Beat* pop star who only a few years earlier had been the heartthrob of every thirteen-year-old girl in America ("I was made for dancing/ All, all, all, night long . . ."), were what I would call part of the Beverly Hills High crowd. They were somewhat outside my incestuous Crossroads group of friends, so to me it was like a new beginning, and a move toward a healthier life.

I have no idea how I first ended up hanging with these two guys by myself, but I'd guess that we had partied together with a bunch of people the night before, and in the morning the three of us had nowhere to go and nothing to do, so we probably decided to keep the party going.

What I do remember about how the day started is being in Leif's 730i Beemer going east on Sunset, following Griffin in his little blue-and-white MINI Cooper. There had been a rare rain shower that morning, and the road was slick with water and oil. At the light at Roscomare at Bel-Air, Griffin rolled down his window and shouted, "Watch this!" The light turned green, and we followed Griffin off the line as we approached the big, wide turn at UCLA. As we made our way around the bank, Griffin, who was about three car lengths ahead of us, pulled his emergency brake and began a slow, balletlike spin around the corner. I watched in horror, disbelief, and awe as he spun around in that little car, somehow not hitting anything, but scaring the shit out of everyone near him. Leif and I looked at each other and rolled our eyes. I couldn't help laughing and somewhat admiring Griffin and his insanity. He was poetic chaos in motion.

So much for trying to take care of myself and being more mature.

At least I wasn't in Griffin's car. I had learned enough by this point not to be in the car with the crazy guy. I was safe in Leif's car. Then Leif casually mentioned that a few years before, while high, he had a horrible accident that had left his best friend paralyzed. He told me he'd grown from that experience and that he was much more careful now about driving and getting high. I was relieved to hear this, since just that morning we all had decided to be sensible and not do ludes—just a few bong hits—before hitting the road.

Leif, Griffin, and I ended up at an arcade in Westwood. Day turned to night, and around seven Terry showed up. Griffin and Leif were also friends with Terry, so I figured that one of them must have told him that we were there. They didn't know our secret history. We all hung out playing Asteroids, Missile Command, and Pac-Man. As time passed, I felt that pull between Terry and me awaken. God, it was crazy. It had a mind of its own. It was as powerful as the gravitational pull of the sun. I suddenly found myself needing him, wanting him, and then, thankfully, I remembered the hell that he'd put me through. I knew that I had to figure out a way to cut the cord, finally to sever it once and for all: I had to sleep with Leif Garrett. It had to happen. I was going to break the gravitational pull of Terry by sleeping with Leif.

In that moment it felt like time stood still and the universe aligned itself with me in my overall purpose to break away from Terry and grow up. It was destiny. In that moment I had turned the corner from being a girl who looked for men to define her, to becoming a young woman wanting to put a notch in her bedpost.

Once we got bored with the arcade, Griffin suggested that we go out to his house in Malibu. Read: Ryan and Farrah's house in Malibu. Perfect. Terry said he had to go home. Double perfect!

I made bedroom eyes at Leif and said what a great idea that was. Leif got the message loud and clear—men are so easy. Even better, Terry got the message, too. Griffin, Leif, and I settled into Leif's Beemer for the ride out to Malibu. Griffin suggested we stop at his dealer's house to pick up some blow on the way. There I was, queen of my world. I was riding on a wave of destiny. Thinking, *I am woman, hear me roar.* As we wound our way on Sunset through the Palisades, I popped in the new Steely Dan tape, and the song "Babylon Sisters" became our soundtrack. Donald Fagen sang about driving west on Sunset and how the evening would be no one-night stand but a "real occasion." I thought, *Yes, Mr. Fagen. You are right. Yes, indeed.*

We eventually made it to "the Boo" (Malibu). Ryan and Farrah were out of town somewhere, so we had full access to everything. I walked in and saw the wall of Farrah I had heard so much about. It was a thirty-foot wall covered with pictures of Farrah in every imaginable size. I was in awe, and I knew that this was indeed a huge moment for me.

Later on Leif and I played footsie in the Jacuzzi, and Griffin began to pout. At some point Griffin pulled me aside to tell me that he was worried about me, and didn't want me doing anything crazy. The champagne nearly shot through my nose. He warned me that Leif wanted to have sex with me, but that he probably didn't want it to be anything serious. He was afraid that Leif was just going to use me. How sweet—Griffin protecting me from Leif! I thought, *These boys are much nicer than the ones I used to hang out with.*

———

Eventually Griffin crashed, and Leif and I barely made it to the couch. I will spare you the gory details of what followed next. But I must say there is not much to spare you from. Even though I was only eighteen, and Leif was only the third guy I had ever been with, there was one thing I knew on that night—he clearly was not, as they say, "made for dancin' all, all, all, all night long"! But who would be after partying all night. If I can save just one woman from one disappointment in life I hope that it is this—that sleeping with a really stoned pop star is not in any way as thrilling as *thinking* about sleeping with a really stoned pop star. Do yourself a favor and satisfy yourself while you keep on fantasizing about Bono, Sting, whoever— you'll get a hell of a lot more bang for your buck that way. Trust me.

The next morning, not wanting Griffin to find us on the couch, Leif and I found our way upstairs, and into Ryan and Farrah's bed. Here in the daylight, with most of the drugs having worn off, we met each other in a very different place. And yes, Leif found a way to redeem himself from the night before. Afterward, as we lay there on Ryan and Farrah's bed, I had to laugh to myself and take in the moment. It was a surreal one for sure. I may have grown up as the daughter of George Carlin and had many a brush with fame, but nothing could possibly top having sex with Leif Garrett in Ryan O'Neal and Farrah Fawcett's bed.

Or so I thought.

Ten minutes later Leif and I found our way to their shower. As the water poured over me, I asked Leif to hand me some shampoo. And he did. Farrah Fawcett's shampoo. No, I mean it. It was Farrah Fawcett *brand* shampoo: Farrah fucking Fawcett shampoo.

And there I was, next to Leif Garrett, washing my hair with Farrah Fawcett shampoo under Farrah's faucet.

CHAPTER ELEVEN

Prince Charming

"DID HE CALL?" MOM ASKED, sounding worried. Dad had called her in Dayton (she was out there visiting her dad) from Toronto the night before, and he had sounded very upset. A movie project, *The Illustrated George Carlin,* that he'd already put too much time and money into had headed in a direction he hated. It just wasn't what he had envisioned, and he didn't know what to do. He cried to Mom over the phone, and told her that he would drive all night to Dayton and see her early in the morning. It was after noon now, and he wasn't there.

"No. No, he hasn't called," I replied, holding back tears.

"I'm going to start calling hospitals," Mom said. "I don't know what else to do."

She hung up. My stomach churned. It was as if I'd been put in a time machine, and it was 1974 all over again. Back then, my dad would disappear for days, no phone calls or warning, doing coke or LSD or God knows what with some group of bikers or fans or whatnot, and then suddenly he'd appear back at home acting as if nothing was out of the ordinary. But now, in 1981, things were supposed to be different. There'd been no disappearing or late-night arguing or major misbehavior for more than five years.

He finally called. He'd been at a hospital somewhere on the outskirts of Dayton. He explained that after stopping by the Toronto comedy club Yuk Yuk's, to watch a few comics and smoke some weed, he'd headed to Dayton with a bunch of beer in the car. He drank the entire way. By the time he'd gotten to Dayton he was shit-faced and plowed his rental car into a ditch. A fire truck just happened to drive by and found him unconscious with his nose smashed up. The first cops that showed up wanted to plant drugs on him so they could bust him. But then a couple of others, who were big fans, came upon the scene and talked their fellow officers out of that idea. The incident was written up as an accident saving my dad from a DUI. Sometimes it pays off to be a counterculture god. When Dad got to the hospital, a plastic surgeon happened to be on duty in the emergency room and put his face back together almost as good as new.

He got lucky.

In the fall of 1981, at age eighteen, when most of my peers were energetically leaping from their families into the world of college and commerce, I needed a nap. After all the chaos in my life, I wasn't up to anything too trying. I wanted some of that "Peaceful Easy Feeling" the Eagles were always singing about.

In high school I knew my job as a teenager was to graduate from high school—simple enough. But now, according to Life Plan 101, I was transitioning into adulthood, and my new job was either to "get a job" or go to college so that in four years I could "get a job." I had only vague ideas about what that "job" would look like—something fun and easy in showbiz? Overwhelmed and clueless about my long-term future, I put off figuring it out. I went to college—UCLA.

My freshman orientation left me disoriented. It was like kindergarten all over again—I craved a lap to cling to and felt like I'd missed the day the "manuals" of life were handed out. As I roamed between seminars, information sessions, and booths from various departments, I looked at my peers and wondered: *How do they have all this ambition, vision, and knowledge about their future?* There were the premed and preengineering students who had known what they wanted to be since they were five. Then there were the kids who for years had been making films, or painting, or dancing, and couldn't wait to immerse themselves even deeper into their artistic passions. And of course there was a good majority of students who just wanted to live three thousand miles away from their parents so they could drink and fuck their way through college.

I couldn't relate to any of them.

The familiarity of the beginning of the school year, with the ritual buying of new clothes, textbooks, and school supplies did help things, but I was still anxious. Most of my friends had dispersed to Ivy League schools that I had applied to but didn't get into (thanks to my fucked-up SAT scores), and with my parents away on a European vacation, I had to face those first few awkward and overwhelming weeks of school alone. Still, I was willing to give it the old college try.

The first few days I was proud of myself for sorting out my schedule and making my way through the maze of almost thirty thousand students on more than four hundred acres of campus with the help of the trusty map I'd glued to the back of my notebook. It wasn't too bad after all. I focused on what I'd be learning, and that kept me excited. But on day four that all changed. When I walked into History 1A: Introduction to Western Civilization, I froze. More than three hundred students scrambled to take their seats. Crossroads barely had three hundred students in total. All these students were smiling and talking to one another. I couldn't breathe. I felt very small, my heart began to race, and I thought I was going to die. I backed out of the class, sat outside for a few minutes to recover, and went home. When I got there I went straight to bed and didn't emerge for a week. When my parents came home from Europe, I told them what had happened. I was sure I'd had a nervous breakdown. They weren't so sure. Whatever "it" was, I knew it wasn't the academics. It was the Okay-it's-time-to-go-out-in-the-world-and-focus-and-figure-out-who-the-fuck-I-am part of it all. I just couldn't cope. My parents didn't seem to have much of an opinion about it.

Well, my mom did.

"You can't just sleep all day," she not-so-helpfully pointed out.

Dad, as always, came to my defense. "No one said she would. Clearly she's been through a lot lately. Let's give her some space. She just needs to find her center again."

I was relieved. Yes, that was it. I just needed to find my center again. "Again"? Hmm—I don't really remember having had one in the first place. In the end neither of them demanded that I return to school, and so I didn't. I quit and did nothing, hoping my center would find me.

What did find me was Andrew Sutton, a twenty-nine-year-old car mechanic who worked at the Chevron station at the corner of Barrington and Wilshire. Technically, Terry, my ex, found him (yes, unbelievably, Terry and I were still hanging out) when he filled up the BMW 3.0 my dad had just given me. Andrew waltzed out to the car, handed Terry his card, and said, "If you ever need a repair, let me know. They're my specialty." Now, in October 1981, I was picking up the car from Andrew after he'd spent a week working on it. As I climbed into the car, he asked, "You wanna party sometime?"

I was a sucker for blue eyes and blond hair. Andrew had neither. But he did have big brown puppy-dog eyes, a confident swagger, and the purest cocaine I'd ever put up my nose. For our first "date," we sat on his bed in his house and did rail after rail of coke. And as often happens when there is a pile of coke and hours of time to fill, much is said, insights are epic, and a cocoon of safety and purpose is created. We poured our hearts out to each other.

I shared with him the feelings I could never tell my parents— how I loved them but that I was really angry that their drug abuse had left me feeling broken inside. I revealed thoughts I could never tell my friends—the deep longing I had to understand life in a bigger way—Why are we here? What does it all mean? I confessed my dreams of wanting to be an actor or a director or a still photographer, but that I didn't have any confidence even to try. I had never shared my inner life with a man in this way.

As the afternoon wore on, Andrew told me he'd felt like an outcast in his own family (he was the stepkid) and misunderstood in the world his whole life—at age nine he could build a TV but couldn't sit down for five minutes to read a book. I felt his pain and loneliness. He explained to me that he was currently married, but that he was divorcing her because she'd cheated on him. My heart ached. I could relate to not being loved by the one you wanted. He said that he'd put a voice-activated tape recorder in her car to catch her cheating. My stomach turned, but I ignored it. He had been wronged, I told myself. He then told me that he and his wife, Stacey, had a son, Elliot, who was a bit of a handful but a real cute kid. He was three. He was born a blue baby, and six weeks later Stacey had taken a bunch of pills, trying to kill herself.

Wow, I thought, poor Elliot, abandoned so young! I was touched by how much both Andrew and Elliot had been through. But at the same time I was suddenly very wary of being in the house of a married man who had a kid, and felt myself quickly erect an emotional wall between Andrew and me. Sensing this, he quickly assured me that the marriage really was over. It was all just a formality. In a few months he was turning thirty and would be getting a trust from his grandmother that he was going to use to divorce his wife. That made sense to me. He had a good plan.

He explained that the reason he was a car mechanic, even though he grew up in Brentwood in a Hollywood family (his dad was a famous character actor, Bert Freed), was that he was on probation for another year for a federal weapons charge for designing and manufacturing silencers for AR-15s (the same guns they used in Vietnam). He immediately reassured me that it was really no big deal because, "I'd only sold them to Beverly Hills doctors and lawyers so they could play with their 'toys' in their own backyards. I like guns. I like to tinker." I took this information in as if he'd told me he'd been volunteering at a soup kitchen, "Wow, that's amazing."

Within two months he was living with me in my bedroom at my parents' house.

The first thing Andrew did when he moved in was chainsaw a hole in the wall of my bedroom.

"You should be able to lie in your bed and see outside," he said while lying on my bed with an ashtray on his chest, acting like he owned the place. My room had an alcove in it where the bed was, so he made a hole in the wall so he could see outside.

While alarmed by his brashness, my dad also saw Andrew's potential. Before I knew it Andrew was fixing all sorts of things for my dad around the house. Need a new fence around the trash cans? Andrew will do it. Need to set up the new satellite TV system? Andrew will do it. Need someone to teach your daughter how to have an orgasm? Andrew will do it. Okay, so Dad hadn't requested that last one, but I must say, it was a real plus. I had been under the impression that the thing that had been happening when I'd had sex with Terry, Mark, and even Leif was an orgasm. I was wrong. Boy, was I wrong!

Even though I knew that Andrew was the most inappropriate boyfriend to have at this time (or any time) in my life that thought got hijacked by the excellent quality of orgasms and cocaine he was providing me. I went with the flow, as did my parents. Neither of them discussed or questioned Andrew's increasing presence in my life. He folded oh-so-neatly into the Carlin familial enmeshment I was so used to.

I attached to him like a barnacle, avoiding the tiny voice within me that occasionally whispered, Save yourself. I allowed his adventurous momentum to lift me up and carry me toward whatever was important to him. I spent hours hanging out with him as he worked at the gas station. So many hours that he eventually bought me my own Chevron uniform shirt to wear. When I was bored, I'd jump up and pump gas and clean windshields. I got a strange kick out of being the rich Brentwood girl pumping gas. It felt almost punk rock to me.

When Andrew wasn't at work, we drove his clients' BMWs, Jensen Interceptors, and Jaguars around the city. He'd trained at Bob Bondurant school of racing and taught me how to drive like a racecar driver. He took me shopping for sexy clothes, took hundreds of photos of me, and told me what a fox I was. He introduced me to people he'd known in show business (he'd worked for a few years on film productions), hoping I'd catch a casting director's eye. I knew he was showing me off like a trophy, but I didn't care. He made me feel like the center of the universe for the first time in my life. I felt beautiful, talented, and loved.

Mostly though, we spent many, many hours holed up in my bedroom having sex and snorting coke. We had so much coke and it was so pure that we'd cut it with mannitol in mixing bowls. I wasn't sure how or where he'd been getting all this high-quality coke on his mechanic's paycheck until one day, when he took me to eat at a Mexican restaurant in the San Fernando Valley. I couldn't figure out why he picked this place, when there were plenty of quality Mexican places closer to home. After we ate dinner we jumped into my 3.0 Beemer and headed back to my parents' house. As we swung onto the southbound 405, Andrew had a sly grin on his face and said, "While we were eating, my client, Joe, put something in our trunk for safekeeping for a few days."

Confused, I said, "Oh, really?"

"It's a kilo of coke," he replied nonchalantly.

My body stiffened. "What?" If I could have, I would have leaped out of that car and run as far away from it as I was able to, but we were going 50 mph on the freeway, so that wasn't a real option. Instead, I asked, "What are you going to do with it?"

"Bury it."

"Bury it? Where?" Thoughts of driving up into the hills of Topanga came to mind.

"Don't worry. I would never think of burying it on your parents' property. I would never risk that." Now I was really worried. He continued, "I'll bury it just off their property line. No one will ever know."

So that's how he got his coke—doing "favors" for his clients with the fancy cars. And that's how a new lifestyle emerged for me—the binge. We'd go on two- or three-day binges, emerging from my bedroom only after my body demanded food. I couldn't go much more than two days without food or sleep, but because Andrew had ADHD, he could eat and sleep after snorting any amount of cocaine. People with ADHD take stimulants to actually feel calmer. But once my body had reached its limit, I needed to refuel. I'd peek out of my bedroom door toward the kitchen, to see if the coast was clear, then I'd dash in to pop a Stouffer's Macaroni & Cheese and Corn Soufflé into the oven, while grabbing a handful of Fig Newtons or Oreos to tide me over until the real food was done heating up.

Scurrying around the house became the norm. I avoided my mother because I didn't want her to see me high, and I seemed to be furious with her all the time now. It had nothing to do with the present and everything to do with the past. All my anger about her alcoholism had finally floated to the surface, and the thought of being in the same room with her disgusted me. I went months speaking only a few sentences to her, and only when I had to. She kept her distance from me, intuiting my need to feel what I did. I avoided my dad because I knew I was out of control. I didn't want him to be mad, or disappointed with me.

He'd gotten mad at me the year before for the first time in my life, and it had to do with drugs. Back in June, before I graduated from high school, my friends and I had bought some coke for the prom. While we were scoring, the dealer asked us if we wanted to freebase some. He cooked some up for us, and had us each take a hit, and then sit quietly. The rush took over my body, and it was the greatest thing I had ever felt. The euphoria expanded me to the edges of the universe. "Magnificent" is too ordinary a word to describe it. A few days later I shared the experience with my dad because it was one of the best moments of my life.

"Don't you EVER FUCKING DO THAT AGAIN," he quickly said. The full force of his rage landed hard upon me. My eyes stung with tears. He continued at full volume, "I want you to promise me you will never smoke that shit again. It is very, very dangerous."

Fighting back a big bellow of tears caused by the shock, I mumbled, "Okay. I'm sorry."

"No, promise me."

Staring down at the ground afraid to look up at him: "I promise!"

He softened, "Okay. Good. Now give me a hug."

We hugged.

"I love you," he added.

"I love you, too," I said through my tears.

Even though I wasn't smoking coke now, I knew I was snorting way too much. I knew it was wrong, but I kept doing it. And hiding from my dad. I didn't want him to find out. I was now the one making up my own version of that homespun Carlin logic I had been so used to: If I'm home doing drugs, then I'm safe doing drugs. And if they don't see me doing drugs, they don't know I'm doing drugs.

CHAPTER TWELVE

I Know I'm in Here Somewhere

"I would like to bring you up to date on the Comedian's Health Sweepstakes. As it stands now, I lead Richard Pryor in heart attacks two to one. However, Richard still leads me one to nothing on burning yourself up! Well, the way it happened was: First Richard had a heart attack, then I had a heart attack; then Richard burnt himself up; then I said, 'Fuck that—I'm gonna have another heart attack!'"
                                                    —Carlin at Carnegie, 1983

In May 1982, I walked out of my parents' kitchen to the driveway and saw a limo pull up. My dad's manager, Jerry Hamza, jumped out and yelled, "George is at St. John's. He's had a heart attack."

Jerry and my dad had been at Dodger Stadium watching the Dodgers beat the Mets (my dad's favorite team) when my dad got hit with an attack of angina. Dad and Jerry immediately went to the first-aid station, but soon realized that the first-aid room at Dodger Stadium was nothing more than a glorified place to get a Band-Aid.

They quickly found the limo and its driver, John Batis, in the parking lot.

"I'm probably not having a heart attack, but just in case, we should probably get to St. John's Hospital as soon as possible," Dad said as they got in the limo.

Because they left before the end of the game, and because John broke every moving violation known to man, they made it to Santa Monica in twenty minutes. When my mom and I arrived, the doctors were not as optimistic as Dad was—it was way more serious than angina. It was almost a full blockage of the right descending artery. Grimly the doctors said that Dad's pulse was around twenty and that we should go in to see him—this could be good-bye.

I was terrified and crying, but Dad was in good spirits and tried to calm me. "It's okay, Kiddo. Everything's going to be fine." I wanted to believe him, but nothing he could say would calm my fear. I thought he was going to die.

After a while the doctors came to a consensus and decided to try an experimental anticoagulant that the hospital happened to have gotten just that week—Streptokinase. They had no idea if it would work. Within minutes the clot broke up, Dad's pulse lifted, and his vital signs stabilized.

Dad got lucky, again.

Six months later, my mom went into St. John's for a routine cyst removal from her breast. Because she had fake boobs, it had to be an inpatient procedure. And thank God it was. If it hadn't been, they might have missed the malignant tumor. After she awoke to the news, they gave her forty-eight hours to make a choice: chemotherapy and radiation or a radical mastectomy. I was terrified that she'd follow in her own mother's footsteps. But Mom had no doubt she was going to live. She opted for the mastectomy and refused the chemo and radiation because she knew that her liver couldn't handle them after all the years of damage from drinking she'd done to it. She'd already had health issues because of it.

A year after Mom got sober in 1976, she had started to have a bunch of weird symptoms that no doctor could diagnose. A few called her crazy, others thought she had some kind of rheumatoid arthritis, but most were just stumped. Finally she was diagnosed with fibromyalgia and non-A/non-B hepatitis (what these days they call hepatitis C). The fibromyalgia attacked the soft tissue in her joints and made my mom tired, achy, and depressed. The doctors had no idea where it came from. But Mom knew exactly where the hep-C came from—the one and only time she ever shot up drugs with an old neighbor. She was sure it must have been a dirty needle.

After the breast cancer surgery, in which they removed her entire left breast, Mom healed at home, and I became her nurse. Whatever anger I had about our past melted away as soon as I saw her now-mangled chest. It was a horror to look at. I could feel myself leave my body when it came time to change her bandages and bathe her. I wanted to run away. But with Dad on the road, there was no one else.

But did the Carlins let a little thing like their daughter dropping out of college and living with an older married man, or a heart attack, or breast cancer slow them down? No, of course not. We were the Three Musketeers—all for one, one for all.

After taping *Carlin at Carnegie* in New York, a year later we all got busy with taping *Carlin on Campus* in Los Angeles. Mom designed the set and produced the show, and I shot all the still photographs for the album cover. We were now a family production company—Cablestuff Productions. Dad bought a beautiful two-story building in Brentwood for our offices. Mom had a big peach-and-light-green office—very eighties; and Dad had the nicest office, but it was one he rarely worked in—he liked to write and keep his stuff at the home office. Jerry Hamza moved his family out from Rochester, New York, and he had the big corner office where he strategized and shaped Dad's career. Ros, the funniest, gayest man I'd ever met (and my mom's best friend from rehab) came onboard as the bookkeeper. Mom's assistant was Theresa, a new friend we'd recently met when Mom, Andrew, and I had worked on a play with the now-heroic limo driver/actor/director John Batis. I took on the role of setting up the press interviews and travel for Dad's touring while I dabbled in photography on the side. And because it just wouldn't be right if anyone was left off the payroll, Andrew was brought on to build my dad a state-of-the-art recording studio. I felt happy because all the people—especially my dad—and areas of my life were connected.

Despite all that was going on, Dad was itching to do even more. In the early 1980s, sitcoms had become *the* avenue for comedians to take their careers to the next level, so Dad developed *Apt. 2C*. With the help of HBO, we shot a pilot about a writer, played by Dad, who could never get his work done because he was constantly getting distracted by his wacky friends, neighbors, and strangers who always seemed to need something from him. Because HBO loved and respected Dad, they gave him complete creative control, which meant he could do whatever he wanted, including casting me. While he was working on the script, I asked him to write me a part. I was ready and could now jump into my "Carol Burnett dream" and try my hand at sketch comedy. Theresa, my mom's assistant, who had become my best friend, ended up writing me a really great part—a punk-rock Girl Scout who came to George's door to sell him cookies.

After a month of casting the rest of the roles, a process I got to be a part of on every level, we shot the pilot at A&R Studios on La Brea, where Charlie Chaplin had built his studio in the 1920s. You could feel the business of show in every nook and cranny of the place. It was heady stuff. While we rehearsed on set that week, I hung out with the cast—Bobcat Goldthwait (wacky neighbor), Pat

McCormick (needy mailman), and Lucy Webb (drunk neighbor). It was amazing. They were all seasoned professionals. I, on the other hand, had no idea what I was doing, but I jumped in anyway, not wanting to show my terror and inexperience.

The day of the taping I was really nervous. We taped two separate shows—the dress rehearsal and the show. Pat McCormick told me, "Just use it—the nerves—use it in your performance." I had no idea what that meant. As I stood at my mark outside the door to "George's apartment," the stage manager, Dency, began counting down my cue, "Five, four, three, two . . . ," and then pointed to me. Bile began to travel up my throat as I knocked on the door to begin the scene. I had no idea what would come out of my mouth: my lines or my lunch. I'm pretty sure that was *not* what Pat had meant by "use it."

Here's the scene as we taped it:

George opens the door to find me, a punk-rock Girl Scout with my hair a multicolored Mohawk, dozens of accessories on my uniform, and an attitude the size of North America.

"Hey, did you order any cookies?" I ask in a thick New York accent.

Confused by my looks, he replies, "Are you a Girl Scout?"

"No, I'm a fucking zucchini. Did you order any cookies or not?" Throwing it right back at him.

"Yeah, I think I had the lemon wafers," he answers.

Giving him the once-over—"Hey, macho guy!"—I go into my bag, "I don't got no goddamn lemon wafers." Holding up a box of cookies, "All I got are ginger snaps."

"Oh, I had those last year, and I didn't like them. They were too hard to chew," he explains.

Dripping fake pity in my voice: "Too hard to chew? I'll soften them up for ya."

I drop the box of cookies on the floor and smash them multiple times with my left foot. I give him one last look as I say, "There's your fucking cookies!" I then turn and saunter away, leaving George with a box of smashed cookies in his doorway. He looks directly into the camera and says, "Boy, scouting sure has changed."

Moments after we shot the scene, Dad walked up to me with tears in his eyes and said, "Congratulations, Kiddo. You just got your first professional laugh."

It felt so good.

When Andrew turned thirty and got the money from his trust, he immediately became the poster child for the saying "He who dies with the most toys wins." Within a year of getting more than one hundred thousand dollars in blue-chip stocks and bonds, he liquidated it all, divorced his wife, and bought a speedboat, a tow truck, a Shelby Cobra Kit Car (which he built with my help in my parents' driveway), a blue-gold macaw named Prudence, two yellow-napped Amazon parrots (one for me and one for my mom), numerous shotguns, rifles, and handguns (in my and my mom's names—he was still not allowed to purchase firearms because of his felony conviction), multiple radio-controlled cars and planes, a full-size dune buggy, a cabin in Big Bear, scuba gear, and a pygmy goat named Toby. All that was missing was the partridge in the fucking pear tree.

Every day with Andrew was Christmas—for Andrew. And just like most kids on Christmas morning, he'd play with the shiny new thing for a little while and then discard it for the next new shiny thing. It makes me think about a line from "A Place for My Stuff" that my dad wrote during this time: "That's what your house is, a place for your stuff, while you go out and get more stuff!"

Speaking of houses, by 1984 Andrew had asked me to marry him, but I had no desire to do that. I'd just turned twenty-one. Who gets married at twenty-one?

I compromised, and instead of walking down the aisle together, we moved into a cute little house in Santa Monica that my dad bought for us—what you could call "marriage-lite." The first thing Andrew did when we moved into the house? Yup, he took a chainsaw to the wall that separated the kitchen from the hallway, and made a refrigerator-size hole in it. He then built a cabinet on the other side of the wall to hide the back of the fridge. Most male mammals mark their territory with urine. Andrew marked his with a chainsaw. The house had been built in the twenties and couldn't fit a modern fridge. No worries. It did now.

Andrew continued his shopping spree, adding, to his already bloated collection of shit among other fine items—a large-scale German train set (complete with village), expensive stereo equipment, something called a Macintosh computer, lost-wax jewelry-making equipment, and even more radio-controlled cars, planes, and helicopters. Every horizontal surface of the house—table, counter, or shelf—was filled with some project of his in process, abandoned, or yet to be started.

Although Andrew had enough money for all his toys (and plenty of coke), he rarely had it for ordinary household stuff. My dad ended up paying for all the things one would need for a house—beds, furniture, kitchen appliances, and so on. Not to mention that he already paid for both Andrew and me to be on his payroll. This financial situation started to weigh on me. I knew I should be pulling my weight by this time in my life, but I was not sure how.

Although I'd been bitten by the showbiz bug after we did *Apt. 2C*, I felt incapable of doing anything serious about it. Yes, I had gotten my first professional laugh, but it'd been in a scene with George Carlin that I had not even auditioned for. I felt like a fake. I had no real acting or comedy training. I felt unprepared to go out and compete against people with real training and real ambition. All I could see was that I was a privileged, spoiled young woman who had never achieved anything without her daddy.

At age twenty-two, I was a Hollywood cliché and hated myself for it.

The minute I'd muster some focus and courage to move forward in my life, there'd be that little pile of white powder on the mirror calling me. I'd snort it, it would feel so good, and I'd feel so connected to the whole world, which was strange because I often didn't leave the house for days on end. And then there was the no-food-and-no-sleep part of it, and then those fucking little birds chirping at the crack of fucking dawn. I'd peek out the mini-blinds and see other people getting up and going to work and having a life. It was so depressing. I'd say to myself, You've got to just try and control yourself and get your shit together! And I'd promise myself I would, and then the thought would pop in my head, *But there's still a little coke left, somewhere. I know where—in the drawer downstairs!* And so I'd go downstairs to the basement and find the drawer, but no coke. Then I'd notice at the bottom of the drawer some coke residue, and I'd collect it very carefully with the edge of a matchbook and scrape it into a little pile, ignoring the fact that there were obviously other particulates commingled with this precious stash. And then I'd snort it. Yes. I. Would.

And I knew, *I knew* I was wasting all my potential. I'd fallen behind all my peers, who were by now getting out of college and heading toward their futures. I'd get clean for a few months even though Andrew continued using, and I'd apply some discipline to my life. Right after *Apt. 2C*, I did just that. I enrolled in an acting class studying Viola Spolin Theater Games, with Stephen Book. I did good work with real working actors. I gained some confidence. Dad saw that I was enjoying myself and getting something from it, so he eventually joined the class. He wanted to expand his acting skills so he could get some parts in films. I was happy we got to deepen our relationship by doing something like this together.

At some point Stephen decided it would be interesting if my dad and I did a scene together. And it certainly was. We did a scene from the play *Rain,* which was about a morally torn missionary and a prostitute in the South Seas. I played the prostitute, and Dad played the missionary who was trying to save me while also unconsciously trying to bed me. Talk about weird Freudian shit. I wanted to be closer to my dad, but this was a bit much.

I'm not sure how helpful this exercise was in the end. The only thing I learned was that I never again wanted to be in a scene with my dad while wearing a skimpy robe over lingerie.

Even though I was able to get to class and focus while I was there, I couldn't translate this into an acting career. I continually found myself distracted by Andrew with his newest adventure, shiny new toy, or pile of cocaine, and his son, Elliot, with his special-education needs and behavioral issues.

The day I met Elliot in late 1981, I thought: I'll be shocked if this child makes it to eighteen. I looked into his beautiful blue eyes and saw a lost soul. He looked as if he had no reservoir of self-preservation, as if he were running on fumes of anxiety and distraction. I'd always felt a bit out of my body, but this little tyke was barely present. My heart ached for him, but from day one I was overwhelmed by his needs. Elliot wasn't a handful; he was an armful. He was hyperactive, unruly, and impossible to placate. Part of me thought he was just a spoiled brat, and the other part thought there might be something seriously wrong with him. The experts told us he was somewhere in the middle. At age five, he was enrolled at a special-education school to help with his impulse-control and rage issues. He was put on Ritalin and then a myriad of other drugs to help him smooth out his moods so he could be in a regular special-education classroom in a Santa Monica public school. I was never clear on the cause of his behaviors. Was it because he'd been a blue baby at birth and had some brain damage? Or that he had attachment issues due to his mother's suicide attempt, or that he had been left in front of the TV at the babysitter's house for too many hours the first three years of his life? When he did allow you to take him into your arms, his little body vibrated with such anxious energy that it felt like his young soul was contemplating whether it was really safe to stick around here on Earth. The only thing that seemed to soothe him was plopping him down in front of a video, or buying him something. I hated that, and did it only when nothing else worked.

Of course I was worried that I was adding to his predicament by enabling his father's behavior. I knew that Andrew and I getting all coked up playing Trivial Pursuit until all hours of the night was not adding stability to anybody's life. But I also thought, *At least we never argue.* Andrew and his ex-wife did nothing but scream at each other when they were together. Our house was a "scream-free zone." And Elliot genuinely liked me. When we were alone with each other, I knew he felt safe around me. Both his teachers and grandma, Andrew's mother, Nancy, felt that I was the only calming influence in his life. But still, that did little to assuage my guilt about the cocaine.

By 1985 I was itching to do something more. I was four years into my relationship with Andrew and felt less and less like I was moving forward. I was bored with managing his needs and living by his whims. I knew that if I didn't make a change soon, my life would become set in stone. I knew I needed to shake it up. I knew I needed to change everything.

So I agreed to marry Andrew.

I knew if I did, he would change. I knew if I did, he would finally grow up, settle down, and get a real job. Which meant that I, too, could finally grow up, settle down, and figure out what kind of real job I wanted. I was ready to quit doing drugs, too. I was tired and burned out by all the late nights and unfilled days. So when I decided to marry him, I made Andrew agree that we would quit doing drugs. I proposed that we make our wedding day the day we quit. He agreed. I was thrilled. I knew that finally my life could start for real.

Everything was set. It was to be a miniseries of a wedding. Mom stepped in as the "executive producer," with the checkbook, and a big notebook filled with lots of tabs marked: "Catering," "Flowers," "Travel," and the like. Part one of our miniseries wedding would be getting legally married in Las Vegas in mid-November 1985 with about twenty close friends in attendance. Part two would be a romantic and beautiful ceremony with just my parents, Elliot, my best friend and Mom's assistant, Theresa, and Jerry Hamza and his new wife, Debbie. The ceremony would be on Christmas Eve at sunset on the veranda of the resort La Samanna on the island of Saint Martin. Part three would then be a big bash with more than one hundred people at my mom and dad's house with all our friends and family in January.

In November, as planned, we went to Las Vegas with our parents and a few friends, and got legally married at the Chapel of the Bells on the Las Vegas Strip. I was now officially Kelly Sutton. We had the Honeymoon Suite at the Flamingo Hotel, and gambled all night at the casino. Every table I sat down at, I won money. I couldn't lose. It was amazing. I took this as a clear sign from the universe that I was on track, and that marrying Andrew was definitely the right thing to do.

For part two of our Let's-Get-Married miniseries we headed down to Saint Martin in the Caribbean, also as planned. For the past few years, we'd been coming with my parents to this resort. It was where the A-list of the A-list of Hollywood vacationed. Our first year there, we had Christmas Eve dinner with Norman Lear, and the next year we bonded with Susan Saint James and her husband, Dick Ebersol, on the veranda outside the bar. It was a magical place where rubbing shoulders with Peter Ustinov, Madonna, Oprah, Mary Tyler Moore, and Ivan Lendl was an everyday occurrence. I was excited to swim in the pristine ocean, eat four-star French food, and see who else would be roaming around the beach that year. After a long fourteen-hour day of travel from Los Angeles, through Dallas, and then down to the island in the Dutch Antilles, I walked out onto the veranda of our little villa to take in the surf and smell the hibiscus. I knew I had returned to paradise. I went inside to unpack.

"What's this?" I asked Andrew, knowing full well what the small burrito-size brown paper bag I had just found in my suitcase was. I began to shake with rage.

"I thought we'd celebrate—" Andrew replied.

I ripped open the bag and saw the eighth of an ounce of coke. Then I saw red. Actual red. There was so much rage in me that I couldn't speak. I was sucked into a maelstrom of anger and insights about him, my life, and my future. I realized that he really had zero respect for my wishes for a new life. I was disgusted that he thought he could just bulldoze me into getting his way by being charming and "innocent" again. I was terrified that he had put this stash in *my* suitcase. But ultimately I was pissed at myself for believing that he could actually be different. As I marched over to the toilet and flushed the white powder down it, I knew that the coke wasn't all that had been flushed away. I knew I'd just made the worst mistake of my life by marrying Andrew, and that he'd never change.

I was fucked.

I should have just walked away then and there. But I didn't. All I could think about was my grandmother Alice saying to my mother after she got pregnant, "You've made your bed, and now you have to lie in it." I had to be a grown-up now. I had to take responsibility for my actions. I had to move forward with my chin up.

I went forward with the wedding ceremony in Saint Martin in my gorgeous off-white lace wedding dress. I smiled at everyone in the hotel restaurant who congratulated me and told me how beautiful I looked. I graciously thanked Susan Saint James and Dick Ebersol for the champagne we toasted with that night. I even laughed and was thrilled when, later that night, I ran into Bill Murray, and he stopped me suddenly in the middle of the restaurant and asked, "Haven't we met before? Oh yes, it was the Pirates of the Penzance."

I did not feel beautiful, or grateful, or thrilled. And I never let it show.

CHAPTER THIRTEEN

Whack! Thump!

I STARTED TO HAVE PANIC attacks. That's inaccurate. I started to have panic attacks every fucking day.

I didn't know what they were, I just thought I was dying—ears ringing, heart racing, a feeling of 25,000 pounds of adrenaline rushing through my body. They had first emerged as a regular occurrence when I was coming down after an all-night cocaine binge. As the morning birds chirped, I'd focus on how stupid I was for letting myself do it again, and then I'd feel my heart start beating way too fast in my chest, and away we'd go, straight into panic-attack land. The good news was that because I feared the panic attacks, my bingeing days became nonexistent. The bad news was that it wasn't only coke that now triggered them.

What tipped them over the edge into a daily occurrence was when it happened one day while I was driving. Thinking that you are about to pass out or die while steering a two-ton object around other moving two-ton objects is some fucked-up shit. And then here is some extra-fun stuff: Once I associated a place or activity with my panic attacks, my mind would automatically trigger another attack when I did, or even just thought about, that activity. All I would need to do was imagine being in my car alone, and, *Boom!* an attack would come on. Good times.

My panic attacks escalated to the point where I could barely leave my house. I could only drive (and when I say drive, I mean white-knuckle-praying-to-the-Virgin-Mary type of driving) in certain safety zones: to my parents' house, to my shrink, and to the market. Nowhere else. I could no longer drive to the San Fernando Valley, or Beverly Hills, or any other part of the city that was not in my safety zone.

I was a crazy person.

When Andrew and I went on car trips to Big Bear or San Diego, I would silently look for signs along the freeway that identified where the hospitals were in case I needed one (I always felt like I needed one). I avoided stairs and hills when I walked because they would raise my heart rate, and then I would think that I was having a heart attack, and this would trigger another panic attack. If I managed to make it to the supermarket along my prescribed route—go up Twenty-third Street, take a left on Montana, drive straight into the parking lot—I would then find a person inside who I believed looked like a doctor or a nurse, and then follow him or her around while I shopped. I assumed that if I did happen to pass out or die in the produce section, they would be there for me. I guess that was part of my fear—no one would be there for me.

And yet I never actually gave anyone a chance to be there for me. I didn't tell a soul about what was happening to me, especially my mom and dad. I could be around my mom and fake it a bit, but I was afraid to be around my dad, so I avoided him most of the time. I was too ashamed to admit that all this was going on. Deep down inside I knew that it had to do with my marriage, but I thought, *I had made this bed, and I was going to lie in it.* Dammit. I could never admit what a horrible mistake I had made by marrying Andrew. I was in too deep.

Dad's career was undergoing a bit of a rebirth (something I could have used a bit of). He built on the momentum of his earlier HBO shows by doing a fifth one—*Playin' with Your Head* in 1986. And then in 1987 he got his star on the Walk of Fame in Hollywood, on the corner of Selma and Vine Streets, right near the very building where he and Jack Burns had done their first radio gig in Los Angeles. Dad loved that bit of synchronicity. His concert life was renewed, and he began to fill large theaters again.

The biggest thing for him, though, was his acting. He costarred in *Outrageous Fortune*, with Bette Midler and Shelley Long, and then starred, with Molly Kagan, in a Disney TV movie *Justin Case*, directed by the incomparable Blake Edwards. I remember visiting both sets. Arthur Hiller directed *Outrageous Fortune*, and the day I visited, he let me follow him around all day. This was the man who had directed *Love Story*, *The In-Laws*, and *The Hospital*. Arthur put his arm around me and said, "Let me show you how it's done." He was a total sweetheart. I was in awe.

When I visited the set of *Justin Case* I met Blake Edwards briefly, but mostly hung out with the young woman, Molly Kagan, who costarred with my dad. She was about my age, and I was so envious of her. Not only was she a functioning person, but she was a young woman pursuing her art by working in a real movie—with my dad and Blake Edwards.

After doing *Apt. 2C* a few years earlier, I had similar ambitions and got my head shots and even went out on a few auditions, but I couldn't hack the audition process. It seemed I was always up for the young ingenue role. I'd walk into the casting office and find myself surrounded by a room full of bimbos. I didn't know how to play bimbo, so I gave up.

As Molly and I talked about the business, I shared with her my view about it all:

"This business is so full of shit. There's no real respect for artists or women or anyone who doesn't fit the mold. I thought I wanted to work in it, but then I realized that it's all about using people to make money."

"Wow. That sounds rather bitter," she replied.

I was shocked by her comment. I thought I was so sure of my point of view. "No. I just know what I don't want," I said, covering my shame. But now I was really unsure about what I'd just said.

"Good luck with that," she said, and went back to her work.

I wanted to crawl under a rock. But my dad had always taught me that if you let "the man" fuck you, "he" will. I built my story about the world to fit that picture. I convinced myself that I wasn't pursuing a career in showbiz because I didn't want to be a cog in the machine. I guess it was easier to believe that than to admit that I was afraid and had no confidence. It's always easier for me to reject something than have it reject me.

During this period my mom was also forging a new path. She'd opened an Equity-waiver theater with our family friend John Batis (the limo driver/actor/director who'd saved my dad's life back at Dodger Stadium). I decided that in that safe environment, I'd give performing another shot. I joined Mom's Park Stage Theater troupe, and wrote and performed a monologue for our premiere show. It was about a Beverly Hills teenage girl who'd run away and become homeless in hopes that her rich and successful parents would realize that she was gone and come looking for her. Can we say a cry for help?

Right before I took the stage on opening night, I had a panic attack and peed my pants a little. For the entire eight minutes on stage, all I could think about was if anyone could see the pee stain on the back of my dress. Oh well. At least it wasn't vomit.

After that I quit acting for good. Between my panic attacks, my fear of rejection, the chip on my shoulder, and the pee on my dress, I was done.

After Andrew and I got married, Dad politely pressured him to get serious about no longer being financially dependent on him. Andrew opened a car repair shop in Santa Monica—Automotive Enhancement. Dad "loaned" him the money to open a state-of-the-art, full-service repair shop for high-end cars—BMWs, Jaguars, Mercedes, and the like. It cost more than one hundred thousand dollars to outfit the place with every gadget, tool, lift, and diagnostic machine one could dream of (so much for that "financial independence"). I was excited because it was exactly what Andrew needed—a regular job where he had to focus and be responsible. I knew if he just put his time and energy toward something, he would be successful at it. He was so damn intelligent and could build or fix just about anything. I did everything I could to support him by becoming the bookkeeper and shop manager. We opened our doors in the fall of 1986, and things went well. Andrew seemed to be keeping his nose clean—literally—and I no longer felt like a freeloader.

After about nine months of things humming along, Andrew began hanging out with a new client who owned a Bentley. I began to notice some new behaviors, like Andrew closing the door to the office more often, staying late with this new client, and lying about little things. It was funny that he actually believed that, after all these years, I couldn't tell when he was high or lying. But what was happening really wasn't funny. I couldn't believe that after finding some sense of stability and normality in our lives, he was starting to use again.

I had already quit doing coke full-time. I'd had a few slips here and there, but between my panic attacks and trying to manage Andrew, Elliot, the business, and the house, quitting cocaine forever was a walk in the park. Because I now wanted to stay clean, I spent less and less time around Andrew and our business. But this only gave Andrew more freedom to do what he wanted, and his using escalated. I confronted him about it, but he played the whole thing down. I felt my future slipping away, and so I began to fight for my life. I screamed at him. I cajoled him. I bribed him with sex (which was really difficult since I was beginning to hate him). I even threw dishes a few times. Nothing reached him.

Feeling hopeless and crazy, I found my only haven at my parents' house, away from Andrew. But because I wasn't willing to tell my parents what was really going on, it wasn't much of a relief. It was still better than being at my own house. Things had never been perfect at my house, but now, by the end of 1987, they'd become unbearable.

I'd always been the one to clean, shop, cook, and care about how our home looked. Andrew never lifted a finger to do anything. He treated me just like he treated every waiter or clerk he ever encountered—he told you what to do or what he wanted, but he couldn't be bothered to do it himself. There was rarely a "please" or "thank-you" involved, only entitlement.

Andrew also never felt it necessary to actually get up and throw anything away. He either didn't throw the thing away (meaning it would sit eternally wherever he had left it until I did something with it), or he would toss the thing from across the room into the trash. The second technique was his favorite, especially in the bedroom. From a lying-down position in bed, he would toss a half-full can of Diet Coke into the trash. This would result in the can banking off the wall, leaving a patina of Diet Coke on it.

Most people would see this as disgusting and do something about it. And in my own way I did. I'd clean the wall. I'd move the trash closer to him. I'd suggest that maybe he could get up and throw it away. In the end nothing worked, and so I learned to endure the sound of the can hitting the wall—*Whack!*—and then falling into the trash—*Thump! Whack! Thump! Whack! Thump!*

I didn't know what to do. I couldn't use. I couldn't leave. I couldn't run to my parents. So I ran to Shirley MacLaine.

I began searching for answers, and thankfully she had them. After reading her book *Out on a Limb*, I saw how simple it was to change the world around me—just think different thoughts about it. While Shirley was on an airplane in bad turbulence, all she did was picture the turbulence ending, and it did. If I thought enough positive thoughts about my life with Andrew, I could change him and myself and really get somewhere. This haunting feeling inside me that Andrew was crazy and I needed to get away from him—that wasn't real; it was just an illusion, a symptom of my own inability to cope with the choices I had made. I just needed to change my thoughts about the choices.

I went to the Bodhi Tree Bookstore looking for more answers and bought lots of books. Initially I was attracted to the Zen—or, as they say, the "chop wood and carry water"—philosophy because it was a path that uncluttered one's mind and life. With all the stuff in our house, I longed to be uncluttered. But I soon discovered that that kind of life took presence and consciousness, and I had neither. What I wanted was a magic wand. I became fascinated with Richard Bach and his book *Illusions*. I figured if he could learn how to walk through walls and understand that it's all just an illusion, the least I could do was walk through my life and see it all as an illusion. I studied Shakti Gawain's book *Creative Visualization* and attempted to creatively visualize my way out of my pain and confusion. I had my aura cleansed and my chakras balanced, but still felt the oppression of my marriage and life. I concluded that there must be something inherently wrong with me, so I went to a Rolfer.

A Rolfer is a body practitioner who manipulates and reshapes the soft tissue of your muscles in order to release locked-in emotions and habits of being. I understood the mind-body connection, and thought I'd give it a try. But, it was such a weird thing, really—you go to an office and pay another human being to push and rub on your naked body until you scream and cry, and the screaming and crying doesn't stop him like it should; oh no, it only encourages him because then he thinks he's getting the really bad stuff out. I really wanted to believe that if I screamed and cried enough, he would release every bad thought and feeling I ever had about myself and my life.

But there was just one problem: I was too embarrassed to scream and cry in front of him.

I had no idea how I had allowed all this stuff in my life to go on and to happen to me for so long. I knew I'd forsaken so much of myself for too many years. I'd even stopped listening to music for the last four years. I was brought up on the music of the sixties and seventies by my father, and it was that music that had bonded us so much at that time. Music had been a guide, a friend, and a teacher to me my whole life, and now it was gone. Today when I hear songs on the radio that are now considered to be eighties classics, I feel like I must have been in a coma or a kidnap victim—I've never heard these songs even once. In the late eighties, there was no music in my life.

About six months after the client with the Bentley showed up, Andrew went officially insane. He was so paranoid that he walked around our house wearing two handguns in holsters underneath his bathrobe. Years later, when I saw the scene in *Boogie Nights* with Alfred Molina playing the coke dealer walking around his house in a bathrobe, I turned away. There was Andrew. There was my past. Of course my past did not include a crazy Asian man lighting firecrackers in the living room. No, instead it included Andrew wearing his guns, with his entire body covered in scabs because he believed there were worms growing in it and he needed to dig them out.

And still, I told no one what was going on.

One week in early 1988, it all came to a head. Andrew and I'd been arguing for days because he wanted to lend his Bentley friend five thousand dollars to make a drug deal.

"We'd get the money back immediately," he told me.

I replied, "No fucking way. That money is my savings, and I don't trust him or you." A few days later he went ahead and did it anyway. I went to the shop and confronted him. He denied knowing anything about it.

"That's it. I'm out of here," I said as I walked toward him to head out of the shop.

He pulled out a gun from I-don't-know-where, pointed it at me, and said, "You can't walk out and leave me."

I looked straight down that gun barrel, froze, and pissed myself.

When he realized what he'd done, he put the gun down. I collapsed onto the floor. My legs had given out. He ran to me and apologized profusely. I pushed him away.

I had been cut in two at that moment, even without a bullet.

I knew it was time to leave.

CHAPTER FOURTEEN

"Mother and Child Reunion"

FOR THE SEVEN YEARS I'd been with Andrew, I'd never been away from him overnight, or out of contact with him for more than three or four hours. Over the years he'd say things to me like, "I could never love another;" or "There will never be anyone who could love you as much as I do"; and let's not forget the always-popular, "I don't know what I would ever do if you left me." This never made me feel loved. It just made me feel trapped. I was too afraid to leave him. Would he become one of those men who shot his wife, her family, and then himself? I knew that *if* I were ever going to leave, I'd have to do it cautiously. But I knew that I had to begin somewhere.

In the spring of 1988 I reapplied to UCLA, and got in. In January 1989, winter quarter, I'd become a full-time student. Knowing that I'd be reentering the world of reading, writing, and studying, I felt hope I hadn't felt in years.

I wasn't the only one. In 1988 my dad took an evolutionary step with his stand-up. In his sixth HBO special, *What Am I Doin' in New*

Jersey?, Dad included plenty of the standard Carlin observational routines like "Keeping People Alert" and "More Stuff on Dogs and Driving," but where he stepped into new territory was with "Reagan's Gang, Church People, and American Values" and "People I Can Do Without." He'd always been a social commentator, but with these new bits, he'd found a new energy and intensity. Surviving two heart attacks and turning fifty gave him a new courage. Having endured the Reagan years of the 1980s gave him a focus for his outrage. When I watched the premiere of the show, I felt that something new and exciting was happening in his work. I was deeply proud and inspired.

On April 8, 1988, for Andrew's thirty-sixth birthday, he and I went out to dinner at a nearby German restaurant with a couple he'd been hanging out with lately. I think their names were Steve and Melinda. Andrew's newest toy was a Harley-Davidson, and he'd met them at some Harley event. They weren't hard-core bikers, but they certainly liked to party.

Andrew rarely drank alcohol (it wasn't his drug of choice), but on this night he ordered a schnapps, a gin martini, and a glass of white wine, all before dinner. By the entrée I was ready to walk out. At this point being with Andrew was difficult enough for me. Add a few too many ounces of alcohol, and it was as if his character flaws got turned up to eleven. He was intolerable—arrogant, pushy, and rude. The minute the check dropped on the table, I left and went to my mom and dad's house.

Around midnight Andrew called. He was in jail at the Santa Monica Police Department and wanted me to bail him out. He wasn't forthcoming about what had happened, and the turn of events didn't become clear until Steve called me to tell me the whole tale. He said that after dinner, while the three of them walked toward our house, Andrew went ballistic about my leaving early, and vandalized a street sign. Steve, wanting to calm him down, agreed to go with him to our automotive shop. He thought they'd hang out there and cool down. But when they got there, instead of Andrew opening up the gate, he pulled out a handgun and began shooting at the front of the business. After he'd emptied a clip of bullets into the garage door of the shop, Steve persuaded him to get back into the car. As they drove away, a Santa Monica police car, on its way to check out the "shots fired" call, drove toward them and made them stop. Andrew had gotten friendly with a few officers from SMPD over the last few years (gun nuts love gun nuts), and told them what he'd just done. A sergeant friend of Andrew's arrived and quickly took over. He arrested Andrew for drunk driving and discharging a firearm but was nice enough to throw away the cocaine he'd found on him.

When Steve was done, I hung up the phone and told my mom the whole story. We both agreed that we'd bail him out of jail only if he went straight to rehab. I called Andrew, told him the conditions, and he agreed.

When I saw Andrew swagger out of the station, I knew it meant trouble. He got into the car.

"Take me home," he demanded. No "Thank you" or "I'm sorry."

"You're not going home. You're going to St. John's CDC," my mom calmly replied.

"No I'm not. I need to think about it. I need to go home first," he countered.

"I can't take it anymore," I tried to explain. "You have to go. You are not going home. We're going to St. John's."

"Stop the car," Andrew demanded, as he opened the door while the car was still moving. He got out blocks away from the hospital and our house, and started walking. Mom and I sat there and watched him.

"He'll go," Mom said as she pulled away and drove toward her house.

About an hour later Steve called.

"He's trashing the house. Throwing shit everywhere. I think you should come home."

"You can tell him I'm not coming home. I'll only come home after he's gone to St. John's." Of course, deep down inside, I hoped he wouldn't go so that I would never have to go home.

An hour later Andrew called, demanding I come home. I reiterated that I would not be coming home unless he went to rehab. He then said, "Well, if you don't come home now"—and then I heard the sound of a shotgun being cocked—"I'm going to shoot Jeremy." Jeremy was my eight-year-old black Lab.

I said, "That's nice." And hung up the phone.

A few hours later Steve called to say that Andrew had taken some Valium, calmed down, and was ready to go to rehab. Jeremy was sound asleep, too, oblivious to the drama that had unfolded all night.

Five days later, after Andrew's detox period, I found myself in my first group therapy session at St. John's Chemical Dependency Center, with the spouses and significant others of the rehab patients. We would undergo our own rehab program, learning about addiction, how to live with people in recovery, and of course, our own issues.

"You know you're more insane than he is," the therapist, Berenice, said to me.

Excuse me? I had just poured my heart out to her and the group, sharing all the insanity, chaos, and emotional turmoil that Andrew had created in my life over the last seven years, and I was the insane one?

She continued, "You stayed with him. You enabled him. You ignored your own needs, and you expected him to change. That sounds pretty insane to me."

I didn't want to hear a word of it. I didn't want to hear the truth.

This "tough love" thing was a bit too tough for me. And yet, somewhere deep inside, I felt the love behind it, too. I was actually relieved. She was the first person in my life ever to talk to me like this. She was not afraid to confront me on my denial and bullshit. She became my therapist for the next ten years.

Once Andrew was out of rehab, our life together was amazing. We both went to meetings—Alcoholics Anonymous, Narcotics Anonymous—and I to Al-Anon, where we made a bunch of new friends. We immersed ourselves in the twelve-step culture and learned how to live in a different way. I realized that my needs and feelings were separate from Andrew's, and that I had the right to ask for what I wanted and needed. Of course, having been expertly trained since the age of three to take care of everyone else's feelings before mine, I found that unlearning this habit was challenging. I felt intense pangs of guilt when I put myself first, but I soon learned that no one died when I abided by my needs instead of others'. Baby steps, yes. But even these baby steps created more space within me than I'd ever had.

Andrew became more honest, accountable, and productive. The house stayed cleaner longer. When he said he was going to do something, he actually did it. He became willing to listen to others and let go of the belief that he knew everything. (I even glimpsed a small sliver of humility one day!) We sold the auto business (too many bad memories and baggage), and he decided to open a new business—a small hobby store that sold radio-controlled helicopters. For him it was a transformation. There were moments when I felt we just might be able to live the life that I had always imagined we were capable of living.

In January 1989 at the age of twenty-five, and despite the fact that my panic attacks were still in full swing, I finally began school at

UCLA. I was excited to fill myself up and move toward a real future. After seven years with Andrew, who had no interest in learning about anything because he felt he already knew it all, being in an environment that invited my curiosity, independent thinking, and creativity was like drinking at an oasis. I could actually dare to ask myself, What do I want to make of this one precious life?

My dad loved that I was in school, not just because I'd be the first Carlin ever to graduate from college, but because he got to hear about everything that I was learning in classes like Astronomy, Oceanography, and Anthropology. He even intimated that he was a bit envious of my chance to soak in so much about the world. He wished he could join me.

It was so nice to be able to share my life with my dad again.

Because I'd been out of school for seven years, I was required to take a Remedial English class my first semester back. One day the instructor, a cool thirty-something guy, brought in what he called the perfect essay that reflected the "compare and contrast" style of writing that we would be expected to use in our future studies. He put a boom box on the desk, pressed PLAY, and my dad's voice came out of the speakers: "I'd like to talk a little bit about baseball and football. Starting with baseball; baseball is different from any other sport in a lot of different little ways. For instance, in most sports, you score points or you score goals. In baseball, you score runs."

I guess Dad made it to class after all.

I swelled with excitement. After class I told the instructor who I was. He nearly fell off his chair. For a flash I felt that old flood of "specialness" that I used to feel backstage with my dad, but mostly I felt a rush of pride for the force my dad had become in the culture. He'd been doing comedy for almost thirty years, and he'd made a real mark. I could feel my own aspiration rise within me. I, too, wanted to make a dent.

But before I could make that dent, first I needed to make it to class. My anxiety and panic made getting to class a bit like an obstacle course. I feared walking up the big hill in the middle of campus because it raised my heart rate, and that always triggered a panic attack for me. My solution was to go into Ackerman Union (a huge building that housed the bookstore, auditorium, and food court), take the elevator to the third floor, and walk through the coffee shop. This would situate me nicely three-quarters up the hill.

On the outside I looked like any other student making my way through the building, but on the inside I was a secret agent searching for the earliest sign of racing heart, tingly hands, and spaced-out head. Once I'd get to class, I'd casually put my finger on my neck, checking my pulse every five minutes, making sure my heart was still beating.

I have no doubt this is what an insane person looks like.

And of course I still told no one. Why break with tradition at this point? I suffered silently. Eventually my mom, who had suffered from panic attacks in her twenties, too, figured it out. But instead of talking about it head on, she just asked, "What do you need? Would you like me to drive you to school today? Come onto the campus with you?"

Quietly I replied, "Yes."

Sometimes she'd drop me off. Other days she'd bring a book and find a table or patch of grass and read while I went off to class. Every once in a while, when I had a big lecture, she'd join me and come to class and pretend that she was just another student. There I was, twenty-six years old, in American History 101 sitting next to my mommy. Life had worked itself out in such a way that I could finally be the "helpless child" and she the "nurturing mother" that neither one of us was able to be during her alcoholism. It's amazing how a simple gesture can heal so much.

About eighteen months after Andrew got sober, the magic spell of sobriety wore off, and he returned to his old Andrew ways. He wasn't using, but he became what they call a "dry drunk"—doing all the dishonest and manipulative behavior of an addict without the drugs or alcohol. It's kind of like memory foam—no matter how much you try and change its shape, it will always return to its original form. He was once again arrogant, controlling, and a liar. He went to fewer and fewer meetings and stopped calling his sponsor. Once again he believed he knew better than everyone else. All the patience and understanding that had been restored in me quickly dissolved. I knew for sure now that my future could not and would not include Andrew. For now, it was all about school.

Eventually every college student must face the question: What the fuck do I major in?

I myself dabbled with the idea of anthropology until I realized that every professor in the department was nine thousand years old. I thought maybe English would be a good fit, but English seemed like the default major for the completely lost—athletes and stoners. I didn't want to pick just anything. I wanted this time at UCLA to really count.

When I was eleven years old, my dad had taken me to the UCLA Mardi Gras, and we'd gone to a booth that played short films by UCLA film students. After watching them I turned to my dad and said, "I want to do that." But now that I was at UCLA and faced with the opportunity to actually apply to that very same Film Department, I balked. I feared being rejected so much that I did it for them by not applying.

In the fall of 1990, the beginning of my third year, I took a rather famous class at UCLA: Communications 101 with Jeff Cole. He was a rock star of a lecturer in the Communications Department. He was funny and cool, and he talked about popular media culture in a way that allowed you to feel like a fan and a scholar at the same time. He was voted favorite lecturer a number of times during those years. We watched everything from *All in the Family* to the famous 1960 Nixon-Kennedy debate. The class was the perfect blend of entertainment and sociology—basically what my father had been doing his whole career. I saw how the media subtly shape our world-views. This enabled me to see below the bullshit that they try to feed us. It was like learning how to read the secret code of our culture. I immediately applied to get into the department and was accepted.

I thrived. I loved the classes and the camaraderie of the professors. The department was more like family than school. I created a circle of friends who were smart, curious, and full of life, and I kept all this very separate from Andrew. I never invited people to my house or talked about him to my friends. Not surprisingly, this new separate life fed Andrew's jealousy and paranoia, and I'd dutifully have to check in with him every few hours. But I didn't mind. I knew I was biding my time.

The first quarter in my new major, I took a class that focused solely on First Amendment issues—something I was already passionate about because of my father. The first day, the lecturer, Geoff Cowan, told the one hundred or so students, "My favorite part of this course is teaching the famous First Amendment case called *Pacifica v. the FCC*. The reason I love teaching it is because I get to recite George Carlin's famous 'Seven Words You Can Never Say on Television.'"

I was the one who practically fell out of my chair.

After class I introduced myself to Geoff. He asked me if my dad would like to come to class to discuss the case. I asked my dad, but he declined. He felt out of his element, and knew nothing about the law behind the case. I tried to explain to him that no one expected him to argue the case. They just wanted him to talk about the comedy that inspired it. He still said no, but a few quarters later he did accept another invitation—to be part of a forum I organized, in conjunction with Geoff and the department, about the chilling effect of politically correct speech on campuses. Dad was genuinely thrilled to participate, and after the event, I could tell he was even a bit in awe of my new scholastic career.

Although I was now president of the Communications Students

Club, I still had no idea how any of this would translate into the real world. Some people went into advertising, others into Hollywood agencies or studios, but I knew those were not options for me. Those felt like selling out to me. I needed to find my way.

I nervously signed up for a writing class, afraid of being critiqued but wanting to find my voice. The class was about learning how to write in the more personal reportage style that Hunter S. Thompson had created and made famous, and I thought it was something I'd be good at. When I got my first graded paper back, I could feel my stomach tighten. I slowly peeled the pages back to the last one to see my grade and comments. "A—Kelly, you need to pursue writing. I can tell you have a lot to say and a great way of saying it. Keep on writing!"

"Keep on writing!" Tears came to my eyes when I realized that I might just be able to carry on the Carlin family's gift of the gab. I saw a future for myself.

When I got home I immediately called my dad to tell him about the comments. He said, "Congratulations, Kiddo. You're on your way!"

I was on my way! On my way! On my way where? Back to Andrew? Ugh.

This newfound vision for my future made my daily life with Andrew even more oppressive. Being in his presence began to physically repulse me. Everything he did reminded me of the self I was when I picked him as my partner—wounded, naive, and desperate for love.

He once again never cleaned up any mess, so his shit took up every square inch of open horizontal space. His personal hygiene was horrific. Because he was diabetic he'd sleep-eat in bed. Because he'd snorted way too much coke for all those years, he'd created a hole in the cartilage between his nostrils; there were unmentionable disgusting ways he would deal with that when he had a cold. In the past, because I was an insane person sharing his space, I somehow tolerated it, but now all I could see was the hell I'd constructed for myself. I spent as little time as possible at home. I led a double life, pretending to the outside world that everything was okay, but also hiding from Andrew the joy and sense of purpose I got from school.

I spent almost all the free time I had with my mom. Many days her fibromyalgia symptoms—deep aching of her joints and fatigue—kept her from getting out of bed. I'd bring my home-work over, and we'd while away the hours watching bowling, ice-skating, and poker on TV. That's when we hatched a plan to go to Big Sur for Easter vacation in 1990.

It was heaven. Since I hadn't taken a trip without Andrew for the last nine years, I was amazed at the freedom I felt. With each mile that ticked farther away from Los Angeles, I could feel myself relax into my body in a way that I had never known. The unsurpassed beauty and raw nature of California's Central Coast settled into my bones. So many people had come to this very place for enlighten-ment and clarity, and I wanted some of that, too. We stayed at the famous Ventana Inn, ate cheeseburgers at Nepenthe, and bought pottery at the Coast Gallery—it was the quintessential Big Sur vacation. We soaked in the peace. We made it an annual tradition.

On our spring trip two years later, in 1992, as I settled onto the deck of our room at the Ventana and stared out at the Pacific, I knew it was time to leave Andrew. I felt the truth of this in my bones. It was time. Of course this put the fear of god into me. I feared An-drew's anger, his guns, and his intense jealousy. He was a profes-sional victim and wore these scars loud and proud.

I told my mom that I was going to leave him, and she asked me the strangest question: "Are you sure?" To this day I am not sure what she meant by asking that question. Maybe it finally occurred to her to ask me the question she should have asked when I said I was going to marry him—like some kind of bizarre, delayed reaction.

I knew there was no other option. It was either leave him or kill myself.

On April 29, 1992, a full month after I had returned from Big Sur, I finally mustered the courage to tell Andrew it was over. I walked into the living room ready to sit him down to explain that I needed to separate from him for a month and "find myself" (this was my way of letting him down slowly). Instead, I found him standing in the middle of the room glued to the TV. It seemed that at that very moment, Los Angeles had decided to erupt into a maelstrom in reaction to the Rodney King trial verdict. Andrew paced around the house and then came back into the living room. He slammed a shotgun onto the coffee table and said, "They're coming for our stuff."

Oh, if that were only true!

I found myself in a surreal world the next few days, going to school by day, knowing that only a few miles away people were going berserk on the streets while classes went on as usual. And then by night, the city went on lockdown, and no one was allowed out after dark.

Finally, weeks later, with the shotgun safely stowed away, I sat Andrew down and told him I was leaving. He was shocked. He said he had no idea anything was wrong. I was on the verge of suicide, and my husband had no idea anything was wrong! For the last two years I had been gone fourteen hours a day, had not slept with him in more than a year, cold-shouldered him when I was with him, and all he could say was that he had no idea anything was wrong?

And so I left. I just left all of it. On May 11, 1992, I walked away from the house and the piles of crap that were stacked up in every room. I walked away from Elliot. And I walked away from Andrew.

CHAPTER FIFTEEN

A Slice of Patty-Cake

TWO THINGS HAPPENED upon leaving Andrew—I slept with a gun under my pillow, and I got laid.

No. Not at the same time.

Terrified that Andrew would become unhinged and use one of his many guns to kill me, my parents, and then himself in some kind of If-I-can't-have-you-then-no-one-can-have-you frenzy, I slid the bull-nosed Smith & Wesson pistol that he'd bought me on my twenty-fifth birthday under my pillow so I could sleep soundly.

Initially I'd told him that I was only leaving for a few weeks to think about what I wanted for my future. That was a lie. I knew my future was without him, but I was too afraid to tell him that. In order to have the space to figure out what to do with my life, I asked him not to communicate with me during those first few weeks. He gave me three hours. He called my parents' house five, ten, twenty times a day, and every time he did, my mom or dad would say, "She's not ready to talk to you. You need to give her some space. Do you really think this is helping your case?"

After almost three weeks of this, I finally sat him down and told him that it was over. Forever. I was not ever coming back. Thus the gun under my pillow. I really had no idea what he'd do or how far he'd go. I even contemplated changing my name and moving to another city if I had to. Mercifully he slowly accepted our new reality, the phone calls died down, and we began that awkward, predivorce time in our relationship.

Unchained from my old life, I walked among other humans feeling as if it were my first time on Earth. Everything seemed fresh, like a new coat of paint had washed over life itself. Every moment was filled with possibility. I could do and be anything I wanted. My whole life was ahead of me. All the dreams I'd been bottling up for years could now be realized. Creative dreams, career dreams, feeling-like-I-can-finally-breathe dreams—all there for the taking.

But first things first—it was time to get laid.

It had been more than two years since I'd had any sex, and probably five since it'd been anything more than obligation of my wifely duties. Although I'd built a life separate from Andrew, cheating was not an option for me. I'll admit I'd done my share of fantasizing over the young, hard bodies surrounding me at UCLA, but now that I was free to pursue them, I couldn't see myself going to a frat party to get laid. I decided to turn to what I knew.

During the previous year, I'd been hanging out on Friday nights with my old boyfriend, Mark Lennon, and our friends Billy and Susea at Capri, a small Italian restaurant on Abbot Kinney in Venice Beach. We spent hours immersed in great conversation while noshing on plates of caprese, bruschetta, and butternut squash ravioli. It was a bastion of comfort. I'd often glance over at Mark and think, *What if?* So now that I had the chance to really ask the question, I did. I mustered up the courage one night to give Mark a booty call.

"Hey, whatcha doing?" I asked with a perky casualness.

"Nothing really. Just hanging out," he answered.

"Cool. Any plans for later?" I was never one for direct communication. How does one actually go about saying, "Can I come over and fuck your brains out?" without saying it?

"No, not really," he replied.

I saw my opening, and boldly I continued, "Could I maybe come over?"

"Uh, sure, but I need to tell you something."

"Okay—" I said, but thought, *Shit! He's got a girlfriend I didn't know about. Dammit. I knew it. I* knew *it!*

"I'm gay."

Whoa. I didn't know *that*. My head whirled. My stomach clutched. The floor dropped a few inches beneath me.

"Oh," was all I could manage. He told me how he'd come to this realization, and how he was slowly coming out to friends and family. But as the information trickled into my psyche, it made sense. Even when we'd gone out, we'd always been more friends than lovers. I began to cry. I knew that it wasn't about Mark. It was that I finally felt my aloneness. There was nothing familiar about where I found myself after leaving Andrew. I realized that I was looking for a safe place to land, and I thought Mark's arms were it. I saw now that there was no going back, just moving forward. My new life alone was now real for me, too.

A few weeks later, my best friend, Theresa, was having a barbeque down at her place in Playa del Rey. I thought, *If there is a cute guy there, I'm going to get laid.* Screw landing in a safe place. I wanted adventure.

At the party, there was a cute guy that I knew from Theresa's office—Bob McCall. We'd met the summer before when I'd done some temp work there. In fact, we'd not only met, we'd had lunch together and talked about music, films, and what was happening in the world politically. It was so different to talk to Bob. Andrew shoved his opinions down your throat and made you feel stupid for having a different thought than he did. But with Bob, it was a natural back and forth, a building on each other's thoughts and ideas, an organic weaving. I remember thinking: *So this is what it feels like to have a conversation with a normal guy.*

Now, a year later, unshackled from my need to be a good wife, I had only myself (and my loins) to be loyal to. Bob and I began to talk in Theresa's kitchen, and I remembered how smart and funny he was. And he had blond hair and blue eyes. I tried on the idea of being with him. After eleven years with Andrew, it was such a foreign concept. We continued talking and flirting. Here was my idea of flirting—I taught him how to patty-cake.

I guess the last time I had flirted was in the fourth grade. But it worked. We were hitting it off. He was a bit tipsy, and we kept having to start over and over again.

"Miss Mary Mack, Mack, Mack," I said as I showed him the moves. "All dressed in black, black, black." Our hands missed each other's on the last beat. "No, it's clap once, then both our hands come together . . ."

As all the other guests were outside drinking and eating on the deck, Bob and I were reliving recess by ourselves in Theresa's kitchen. Her sister, Mary, looked inside at one point, saw us laughing and patty-caking, and said to Theresa, "Well, will you look at those two."

After we had exhausted the basics of patty-cake, Bob and I talked and talked the night away. After all the guests had left the party, we both stayed to watch *Saturday Night Live* with Theresa. We were both being cautious, but I could feel the chemistry building between us. Just as we were getting comfortable on the couch, Theresa's phone rang.

"Hello," Theresa said. Then she looked at me, covered the mouthpiece, and whispered, "It's Andrew."

Terror shot through my body. *Does he know what I'm doing? Is he stalking me? Is he really psychic like he once claimed? What the fuck?*

I took the phone and turned my back on the room.

"What do you want?" I asked as coldly as possible.

"I'm at Santa Monica Hospital. I had an incident with my blood sugar," he replied.

"What do you want?" I repeated in the same tone.

"I need a ride home. They won't release me unless I have one."

"Call Steve," I suggested.

"He's not around. He's out of town. They won't let me take a cab," his voice getting more desperate.

My heart ached with guilt. "I don't know what to say."

"You're still my wife," he threw into the quiet space between us.

I didn't reply at first. I didn't believe that he'd had "an incident" with his diabetes. I didn't believe a word of it. But I felt his pain. I felt my guilt. I knew I should just hang up.

"I'll be there in twenty-five minutes," not believing the words even as I said them.

I got off the phone and told Theresa and Bob that I had to go— family emergency. As I drove toward Santa Monica Hospital, I roiled in rage and decided that this was the very last act of charity I would give to Andrew Sutton for the rest of my life. I was done. I found him outside the emergency room on the sidewalk waiting for me, and silently drove him home. I couldn't speak. There was nothing to say. I wouldn't speak. It was the beginning and end of some kind of standoff. I had succumbed to this wish, but my silence said I would never grant him another. Whatever he'd tried to do had not worked. I was not going into the house with him. I was not coming home.

I drove away, furious with myself for having given in to him one more time, but more determined than ever to protect the stand I had taken for my life.

While I was clumsily taking a stand for *my* life, my dad was boldly taking a stand for his art. Like the great artistic leap he had made in 1969 when he went from clean-cut comic to counterculture co-median, he evolved once again. During that spring of 1992, he taped his eighth, and what was later considered his most groundbreaking, HBO show, *Jammin' in New York*. Years later, when he talked about this show in interviews, he often said, "After thirty years of doing stand-up comedy, I'd finally found my true artistic voice."

Although he did some classic Carlin material like "Airline An-nouncements" (my favorite line being, "Tell the 'captain,' Air Mar-shal Carlin says, 'Go fuck yourself!'"), the show overall was a huge change for him. The most controversial and famous piece that emerged from the show was "The Planet Is Fine." In it he de-clared:

> *The planet is fine; the* people *are fucked. . . . The planet has been through a lot worse than us. Been through all kinds of things worse than us. Been through earthquakes, volca-noes, plate tectonics, continental drift, solar flares, sun spots, magnetic storms, the magnetic reversal of the poles . . . hundreds of thousands of years of bombardment by comets and asteroids and meteors, worlwide floods, tidal waves, worldwide fires, erosion, cosmic rays, recurring ice ages. . . . And we think some plastic bags and some aluminum cans are going to make a difference? The planet—the planet— the planet isn't going anywhere. WE ARE!*

These days, some climate-change deniers love to quote his line about the plastic bags and aluminum cans to justify their position. They don't understand what he really meant. That line was an at-tack against yuppies—a group of people my father hated because they claimed to be altruistic when in fact they were only saving the planet to save themselves from the inconvenience of climate change. It was an indictment of the 1980s Reagan era that had turned a whole generation, the Baby Boomers, away from the common good and toward NIMBY—not in my backyard—thinking.

That aside, the main punch line of the piece hit many, including myself, in a profound way.

He continued:

> *We're going away. Pack your shit, folks. We're going away. And we won't leave much of a trace, either. Thank God for that. Maybe a little Styrofoam. Maybe. A little Styrofoam. The planet'll be here and we'll be long gone. Just another failed mutation. Just another closed-end biological mistake. An evolutionary cul-de-sac. The planet'll shake us off like a bad case of fleas. A surface nuisance.*

Here was a hero of the counterculture taking a stand, not for the progressive Left's party line about environmentalism, but for the planet itself. He invited us to step away from our entrenched daily political struggles, and join him in a new perspective where we could see the much bigger picture—floating in space looking back at Earth. He had found a place where we could detach from the Sturm und Drang of the second half of the twentieth century and find some peace.

He finished with:

> *See I don't worry about the little things: bees, trees, whales, snails. I think we're part of a greater wisdom than we will ever understand. A higher order. Call it what you want. Know what I call it? The Big Electron. The Big Electron . . . whoooa. Whoooa. Whoooa. It doesn't punish, it doesn't reward, it doesn't judge at all. It just is. And so are we. For a little while.*

As I sat alone on the couch in my old room at my parents' house (I had not gone to New York to see it live), watching this unfold before my eyes, I was terrified, stunned, and in awe of his proclamation. I felt the truth in it. I felt the freedom in it. But I wasn't ready for it.

I felt like I had finally joined the world. I didn't want to leave it now. I wanted to step into the fray, pick a side, take a stand, and make some noise for a cause. I wanted to chain myself to a tree, defend a women's clinic, or register voters in South Central Los Angeles. I wanted to use my heart and mind to evolve the world forward. But there was my dad, my hero, now telling me to fuck hope. I was confused and startled. And yet I was also awakened, as if I were a bell that had just been rung.

Three weeks after I left Bob on Theresa's couch, we met again. Bob had told Theresa that he wanted to see me again, and so she invited me to *Inside Edition*'s end-of-season wrap party (she was the production manager). I felt like a giddy teenager. Which made perfect sense, seeing how the last time I had been with a man other than Andrew was when I was eighteen.

The party was held at a bar in Brentwood. I walked in and found Bob hanging out with Theresa. He looked as cute as I'd remembered. We tried to talk over the music and din of the party, and then moved to a back area where there was an arcade and some semblance of quiet.

Within twenty minutes, we were making out against the Pac-Man machine. We couldn't keep our hands off each other. Someone told us to get a room, so we made our way out to the parking lot. After making out there for twenty, thirty . . . well, maybe forty minutes, we decided we probably *did* need a room. Breathless, we each got into our respective cars and headed to his place in Playa del Rey. We made out on his couch for another hour. When his roommate walked out of his bedroom on his way to the bathroom, Bob asked me if I wanted to move to his room. I said yes faster than I probably should have. I sort of made up for it by asking him, "Will you respect me in the morning?"

He breathlessly replied, "Yes, of course." Don't they always say that?

Bob and I stayed in his room for three days, taking breaks only to walk down the street to Blockbuster to rent foreign films and buy food at Hank's Pizza. I was the happiest woman on earth—food, film, and fucking.

On day four Bob got up and started to pack an overnight bag. As I rolled over, I nervously asked, "Where you going?"

"To my brother's place in Lake Elsinore for the next week. He's going to help me fix my Camaro," he replied.

"You're leaving?" I tried not to sound too panicked.

"Yeah, we've had these plans for weeks. It's the only time he has free."

"Where's Lake Elsinore?" Knowing already that it was probably not close by.

"About seventy-five miles east of here, near Riverside."

How could he leave? Who was this guy who could leave a naked and willing girl in his bed to go fix his car? I had only ever known the attached-at-the-hip kind of relationships. I also had stuff to do at this point, like study for a final I had that Tuesday, and to proctor another one Friday. But, if I was called to, I was ready to drop all my needs, duties, and appointments to disappear into his life.

Not wanting to appear too needy, I got dressed, and we made plans to see each other when he got home. And then I left.

While thoughts of Bob—how he smelled, how he felt, how he made me feel—cluttered my mind, I distractedly studied for and took my final on Tuesday. By Thursday I couldn't take it any longer. I needed to see him. I called him at his brother's house and asked if I could come out and see him. He quickly agreed. He did warn me that it wasn't very exciting out there. I didn't care what was there, as long as *he* was. The last time I had felt this euphoric was eight years earlier when I had seen a very large pile of pharmaceutical cocaine on a mirror on the coffee table in my bedroom. I was happy, happy, happy. I told him I'd leave UCLA on Friday afternoon around two, and he began to give me directions.

He began with "Take the 10 East to the 110 South to the 91 East. Take that for about thirty miles—"

My stomach did a somersault.

"The traffic will be horrible on a Friday," he continued.

My lips began to feel fuzzy, as did my head.

"Uh-huh," I said casually, trying to mask the rising panic in my chest. I finished up the conversation pretending to be the kind of person who could easily drive seventy-five miles by herself in a car without thinking that she's dying from a heart attack or having a stroke. I couldn't let on that I was in fact a crazy person who hadn't driven more than seven or eight miles away from my home in more than six years. I wouldn't let myself fuck this up.

After I'd proctored the final on Friday, I headed east on the 10 freeway. I threw Tom Petty's *Damn the Torpedoes* into my cassette player, and distracted myself by singing along. I made it down the 110, "You see you don't have to live like a refugee/(Don't have to live like a refugee)," and then found the 91 East with ease. I was a road warrior!

But as I ventured deeper east, the highway began to fill with traffic and we slowed down to a crawl of ten miles an hour. I found myself surrounded by semitrucks, locked inside a canyon of eighteen-wheelers. The bile began to rise in my throat, and my guts cramped. "Don't do me like that. Don't do me like that/What if I love you baby?/Don't, don't, don't, don't!"

I was convinced that I was about to throw up on my steering wheel and shit in my pants at the same time. Then the adrenaline hit and rushed through me like a freight train. Breathing became more and more impossible. My head got light, and I was sure I was dying—absolutely positive. I saw a hotel at the next exit and got off the freeway, into their parking lot, and quickly into the lobby. As I searched for the bathroom, my limbs felt heavy and my tongue was like a sponge in my mouth. Once safely ensconced inside the stall, I took deep breaths, attempting to collect myself. Thoughts raced in my head—*Fuck you. Fuck you, fuck you, body. I fucking hate this shit! Why can't you stop doing this? Why am I so fucking crazy?*

I knew the one and only thing that could save me—I needed

to talk to someone while I drove. It helped me to feel tethered to something sane. I usually called my mom, but I didn't really want to explain to her where I was. I'd told her that I was spending the weekend with Theresa and friends. I wasn't ready to tell either of my parents about Bob.

After grabbing a Snickers bar at the hotel gift shop to stave off the feeling that I was passing out from low blood sugar (another fake symptom brought on by the panic attacks), I got back in the car and weighed my options. I took a deep breath and called Bob.

"Hello," a male voice answered.

"Hi, this is Kelly. Is Bob there?" I asked.

"Sure, one minute," the voice replied, and I could hear the sound of the phone being put down. "Bob. Phone. It's Kelly." I heard a door open and shut, and the phone being picked up from the counter.

"Hey, where are you?" asked Bob.

"Somewhere on the 91. I think Bellflower?" I replied nonchalantly.

"Oh, okay," he said, sounding a bit confused.

"I'm calling because—well, I have a little problem. You see, I have this thing called panic-attack syndrome. Do you know what that is?"

"No, not really," he said.

Of course he didn't know what it was. He was a normal person who came from this really normal background, with a family that was really normal and far, far away from the crazy life and things that I had seen and done.

I was a freak. And now he was going to find out.

I continued. "Well, it's this weird thing that happens where I feel like I can't breathe, and my head gets a bit spacey, and I feel like I'm going to die."

"Okay," he replied.

"And, well, it's happening right now. It happens a lot when I'm in the car. I just need someone to talk to me for a few minutes while

I drive so I don't feel so alone right now." There, I'd done it. Now he knew I couldn't drive by myself without thinking I was going to die. I felt alone, and stupid, and broken.

"Okay, so where are you right now, and what do you see?" he asked me.

And for the next twenty-five minutes, this really smart, funny, soulful, cute, normal guy talked to me, asked me questions, told me about his car, and made me feel not too crazy.

I was in love.

This was crazy. It had been only about two months since I walked out of my eleven-year marriage, and I knew what I was supposed to do—learn to be single, forge a path by myself, be like Mary Tyler Moore and have an apartment in the city, a career I could find myself in, and fling a hat into the air. But there was Bob with his grounded perspective, his commitment to doing a job right, and his normal family. He loved Japanese films, knew all the words to Tom Waits's songs, and could cook a damn good marinara sauce from scratch. He was the kind of guy who would rescue a dog wandering in the street and find its owner and make sure it got home safe and sound.

There he was—the man of my dreams—something Mary Tyler Moore had spent seven seasons searching for—right in front of me. How could I turn my back on all that?

Once my mom found out about Bob, she was not shy about sharing her opinion about the situation. "You need to be dating lots of men. Play the field. Find yourself. I mean you JUST left Andrew!" On paper she was absolutely right. No doubt about it. She spoke from experience. She'd been with my dad for thirty-two years, since she was twenty-one, and never really had a life unattached to a man. She'd spent most of the last three decades mostly alone, while he was on the road, and she'd never had a whole world to herself. She wanted that for me.

My dad, as usual, took my side.

"But he's not Andrew, he's a good guy—solid, self-sufficient, no bullshit, treats her well. Who says there are rules about this kind of thing? She's happy for the first time in a long time. Let her be happy."

The good news was that I didn't have to choose between happiness and independence. I found that with Bob I had no choice but to have both. The minute I'd toss any of my unconscious codependent bullshit behavior toward him, he wouldn't swing at it. He didn't even know how to play the game.

One night about a month into our relationship, he'd made plans to go and hang out with his guy friends at a bar. When I asked if I could go, he said no. He wasn't hurtful or cold, just calm and matter-of-fact about it. I started to cry. I felt rejected, ugly, and worthless. He looked at me like I was crazy (because I was) and told me that it really was okay to not be together 24/7, that we could love each other *and* have independent lives. He suggested I go out, make plans, and do things without him, too.

I had no idea how to do that. I didn't know how to pick what movie I wanted to see, or what meal I wanted to eat, or what career I was supposed to have, without sending any thought I had through the what-would-Andrew-or-Bob-or-my-parents-think? inner filter first. Although I'd lived a life attempting to be separate from Andrew for the last few years, I'd still been doing it in reaction to him. I hadn't done it *for* myself; I'd done it *against* Andrew. I knew there was supposed to be a separate Kelly in there somewhere, but I didn't have a clue how to find her.

CHAPTER SIXTEEN

Right Foot Forward, Left Foot Back

BY 1994 MY DAD had been on the road for more than thirty years. He was tired—tired of having to squeeze his home life into a few days a week; tired of the asshole businessmen sitting next to him on airplanes; and tired of bad hotel turkey sandwiches. He wanted to do something that wouldn't take so much out of him.

What he got was a sitcom—*The George Carlin Show* on Fox TV. Dad played George O'Grady (his grandmother's maiden name)—a much-less-enlightened, not-quite-as-worldly, and way-more-cynical version of my dad, who would've become a New York cabbie instead of a comedian. Dad was excited to be off the road and to get a chance to stretch himself by writing solely for this curmudgeonly character while immersing himself in an ensemble of comedic actors. He'd always yearned to be part of something, contrary to his very public stance about groups: "People are wonderful. I love individuals. I hate groups of people. I hate a group of people with a 'common purpose' 'cause pretty soon they have little hats. And armbands. And fight songs. And a list of people they're going to visit at 3:00 A.M. So I dislike and despise groups of people, but I love individuals. Every person you look at, you can see the universe in their eyes, if you're really looking."

Mom was also thrilled about the Fox show because she would finally get to spend more time with Dad. She had been a latchkey spouse without a partner to play with for decades, and she was tired of it. In the early 1980s she was so lonely that she considered leaving him. When he realized that she was serious, he started making more of an effort. Suddenly there was a whirlwind of dinner dates, movie dates, and trips to exotic places like a cruise on the Mediterranean and the Nile. But it could never be what she wanted. How could it, with my dad always catching another flight on his way to another gig to catch up with the everlasting back taxes he perpetually owed the IRS?

This TV show just might solve all that.

I, too, was happy that my dad got the show, and not just because I'd get to see any number of movie stars roaming the Warner Bros. lot where the show was taped. It was pretty much the best day of my life when, one afternoon, Warren Beatty rolled down his window to check me out while I stood outside the commissary—that's bucket-list material. But mostly I was happy for Dad because he deserved the financial reward and success of a Roseanne Barr or a Jerry Seinfeld. I was conscious of how hard all the traveling was on him, especially on his heart. I was always worried about his heart. Three years earlier, in 1991 in Las Vegas, he'd had a third heart attack.

I said to him as he recovered in the hospital, "You know, Dad, you could just move to Big Sur, write books, and sit with Mom and stare out at the ocean for the rest of your life if you really wanted to." He smiled his sweet I-know-you-love-me smile and then patted my hand as if to say, That's a nice thought, but you know it'll never happen.

Even though this sitcom wasn't close to allowing him to retire in Big Sur, I thought that if the show was a hit, he could slow down eventually and just maybe live a little longer.

Selfishly, I was also excited about the show because I wanted to be part of it. At age thirty-one, I was ready to assert myself in the world and catch up to my peers careerwise. I was really behind. My fellow Crossroads graduates were eight years ahead of me and fully immersed in success. I'd thrown a whole decade away shoving coke up my nose, mothering Andrew, and having panic attacks on freeways. I wanted to prove to the world that I was not the lost child I felt like, but an adult with talent and something to say. I needed a break, and quietly, in my heart, I hoped that this show could be that break.

The year before the Fox show, in June of 1993, I graduated from UCLA and turned thirty all in the same week. My mom threw me a huge surprise party on a boat in Marina del Rey, which she filled with friends from every decade of my life. I felt like a debutante (sans tiara and crinoline), like I'd finally arrived. Where? I did not know. I still had no idea what I wanted to be when I "grew up." I knew that I wanted to write, but I didn't know what that meant. I toyed with the idea of advertising (potentially lucrative but too soul crushing), journalism (not lucrative enough and possibly soul crushing, or soul affirming), short stories (likely soul affirming, but zero chance of being lucrative), and screenwriting (potentially very lucrative and soul affirming if I ignored the thousands of unproduced screenplays being written by people in coffee shops all across America).

Around that time Bob's best friend, Tom, moved to Los Angeles, and the three of us often sat around, dreaming up ideas for sitcoms that my dad could star in. It was the golden age of sitcoms— *Seinfeld, Mad About You, Home Improvement, Roseanne*. If you could find the sweet spot of a great premise with quality writing and acting that tackled social and domestic issues, you could win the Hollywood lottery. Every young comic in town was honing their stand-up act or doing one-person shows in hopes of being snatched up by the sitcom gods.

Bob and I began to write sitcom spec scripts together. The spec script is the foot-in-the-door-please-notice-me work to show agents and show runners that you are funny and understand the format and characters of the show. Bob, having come up in the world of TV news production, didn't have much experience in that world. When I met him, he was a sound guy, and by 1993 he had become a camera guy. But he was smart, well read, watched lots of films, and had a wicked sense of humor. We figured if we could make each other laugh, we had a good chance at making others laugh, too.

When *The George Carlin Show* went into preproduction, Sam Simon (*Cheers, Taxi,* cocreator of *The Simpsons*) became the coexecutive producer along with my dad and Jerry Hamza. As the show runner, Sam's job was to run the writers' room and help shape the overall feel and story arc of the show. Sam was the cream of the crop. When he moved into our Brentwood offices to begin working on the show, Bob and I were very excited. We wanted guidance and really wanted to learn. Sam was gracious enough to oblige, and he read our spec scripts and gave us honest feedback. It felt great to have him in our corner. When there was free time during his workday, he'd regale us with his tales from showbiz and his life. My favorite was the one about how, when he was a kid, he walked in on his mom screwing Groucho Marx.

Being around the office, hanging out with Sam and my dad during those preproduction months, made me feel like I was a part of something again, like when Mom and Dad and I had been on the road in the seventies, and doing the HBO shows in the eighties. It was nice to be in the family business again.

Mom and I were not technically part of the show. She was not attached as a producer like she'd been on the HBO shows, and although I was working part-time for my dad, it was only to book interviews and travel for his concert gigs. But Dad made it clear that Mom, his brother, Patrick, and I were an essential part of his emotional support team. We were welcome anytime to hang out and watch the process.

In the fall of 1993 the show began shooting on the lot of Warner Bros. Studios. The first day I went there was to watch the table reading of the first episode. As I walked across the lot, there was a palpable buzz in the air. This was the home of Humphrey Bogart in *Casablanca*, Joan Crawford in *Mildred Pierce*, James Cagney in *Yankee Doodle Dandy*, and Bugs Bunny! Most people think growing up in Los Angeles around famous people makes you jaded. That's not the case, at least not for me (or my dad, for that matter). Because I had showbiz ambitions, this kind of stuff affected me even more. These were what my dreams were made of. And here it was right in front of me.

As Mom and I arrived at Stage 17, Dad excitedly introduced us to all the actors, writers, and some of the crew. There were also some suits from Fox. When Sam came around, I said hi, but he ignored me. I thought little of it. But then the next day, when I went to watch rehearsals, the same thing happened. He walked right past me with no "Hello" or "How ya doing," just a neutral look on his face, as if I were invisible. This kept happening for months. I saw him joke around with the actors, the writers, his assistants, but not me. All the warmth we had shared was gone. Was it something I'd said? Something I'd done? I searched my mind for anything that would have caused him to give me the cold shoulder. It turned out it wasn't something I had said or something that I had done. It was something I *was*: George's daughter.

Maybe it was weird that Mom and Pat and I *were* there hanging out. Maybe he wasn't used to our brand of family. But that's how Dad did it—we were part of his life—all for one, one for all. Sam, I found out, had a real issue with nepotism, and I guess he didn't want me getting any ideas about writing for the show. At least that's what I heard.

I get it. In some ways I see his point. I remember how I felt after shooting *Apt. 2C*—I felt like a "Hollywood cliché"—empty and worthless. I never wanted any job or opportunity unless I felt qualified for it. I mean, who wants to be a Frank Stallone?

But damm it, I knew I could do this. After a few months Sam finally acknowledged my existence again. He walked by and gave me a slight nod—miracle of miracles!

After the first season finished, Dad became disillusioned with the weekly grind and secretly hoped it would be canceled. He hadn't realized the beast he would be dealing with—eighteen-hour days. In order for the show to live up to his exacting standards, and be true to who he was, he needed to put in a lot of time and effort. He was both writer and actor. It was his name on that show. There went all that free time to be with Mom and have a life. There went him getting to slow down and take care of his heart.

Even more stressful was the atmosphere on the set. He had issues with Sam both creatively and personally. Their meetings were often contentious—my dad felt that Sam saw him as only an actor and not a writer, which led to many disagreements about scripts. In general Dad didn't like Sam's leadership style. Dad liked it when everyone felt welcome in the creative process, and thought Sam liked to play favorites. He was especially irked by Sam's attitude toward my uncle Pat and me.

At the beginning of the second season, Bob and I pitched an idea for an episode to my dad and Jerry. It was called "George Pulls the Plug," and in it, George faced an awkward quandary: When is the right time to take someone off life support, especially when it's someone you barely know? Dad loved the premise. It fitted in perfectly with how the show liked to make his character face moral dilemmas. He pitched it to Sam without telling him that Bob and I had come up with it, knowing how Sam would react. Sam liked the idea and said they should do it. Then Dad revealed to him that we'd come up with it. I'm sure the air in that room was so thick you would've been lucky to cut it with a machete. But, to his credit, Sam agreed to let us write it, and assigned one of the writers, Bruce Helford, to guide us through the whole process. He would go on to be the show runner of *The Drew Carey Show* shortly after this time. Bruce was a doll.

The cast, writing staff, and a few executives flew to Las Vegas for our episode's table read. Dad was away doing a week of shows at Bally's Casino and Hotel. As the reading began I thought I might throw up. I was so nervous I wanted to crawl under the carpet. But then we got a laugh from a few of the writers, and then another, and before I knew it we were through the whole thing, and there was applause. The actors told us what a great job we had done. Bob and I felt validated and excited, and by the big smiles on their faces, I could see that Jerry and my dad were very happy for us. Sam and Bruce thanked us for the great script, and we all flew home.

When we all landed back in Los Angeles, Sam, Bruce, and the writers disappeared into the writers' room, and Bob and I went home. We were not invited in. This was standard practice in the sitcom world—nonstaff writers are never invited into the inner sanctum. At the end of the week we went to watch the dress rehearsal. As scene after scene unfolded, it became clear that very little of what Bob and I had written was still intact. All that was left was the premise and a few jokes—also standard practice in the sitcom world. Though frustrated that we hadn't been allowed to defend our old jokes or pitch new ones, we knew we couldn't do anything about it. At the end of the day we were truly just happy to be there.

The night of the taping, in the fall of 1994, we were told that we would be introduced to the audience as the writers of the episode. I told Sam that I felt weird about that because barely anything we had written was in the script. He leaned over to me and very sweetly said, "Take your bow. This is the way it is. Some nights you do all the work and get none of the credit; other nights you feel like you've done nothing, and yet you get the applause. That's showbiz." I took that to heart and knew he was right. At least I hoped he was.

Since Bob and I now had a produced sitcom episode under our belt, we looked for an agent. In the spring of 1995 we had a few meetings, but no one jumped on our bandwagon. That era was a frenzy of competition. Even with connections and a produced script, it was hard to get even a toe, let alone a foot, in the door.

But then we got a huge break.

We were invited to interview for the Warner Bros. Sitcom Writers Program. This was very exciting. Every year Warner Bros. picked a handful of writers to be mentored by show runners from existing shows. The up-and-coming writers would then be shepherded along until they were ready to be dropped into a writers' room and on a staff. Getting this opportunity was like opening a candy bar and seeing the corner of the golden ticket.

In the interview I did most of the talking, hoping I was charming and affable. I talked about how Bob and I loved to write together and what a great team we made. I shared our long-term dreams of someday making thoughtful films that entertained but also shifted people's minds and hearts—the kind of films that can change a life. Then I began to expound on *my* thoughts about sitcom writing—how it was not real writing, but more like paint-by-numbers formulaic fare that was basically dumbed-down trite for the masses, and used to sell beer and cleaning products. I told the Warner Bros. executive, who had the keys to my future in his hands, that during my career I hoped to someday elevate the genre and be able to write stuff that challenged rather than perpetuated the status quo. I was, after all, a Carlin, and would not be a patsy for corporate interests. The executive politely nodded, as if he agreed with what I was saying, but you could feel the chill in the air.

As we walked out of the meeting, Bob had a look on his face like, What did you just do? This was our big break, and I had just broken it.

We never heard back from the program.

I guess both my dad and I were done with sitcoms. His got canceled due to low ratings around the same time. Dad was happy about that, but I was unsure that I had done the right thing in that meeting with the Warner Bros. executive. To this day I deeply regret not giving Bob and myself a chance to learn the craft, make some dough, and get our foot in the door. But I also know that we both would've been miserable there. Some of the sitcom writers' rooms back then (and maybe now) were run by Ivy-League white guys who loved to lord their intellect and large egos over the room. That atmosphere would have pissed Bob off daily and sent me into an anxiety tailspin. Having just come out of my own personal dark ages, I didn't have the confidence to stand up to the head games and ego brinkmanship in those rooms. I'd barely formed a sense of myself. But still—poor Bob. Here was a man who'd walked away from his day job to pursue writing, and his partner had just killed quite an opportunity.

Thankfully that didn't stop him from marrying me.

By early 1995 we'd been living in the house we'd bought together for more than a year, and we were months away from our wedding. On Christmas Eve of 1994, after formally asking my dad for permission the day before (no urinals involved), Bob poured two glasses of Cristal champagne, got down on one knee, and proposed. I cried tears of joy and said yes. On June 10, 1995, Bob and I got married under the Mexican Wedding Bell tree on my parents' front lawn, surrounded by friends and loved ones. As I looked into Bob's blue eyes, every cell of my body said yes. When I looked into my mother and father's eyes after the ceremony, I could tell that they both felt that I'd finally landed in the safest of arms. And I had. I was now loved and supported, and ready to take the world on even more.

"Well, you can't just sleep all day!" echoed in my head. Those were the words my mom had said to me after I dropped out of UCLA in 1981. I knew they applied even more now. I had to keep moving forward with my career. I'd fallen even more behind my peers by fucking up the Warner Bros. program. And I was no longer working part-time for my dad, but he was paying me like I was. I felt guilty and weak for taking his money, but clearly not guilty enough to look for a real job. (Besides, I don't think the chip on my shoulder would've fitted into a cubicle anyway.)

The foundation of that enormous chip on my shoulder was my trifecta of anxiety around my career: fear of making the wrong choice, fear of failure, and fear of success. What made up most of the fear of making the wrong choice was decades of listening to my dad tell stories about how miserable he'd been in the late sixties because of not honoring his "true self." I was scared of making that same mistake. At thirty-three I didn't feel like I had the time to waste working for ten years only to end up hating my life and having to reinvent myself like he did. He was thirty-three when he did the reinventing. Did I want to be forty-three when I had to do it? No—better to follow the right path from the beginning.

What I'd failed to realize with that inner logic was that to understand what it is you really want, you must first choose a path. It rarely works the other way around. You need to live a little so you can know what's working or not. Then, if need be, you can change course. My dad had chosen his path early—the "big Danny Kaye plan"—and had given it his all. But it was only through being on that path that he discovered who he truly was—a rebel who needed to speak the truth. I'd only heard the part of my dad's story where he was unhappy. He never mentioned the part about the importance of the thousands of hours of stage time he got that allowed him to discover his true self.

Which brings me to my second fear: fear of failure. In order for me to find *my* true self, I needed to be willing to fail—take a wrong turn, fall on my face—and learn from it. But I believed that everything I would do in the world would be a failure no matter what. If it wasn't immediately excellent or approved of, or if thousands of people weren't chanting my name like they did for my dad, it was pointless. I was paralyzed, unable to try things that were creative and risky. Dad's shadow loomed large.

Add to all that the ever-twisted logic of my version of fear of success: If I do well, then my mom will feel left behind, and then she'll get depressed and drink—and, well, you have one helluva drug to induce paralysis and ennui.

And so I dabbled.

Bob and I began to shoot a short documentary about a homeless man named Mr. Wendal, who sold poems on a corner to the rich people of Brentwood. But because I really didn't know what I was doing, I felt overwhelmed by doubt, lack of experience, and inertia, and after a few months I gave up.

Then we produced a short film with a bunch of friends called *Gary's Beer*, but it didn't make it into any film festivals, and in 1996 there were no YouTube or Funny or Die Web sites you could distribute something like that on, so whatever ambition I had around that just melted away.

I knew I had to do something, so I went to lunch with one of my mentors from the Communications Department at UCLA, Marde Gregory. She was a straight-shooting, tough-love champion of mine. She listened to my anxieties, reminded me of my potential, and then gave me the name and number of a friend who was hiring at his documentary TV company that produced *Mysteries of the Bible* and *Ancient Mysteries* for the History Channel, and many *Biography* shows for A&E. Bram Roos, the president of FilmRoos, hired me to be a research assistant. My duties incuded logging interview tapes, doing background research, and then he said, "We shall see where it goes. Maybe we could shoot a biography about your dad and have you help to produce it."

When I told my mom that I'd gotten the job, and that I'd potentially be writing and producing a *Biography* in the near future, she said with skepticism, "Can *you* do that?" I really wasn't sure if I could, and her doubt was like a stake through my heart. But I knew ultimately that she loved me and believed in me. After all, she had once written me a birthday card that said, "Kelly—you are capable of anything you put your mind to, and you don't have to prove anything. If you want to spend the rest of your days staring up at the sky and studying the shapes of clouds, you can. You are perfect just the way you are. Love, Mom." I often wondered if any of the Ivy League universities might offer me a Ph.D. in Pondering Shapes of Clouds.

After I spent a few weeks doing research, Bram moved me to the Development Department with an old acquaintance from Westlake, Felicia Lansbury, and a nice guy named Doug West. They too were from showbiz royalty—Felicia was Angela Lansbury's niece, and Doug was Eve Arden's son. I wondered, *Did Bram put us together so that we might spin some Hollywood success for him?*

Although I knew little about developing TV shows, I knew what I liked, and I loved that FilmRoos cared about making shows that taught history through beautiful images and interviews with experts.

In the fall of 1996, about a week after I'd become part of the Development Department, Felicia and I were eating lunch and talking about our families. She told me she'd just lost her mom to cancer. "It was so fast," she said. "She was diagnosed, and within a few months she was gone."

Every cell in my body tightened with terror. As I listened sympathetically, I thought, *Thank God that hasn't happened to me.*

CHAPTER SEVENTEEN

What It Looks Like
When the Other Shoe Drops

IT WAS OFFICIAL: I was an adult. At age thirty-four I went on my very first business trip. In the last week of March 1997, I flew business class to New York City to pitch documentary show ideas with Felicia and Bram to A&E, Lifetime, and the Discovery Channel. I felt so darn grown-up—at least on the outside. On the inside, though, it was still up for debate. Before I left for New York, I was in a panic. First, I hated flying—too many memories of cocaine-induced panic attacks on planes in the 1980s. And then, to make matters worse, I had to fly into JFK in a snowstorm. To reduce my anxiety, my look-at-me-aren't-I-a-grown-up? solution was to pack a stuffed animal. My flying companion was Celery—a lime-green rabbit my mom had given me for Easter the year before. Because he was like all transitional objects that have been clutched, drooled on, and given godlike powers by toddlers since the beginning of time, I knew he'd make everything okay. And he did. We landed safely. When I got to my hotel room there were flowers waiting for me with a note that said, "I knew you'd make it. Love, Bob." Either he was in on it with

Celery, or I really did marry the right guy. He always knew how to ground me.

For three days I went to pitch meetings. Things went well for me mostly because I followed the advice my mom had given me a few years earlier: Fake it. She told me the secret to any job—pretend you know what you're doing. Everyone else is. As I went from meeting to meeting, I thanked her silently for that advice, and for the suit that she'd bought for me only a week before the trip. I felt her support all around me. We had healed so much.

The flight home was much less anxiety-inducing thanks to Celery—and knowing that Bob would be at the airport to pick me up. As we waited for my luggage, I asked him how my mom was doing; she'd been in the hospital while I was away, readying to have some gallstones removed.

He told me, "They found some spots on her liver. They're doing a biopsy."

That was it. I knew immediately what they'd found. Mom was in her fourteenth year of remission from breast cancer, and here was the other shoe. It had finally dropped.

I hadn't realized it, but I'd been holding my breath for fourteen years.

Although she'd been cancer-free for those fourteen years, she hadn't been well. She'd been suffering from a multitude of chronic ailments: diabetes, hepatitis C, and fibromyalgia. All had their issues, but fibromyalgia was the great debilitator. She was in pain daily and fatigued constantly. There were days when I would look at her face and see the courage it took for her to just get up and go out and have lunch. She was always in far more distress than she ever let on to Dad or me. Although most days she'd rally, get dressed, and go out to run errands, or eat breakfast at the deli at the Brentwood Mart, in the last ten years she also spent a lot of time watching TV in bed. On days when I was down or confused or just couldn't deal with the world, I'd still go over to her house, crawl into bed next to her, and we'd spend the day doing crossword puzzles and watching TV. Our favorite thing to watch? Bowling. We just sat and watched and thrived on each other's company.

That night, after getting in from New York, I went right to St. John's Hospital in Santa Monica to see my mom. I walked into her room and felt a wave of panic. She was yellow—her eyes, her skin, her everything. My mother was yellow. It had only been a week since I'd seen her, and already the cancer had begun to take her. I looked down at the side of her bed. There was a bag hanging off it full of urine the color of maple syrup. I knew. I knew she was going to die. People who are that yellow and have maple syrup urine and three big spots on their liver die. A surge of terror rushed into my body.

The oncologists, knowing that we were all in shock, took charge. Over the next few days there wasn't a whole lot of debate or conversation about the course of action. The doctors told us, "The only option is chemotherapy. Without it there's no chance. We need to get this thing into remission."

The only other option would have been a transplant, but that was off the table since she'd had breast cancer, which deemed her ineligible, even though her liver cancer was not metastasized breast cancer. It was a brand-new cancer, most probably from the hepatitis C.

None of us heard what they were really saying, or thought to ask, What if we don't do chemo? What if this doesn't go into remission? No one said any of that. There was just a silent acceptance of inevitability between my mother, father, and me.

The next day Mom did say to me, "If I only have a few months, I want to know. I want to have time to say good-bye properly."

I choked those words out to our family physician, Dr. Forde, in the hall outside her room. He said he'd tell us if that were the case.

And so we started chemo. It was ironic: Fourteen years before when my mother had breast cancer, she had refused the chemo because she knew her liver was too damaged from all the drugs and drinking to handle it. She thought it would kill her, and now she *had* to have it—there was nothing else that could save the very same damaged liver she so vehemently protected so long ago.

Once Mom left the hospital, an oncology nurse came to the house to help us out. The side effects of the cancer undermining Mom's liver progressed quickly. She was weak, bloated, and in pain like she'd never been before. Because of the fibromyalgia, this woman knew pain. A machine was delivered to administer the morphine drip that would ease her pain. The first day the nurse took me aside.

"I'm going to teach you how to override the machine so you can allow your mom to have as much as she wants," she said. I stiffened at her bluntness. I didn't want to hear this. I didn't want to learn how to override the morphine machine. I didn't want any machine in my house, attached to my mother. I wanted all this to go away. But I dutifully listened, and watched as she showed me which buttons to press, and in what order, because I certainly didn't want my mom to be in pain. But really, I didn't want to realize why the nurse was doing this—this nurse knew more than we did about how bad it really was. We still hoped this care would help to save her life. The nurse knew this care would only help to ease her death.

At the exact time all this was happening, my dad's first book, *Brain Droppings*, was about to be released. It had been in the works for more than a year. This book was a huge thing for him and Mom. If it did well it would give them some financial breathing room for the first time in twenty years. But in order for it to do well, Dad needed to promote it. That meant he had to leave. It was an agonizing choice, but really he *had* no choice. Canceling the book tour and the concerts he had lined up that month would have meant financial ruin. There were endless contractual obligations, and Dad still had that tax bill hanging over him from decades ago. Every quarter, the IRS threatened to seize assets and take away the house. If this book was a success, all that would go away.

Mom, Dad, and I had a family meeting to figure out how to

handle this. First we decided to cancel the sixtieth birthday party Mom was planning for Dad. His birthday was May 12, but we decided that we'd delay it till the fall, when Mom was feeling better. Then Mom and Dad agreed that he should keep his concert and book commitments, which meant I would take care of Mom. I decided to quit my job. How do people go to work when their loved ones are dying? I couldn't imagine it. I could barely see straight. And so we all agreed that all this was the best plan we could come up with, given the circumstances, even though I could see in Mom's eyes how scared she was and how sad she was that my dad had to leave. I went along with it all even though I was scared, too. I didn't know how to take care of someone who was yellow and was on a morphine drip twenty-four hours a day.

And I was pissed. I couldn't believe this was happening—Dad's work was taking him away again. I wanted to ask him, What could *possibly* be more important than staying home with me, and taking care of Mom?

But I couldn't say those words to my father. I didn't know how.

As the next few days went by, no one talked about what we were feeling or what we all knew was going on. The only time we acknowledged it was that first weekend, when they had found the spots. Dad and I had talked on the phone.

"This doesn't look good, does it?" I said, crying, as I sat on the floor of my bedroom as the shock of the news hit me.

"No, I'm afraid not," Dad replied quietly. I could feel the weight in his voice. As if the news were too much to take in.

Other than that brief exchange, there were no frank discussions about death, or what we were all feeling, or even last-minute instructions from Mom about our future without her. It was just about getting through it. But for what? What comes after the getting through it? Life? Yes, ours, but not hers. Hers was soon to be irretrievably gone, and none of us had the courage to say anything about it.

It's not like it is in the movies. There is nothing warm and fuzzy about this death shit. It is unreal. It is in slo-mo. It was a slippery slope, and I was falling down it. I had just enough strength to be there.

I quit my grown-up "executive" job. I tried to take care of Mom, but it was overwhelming. My main task was to monitor how much she was peeing versus how much she was drinking. Every day it got worse—she took in more than she was releasing. The liquid stopped going through her body, and instead it accumulated in her body, and she got a huge bloated belly. On top of this I had to try to control her blood sugar.

Mostly I felt that my job was to keep her occupied with movies and chitchat. We didn't spend afternoons rehashing the past. She didn't regale me with great stories about her childhood or family. We didn't say much to each other. What I really wanted to say to her was, Mom, don't—don't go. Not now. I'm not ready. But we didn't have conversations like that. We just sat in bed and watched the world go by on the TV. We no longer limited ourselves to watching bowling tournaments. We now watched anything. There was no sense of what was actually happening. The day was about getting her to drink four ounces of Ensure every few hours, wondering what time the night nurse would be there, and waiting for Dad to call and check in.

The first few weeks Dad would come home every few days, but then he'd have to leave again. Even though he was chartering planes to be home every available moment he could, I deeply resented him leaving me in charge of Mom. It felt all too familiar—Mom's existence hanging by a thread, and me feeling ill equipped to handle it. I was eleven and we were all living on Tellem Drive again.

When he did make it home, it was always a huge relief. He was the most attentive I had ever seen. He checked in on the nurses to make sure Mom was getting the best care, and even got Mom to eat when she was supposed to. Most important, he got her to laugh.

I didn't think it was possible under the circumstances. She was so tired and in so much discomfort. But he did it. He really was the only one who could.

After being in and out of town for the first month after her diagnosis, he told me he had to leave again for the first two weeks of May for concerts and early book-tour promotions. When the oncology nurse heard about his plans, she said to me, "She won't make it to his birthday."

I didn't want to believe her, so I made my dad call our family doctor to confirm that Mom would not deteriorate and die while he was gone. All the doctors assured us that Mom would be okay when he got home. It made me feel better, but I wasn't so sure. I kept quiet, as did Mom, because by this time everyone had entered the Super Bowl of denial. I pretended that I wasn't angry. Dad pretended he could work. The doctors pretended they were being honest, and so we all pretended that Mom wasn't dying.

And I knew it killed Dad to leave. It killed me to watch the fear in Mom's eyes. We were all dying.

On Friday, May 9, five weeks after her diagnosis, I drove my mom to chemotherapy number three. As the poison dripped into her veins, I worried that she didn't have any interest in watching the *Wallace & Gromit* video I'd brought along to distract her. In the car on the way home, in the middle of a left turn from Wilshire Boulevard onto Twenty-Sixth Street, Mom said, "I'll be really pissed off if I'm going to die soon. I've got too much left to do." I could barely drive with tears now stinging my eyes. It was the first time she'd mentioned the topic. Choking back sobs, all I could manage to say was, "I'm not ready for you to go either, Mom."

The heavy silence of reality hung between us, and nothing more was said about it as we made our way home.

When I was young, taking care of my mother was a traumatic and overwhelming burden. But on that day I felt connected to the natural order of things, and knew that easing my mother's pain and simply being with her during this time was a profound privilege.

Death. How real, and yet, how unreal this visitor was. The experience forced me into two worlds at once. Nothing was conveniently black-and-white any longer. Normally the light of life was in the here and now, while the shadow of death was over there, somewhere far, far away. But now they had converged and life was gray. In this gray I fought to keep my mother alive for another day with chemotherapy and morphine. I volunteered to be my mother's caretaker while I dreamed of running away to some nonexistent paradise where I could desert this wretched duty. In this gray I was the daughter *and* the mother of my mother.

The next day, Saturday, it was just the oncology nurse, Mom, and me in a very quiet house. Mom mostly slept. That's all she'd been doing the last two days. I went into her home office to rummage around for magazines to cut up for a collage. Mom and I had a long tradition of collage making together, and I wanted to make her one for Mother's Day, which was the next day. This gesture of love felt both essential and impotent; essential because my mom lay in the other room dying of liver cancer; impotent because my mother lay in the other room dying of liver cancer.

While in my mom's office rummaging for collage supplies, I came across a yellow three-ring binder full of writings. They were my mother's writings—some handwritten and others typed. I found a corner of the couch and began to read. I felt uncomfortable plunging into this private material, but with the strange visitor of death in the house, I felt all the rules had already been broken. I quickly realized that some of the writings I had seen, but others I had not. I found an essay called "My Race Against Time" in a separate portfolio. It was typed on that thin onionskin paper that I remembered so well from childhood. I began to read:

If we could live our lives to their fullest and never have to face any kind of crisis or tragedy, I know we all agree it would be a beautiful experience. Unfortunately, life isn't meant to be that perfect, and at one time or another, we must all meet our own personal challenge. Two years ago I learned what it was like to grow up overnight, and I lived in a nightmare of conflicting emotions. At that time, I was twenty-three years old, and I felt I had already reached a level of maturity . . . until I was put to an extreme emotional test. Within a period of six weeks I had to face the death of my young mother and the birth of my first child!

My breath stopped. I felt like there was something else in the room with me, watching me, sitting with me. I began to cry. The words confirmed everything I'd been holding at arm's length. I now knew without a doubt that my mother was going to die. All the pretending, all the busyness, and all the denial that kept that impossible reality from me vanished in a flash. And I knew that what I was reading was exactly what I needed in this moment. Not what I wanted, but what I needed. What I wanted was the fairy tale with the happy ending, not the part where you have to face the ogres and witches of the dark forests.

Here in my hand was a map, my mother's emotional map of the territory of her own broken heart from her own mother's death thirty-four years earlier. This map was the bread crumbs from her life that could safely usher me through the dark forest of death. I slowly took in all that it had to offer. I read and then reread her sentence, "Within a period of six weeks I had to face the death of my young mother," and I realized that on this day in May it had been six weeks since my mother was diagnosed. As I read further, I took in how she'd had to cope with her grief while my dad was on the road, not able to physically support her during that time. And I took in that she, too, had felt a need to keep a show of "cheerfulness and hope for mother's sake because that was what she wanted." I sat with all the strange parallels and let the weight of their truth offer me a glimpse of the comfort and power I would need in the months to come. I knew that those words let me know that somehow I would survive this impossible ordeal.

After I finished reading her essay and creating her Mother's Day collage, my mom woke up and needed to go to the bathroom. The chemo had so ravaged her body that she could no longer walk on her own. The nurse and I began to practically carry her to the bathroom, when her body went into a violent fit of convulsion—her legs shaking uncontrollably. Then every part of her convulsed, and she screamed out, "Help, help me, I can't—I can't stop it! Make it stop!" We almost lost our grip on her but managed to get her back to bed. She was ashamed. I was ashamed. There was no control.

The next day, Sunday, May 11, was Mother's Day. I was exhausted, spent, and emotionally drained. Mom had sunk into some kind of childlike state that I couldn't identify. She acted and spoke like she was a three-year-old child. I wondered—does anyone come back from a state like this? This panicked me, but all I could think about was that I had to get her to eat or drink something—anything. She hadn't in two days. She couldn't. The chemo had ravaged her far worse than the cancer on her liver.

Dad was somewhere else—New York City. He still thought he was there for their future. But there was no more future for Mom. There was only that moment—me sitting on the end of her bed begging her to just take a sip of the orange juice. Her blood sugar was dangerously low. Like a bratty child she shook her head and refused. I couldn't blame her; she probably couldn't taste anything anyway. I doubt she could even have kept it down.

But I begged anyway. "Please, Mom, please, just a sip."

"No!" she cried, and clamped her mouth shut.

I acted strong. "Well, if you can't drink your orange juice, I'm going to have to call the paramedics and take you to St. John's. Is that okay?" After a moment she nodded her head yes.

That was the last thing I said to her. Well, probably the last thing she remembered me saying to her: "Drink your orange juice, or I'm calling the paramedics." Not what I had wished as my last words to her. But that's the thing with being in the middle of a crisis; there is no grand moment or time to reflect—it's just *do*. Do now what needs to be done in this moment. And in this second I believed, or at least wanted to believe, that getting her to drink some orange juice would make it all okay.

The nurse called an ambulance. Mom rested with her eyes closed. I didn't know if she was conscious or not. I cried as I called my dad to tell him that we were taking her to the hospital. Things were bad. I told him to take the next flight out.

I followed the ambulance to the hospital. Have you ever been to an emergency room on Mother's Day? There are children. Many, many children. And that morning they have all been making Mommy breakfast, and they have all burned or cut or scalded or scraped themselves in the process. By the time the tired, over-worked ER resident got to my mom, he was in way over his head, because she was going down, and going down fast. One minute we—Bob, our dear friend Theresa, and I—were all standing in the cu-bicle with Mom and she was alive, not conscious but alive. The next minute bells on machines were going off, alerting all that her blood pressure was dropping, heart rate was racing, and pulse rate was plummeting. They moved her quickly to a private area to get con-trol of the situation. We waited outside the room.

"Code blue! Code blue!" came over the intercom. A rush of doc-tors came at us, shouting instructions at each other. "Code blue!" Nurses rushed by. I watched all this from about ten feet away. It was all in slow motion—nurses racing in with carts—more shout-ing, words, motions. I turned around, walked through the doors outside, and screamed,

"No, no, no!" I collapsed against a wall. I thought, *This is not happening. This is happening to someone else. My mother is not dead. No, she is not dying. This is not how it's supposed to happen. This happens much differently; it's quiet, serene. We're all holding hands, Enya is playing, peace, love. . . . No. Not this. Not now. Not today.*

A nurse rushed out.

"They've revived her. She's on life support. She's alive," she told me.

She was, kind of, but not really alive. It's that place where bodies take on air and blood flows around their arteries, but the person is gone. She was gone.

I wanted to call my dad, but I couldn't. He was already on the plane.

I spoke with the intensive care doctor and told him, "You must keep her alive for six more hours. You *must*. My dad has to say good-bye to her. It can't end like this. It just can't. He has to be with her. He's been gone for so much, he can't be gone for this."

The doctor reassured me that he would do everything in his power. It was like a dream. I was not real; Mom was not real. This hospital was a figment of my imagination.

After a while they moved Mom into the ICU, and a crowd of friends gathered at the hospital. Mom had isolated herself these last five weeks from most of them, not telling many the extent of what was going on. She didn't have the energy to deal with their emotional reaction to what was happening. Most of them were people she had nurtured and sponsored in AA. Some of them believed that they wouldn't be alive without my mother. As word spread among her friends and the AA community, everyone's face told the story of the reality of the moment. I thought, *What are they going to do now?*

What was I going to do now?

At five o'clock Bob and I took a limo to the airport to get my dad. When we got to the gate to wait for him, there were paparazzi. I found a security guy from the airline and told him my situation. He told us that Diana Ross was on the flight, and he'd usher her toward the cameras so that we could make a clean getaway with my dad. He did, and we did.

In the limo all was quiet. Then Dad spoke: "While I was on the plane I watched the moon and Venus rise together, and I knew that it was over. That this was good-bye."

The ICU was not pleasant. Mom was hooked up to every possible device to keep her alive, and her eyes were open in a very disturbing way. She was not looking at anything. She was not conscious. But her eyes were open. Dad had not seen her in more than ten days, and she was very yellow, very bloated, and bald. He tenderly cradled her face in his hand, kissed her, and said, "Oh, Brenny. Oh, Brenny." And then he wiped her eyes with a tissue. Two years later I would find this tissue in a box of mementos with a note in my father's handwriting identifying it as the tissue he wiped her tears with on that last day. His love was huge. My love for him was, too. We spent about forty-five minutes with her. But we knew that Mom was no longer alive. We knew that these machines were the only things keeping some semblance of her physical presence with us. We knew it was time. We said our good-byes.

On May 11, 1997, Mother's Day, at 10:38 P.M. they turned off the machines. We stood above her and cried. About three minutes later Brenda Florence Hosbrook Carlin was released.

CHAPTER EIGHTEEN

"Sunday Will Never Be the Same"

ALL I WANTED, needed, was to sleep. Every cell in my body stung with a hot fire. My mind screamed for relief. I went home to my parents' house to sleep in my old room because I needed to be near my dad and near my mom's things. All I wanted was to fall into the peace of slumber, but my mind resisted because it knew what I'd face in the morning—a world where my mother no longer existed.

Somehow, some way, I fitfully slept. When I awoke, the raw, burning pain was still there. When does this stop? Will I feel this forever? I couldn't imagine a time when I wouldn't. I stepped into the shower thinking that just maybe the water would temper the pain. As the warm water poured over me, my body began to convulse, and I sobbed. I didn't know how long I would have to sob to release even a small fraction of the shock and pain I felt, but I feared it was longer than my lifetime. I wasn't sure if I could endure this ordeal. That's when a pair of arms, my mother's arms, came around me from behind and just held me. My mother's voice filled the space around me: "Kelly, you're going to be okay. You will be fine."

Even though I'd idolized Shirley MacLaine and flirted with every New Age ideology, I had never experienced an encounter with the "paranormal." I was not one to believe in that kind of stuff readily. A part of me wanted to, but there was another part that really wanted to see the scientific proof. Nevertheless, in that shower on that morning, I absolutely felt my mother's presence and her arms around me, and heard her words. She was as real to me as she'd ever been.

As her loving arms held me, I felt a surge of strength in the inner core of my being. It was a strength she'd exhibited so many times throughout her life. It was the same strength she'd used to take that leap in 1960 to be with my dad; the same strength she'd used to support my father when he decided to transform his career in 1969; the same strength she'd used to rebound from alcoholism and addiction in 1975. It was her human spirit, and now it was mine. Her fierce love and warrior courage implanted themselves inside my being, and although the pain, fear, and confusion of loss still flooded my body, I knew that, yes, someday, I would be okay. I would be fine.

Immediately I got out of the shower, threw on some clothes, and ran across the house to tell my dad what had just happened. Like a child who didn't get what he wanted for Christmas, he said, "Fuck, man! Cool shit like that never happens to me!"

Those first few days Dad and I hung out and spent hours playing music—mostly vinyl records, some CDs—and drinking beer in his home studio/office. A clear sign that Mom was gone already: We were both drinking together in the middle of the day. Not heavily, but just enough to soften the sharp edges of the new reality. Dad was making a tape of songs that had some connection to Mom— "Somewhere" from *West Side Story*, Van Dyke Park's "Sail Away," and Doc Martin's "If I Needed You" were a few—songs they'd shared and some that when he'd hear them he'd think of her. I added some songs, too. Mine were from my "broken heart" track list: Nick Cave's "Into My Arms," Iris DeMent's "After You're Gone," and Spanky and Our Gang's "Sunday Will Never Be the Same." Spanky McFarlane, of Spanky and Our Gang, had been a close friend of the family since the 1960s. My mom and dad, with me in tow, often went up to Topanga Canyon to party with her and Nigel Pickering and Oz Bach, the other founding members of the band. The song "Sunday Will Never Be the Same" was part of the soundtrack of my early life. And now, with Mom having died on a Sunday, it was the anthem for my grief.

Hanging out with my dad those first few days after Mom's death enabled me to see a private part of him I had rarely encountered— his sentimental inner life. As each song played, I caught sight of the deep connection that had originally bonded him to Mom, a bond that their thirty-six tumultuous years together had naturally eroded. As he dug deeper into his enormous collection of music, his love for her seemed to be restored to its pristine state.

Something healed between us, too. My father became whole to me. I'd always seen him as the man of great intellect, which he proudly showed the world, but now I witnessed a man of deep feeling and connection, a part that the world knew little about. My dad was now as deep as he was great to me. It scared me a bit. This was uncharted territory for me. The safety I'd felt with my father most of my life had always been based on him being the rational one, not the emotional one. I worried: *Would he know how to venture into this dark place and get out?* I hoped so, because I couldn't be his guide. I had my own dark places to go now.

When we weren't soothing ourselves with music and beer that week, Dad and I were in full planning mode for the memorial. I knew memorials were to honor the person who had died, but I didn't know that they could save the life of the living, too. I'm not sure what I would've done that week without the focus and purpose it gave to me. Although in a surreal daze, at least I had a job to do. I was doing. Next foot forward—music? Pictures? Food? Valet? Words? All were questions that had to be answered.

I'm not into the whole bullshit angel thing, but I'm not sure what else I'd call the people around us that week. We were held up and together by many spirits weaving love around us. People everywhere swooping in to take care of everything for the memorial. It was as if someone threw a huge safety net down to catch me gracefully as I fell from the highest point. Many hands, arms, and faces caught me, and whispered, It's okay. We are here. We are here. The memorial was shaping up to be more than a remembrance of my mother, my father's wife, the friend, confidante, and hero of hundreds. It was becoming a physical manifestation of Brenda Carlin herself. The many hands worked to create something beautiful, something quite real and yet most intangible—just like her spirit.

Wednesday morning I woke up (still sleeping at my dad's house), and it was gray out. It's what we call June Gloom here in Los Angeles, and it fit my mood perfectly—no cheery fucking sunshine to juxtapose against my grief. In the kitchen as Dad made coffee, I said, "Mom would have woken up in pain today because of the gray. I always felt horrible for her on days like this. I'm glad she no longer has to. Is that wrong?"

Dad stared out the window and nodded his head ever so slightly. "No. Me, too. I think it's okay to be glad the bad parts are over."

That wasn't the only relief I felt. Woven between my searing rawness was a sense of expansion, as if there was now more space in the world for me. A chunk of my inner hard drive had been erased—one part held the worry for my mom, but the other part held my need to take care of her self-esteem. I was relieved I was no longer in charge of that. I didn't say a word to my dad about those feelings. I felt too guilty to share that one.

On Friday, Dad, Bob, and I went to the funeral home. Why the fuck do you have to do this just days after a person dies? Isn't it difficult enough to face the big bogeyman of death without having to encounter some horribly sincere yet strangely detached man whose only job is to sell you a fancy wooden box? It felt like too much, but still we wanted to have one last good-bye. Mom would be cremated.

We walked into the room that held her, and there she was—in a coffin. My mom was in a coffin. She'd never again get up; never again fill that chair in the kitchen where she, in her nightgown, ate her banana in the morning; never again lie on her side of the bed, where she'd spend endless hours reading detective novels and watching bowling or ice-skating on TV; never again brighten my soul with that laugh, that spectacular laugh.

I looked at her and thought, *She's not here. She's not anywhere.* I tried to let the surreal be real to me. *This stiff body is my mother.* I touched her hand. *I'll never talk to her again.* I kissed her forehead. *She's not here.* I cried. Again.

I slipped a picture of Bob and me holding each other and smiling beneath her cold refrigerated hands to let her know that I was safe and loved and taken care of now. I did this believing full well that she knew that already, because otherwise she never would have left me so soon.

The day of the memorial was eerie. I'd always imagined that when my mom died, they'd have to sedate me and put me in a straitjacket in a rubber room at UCLA Psychiatric Ward. I just knew that I'd fall apart. For years I had dark images of this scenario creep into my mind's eye while I was driving on the 405. But on that morning, I woke up in a state of complete serenity—the kind Zen masters only dream about. Every cell of my body was alive and twitching, yet my center was as solid as the very earth I stood on. I was the earth.

I gathered our family—my father, Bob, Mom's family from Dayton—my aunt Barbara and my cousins, Ginger and Mindy—and

Mom's closest friends—Ros, Theresa, and Susan—in a circle in the backyard away from the rest of the guests. I knew we needed to ground ourselves before we faced everyone at the memorial. We all held hands, our eyes closed, and I offered a prayer. Since I didn't know any real prayers, I talked about Mom. I talked about her strength, her unconditional love for everyone, and how *we* were now beacons for this love, and that we were to go out there today, for the rest of our lives, and do her work: Love ourselves and all those we touch—just as she would have done. I finished with, "She is no longer here to care for us, so we must care for ourselves now."

It was amazing. I was standing there, my feet firmly on the ground, and my heart wide open. It was real. I was real. I was love.

The memorial was out in the garden of my parents' front yard. The same front yard that Bob and I had gotten married in less than two years earlier. My father with Moe, my mom's Maltese, in his arms, along with Bob and me, joined the guests there and sat in the front row. Amid the hundred or so mourners sat a couple of very special guests: a life-size papier-mâché chimp smoking a cigar, sculpted by the Mexican artist Sergio Bustamante; and an enormous stuffed Easter bunny Mom had bought one Easter to sit at the dinner table with us. Later that week I found out that two neighbors had been puzzled by the chimp and bunny sitting amid the empty chairs before the memorial, but I couldn't imagine the day without them. It was essential that the chimp and bunny be there. They were tangible examples of Mom's spirit—her ability to be silly, even during a great tragedy, even during her very own memorial.

When the services began, I felt the reality of grief grip the air. It was overwhelming. But then Kenny Rankin, who'd opened for my dad in the early 1970s, took the stage and sang "When Sunny Gets Blue." My heart melted. All I could think was, *Shit, man, this is going to be a great fucking memorial.*

Kenny, as requested by Dad, was singing Mom's favorite song for her moments of floating melancholy that she was so prone to. The words filled me with such grief, and yet it was so beautiful and perfect for the moment that an enormous joy entered me. There was that realness, that love, showing up again.

Dad got up to speak. His first words were, "Brenda was a stone-cold knockout." He then told the story of their whirlwind romance, starting at when they met at the Racquet Club. He talked about her taking him home to listen to her "stereo hi-fi," his unexpected arrival to sweep her off her feet and get engaged, and their years before I was born driving to gigs all across America in their Dodge Dart. Although his voice was full of sadness, there was a glint in his eye and warmth in his heart that took us all back to the night their eyes locked at the bar thirty-seven years earlier in Dayton, Ohio. We were all young, fresh, and untarnished with George and Brenda in that moment.

A few friends, the ones who could manage to speak, got up and revealed the myriad ways Brenda had touched their lives: Her ability to have fun almost anywhere; the importance of buying three of anything—pairs of shoes, sweaters, bras—if you fell in love with it; and how you could confess any transgression to her, because she'd receive it without a twitch of judgment.

And then I got up to speak. I spoke about Mother's Day, and how it would never quite be the same for me, ever again. I spoke of love, and how I now knew that it is the only thing that can survive death. I spoke of my mother's philosophy toward life. I used the words of Joseph Campbell, who described it so eloquently. He talked about how the only way to begin to understand and know the wonder and mystery of life is to accept the monstrous nature of it, too. That there is the good and the bad, the beautiful and the ugly, the joy and the suffering, and that's just the way it is. Nothing can change that. And if you think you can change it, you've missed the point. Life is fucked, and the only way to be in this world is to "participate joyfully in the sorrows of the world."

That's what my mother did: She participated joyfully in the sorrows of her world.

As I spoke and looked out at the crowd, I could feel the space between everyone, that unique space that's cracked open by death, filled with an unflinching honesty, and where no one needs to hide. I was filled with such exhilaration because I was so tired of hiding—hiding my voice and truth from myself, and the world. I didn't know how, when, or where, but I knew, as I revealed myself to them, who I really was, and what I was here on this earth to do: to stand in front of others and reveal the rawest truth about life.

It sounds strange, but that day was one of the most beautiful days of my life.

And it was the closest I'd ever come to having a plan.

Those flashes of clarity and strength quickly waned. I was flayed by grief. Everything hurt, nothing felt real, and I felt an eerie separation from the rest of the human race. When I watched TV or went out in the world, I couldn't believe that life still marched along. How dare it? I wanted to stop people on the street and say, My mother is dead. How can you go to lunch or pick up the dry cleaning? My mother is DEAD. Have you no heart? Nothing interested me, felt meaningful or worth an effort. I existed somewhere between the living and the dead. I was beyond the veil.

Bob and I went to someone's birthday party the weekend after Mom's memorial. It was mostly filled with strangers. As people found out about what had just happened, I'd get a blank stare, then a "I'm sorry to hear that," and then they'd retreat. They were afraid it was contagious. I didn't blame them. I'm sure a black hole surrounded me. I wanted to retreat from myself, too.

Six months before Mom died, Bob had signed up for the AIDS ride, a bike ride from San Francisco to Los Angeles encompassing fifteen hundred riders, one thousand tents, and five hundred miles over seven days. I had signed up to be a crew member so that we could do it together. The ride started on June 1, just three weeks after my mom's death. Although it was the last thing I wanted to do, I also knew it would help me survive those days of existential confusion. I would be so preoccupied with *doing* that the emotions I feared would crush me would have to be kept at bay.

But as I got on the plane to go to San Francisco to join Bob, I thought, *What was I thinking?* My only saving grace was that I was not doing any of the riding. I was on the crew. And thank God the universe sent me another angel—the person running the crew was my former sponsor from Al-Anon. I hadn't spoken to her in nine years, and there she was. Not that anyone could really take care of me in that moment, but she gave great hugs.

I was in shock still—a shell of a human being. I was part of that weird club—I'd lost a parent. When I looked at the people around me, I imagined how many other people had lived through this, and realized that a month earlier I'd never even had that thought. But now I looked at everyone and wondered, *Do they know this pain? This loneliness?*

But there's nothing like a thousand gay guys to cheer you up. Every night at dinner there was a cavalcade of drag queens with amazing outfits. *Where did they* pack *this stuff?* I wondered. I barely had enough room for shorts and T-shirts for seven days in the one suitcase they allowed us. How does one pack a different sequined gown and headdress for a whole week?

My crew assignment was easy enough—every day we were to take down the signs, move them to the next camp, and put them up. Or it would have been easy if we'd had the right tools and experience, and the wind hadn't been blowing 20–30 mph most days. We had none of those. Every day we reinvented the wheel. By the third day I wanted to go home. Sleeping in a tent city, peeing in overflowing porta-potties, and worrying about Bob being mowed down by semitrucks on the highway was taking its toll. More than once I thought about using the dead-mother-get-out-of-work card so I could leave, but then I'd see some guy with HIV get on his bike to ride another seventy-five miles, and I told myself to hang on.

On our second-to-last night at Lake Cachuma, we were all physically and emotionally stretched. I was standing in line for dinner when a woman came up to me and told me that my dad was looking for me. I frantically searched through the camp looking for him. I scanned the tent city, the dining hall, and then ran out to the lake's entrance, but he was nowhere. I had missed him. He had looked for me for more than an hour in the sea of people and tents, and never found me. This was one of the biggest acts of love I'd ever felt from my dad. He rarely gave up his day for anyone else, and never did anything spontaneous, and yet he had on that day, just to say hi. I burst into tears when I realized that I had just missed him.

He missed me. He needed me.

A week later, when my dad told me that he needed to travel to Boston and New York for a few weeks for his book tour, I knew I had to go with him. On the outside I was a thirty-four-year-old married woman. On the inside, I was a lost little girl who needed her daddy. I wanted to be near him, hear his voice, and witness his thinking. Soak in his daddyness. The three-, seven-, and ten-year-old who had felt abandoned by him all those decades ago needed to clutch at his presence. I felt like I would finally get the time with him I'd always craved, and that this was my path to finding my way home to myself.

While on the trip, I escorted him to radio shows, morning talk shows, and book signings. I felt one orbit closer to him. Sometimes we talked about Mom, other times we watched TV together, but mostly we took in each other's presence and allowed it to heal us. I almost felt like his equal. Although my mom's presence was palpable in every breath I took, his daddy glow felt like it was keeping me from falling apart completely. I let it fill me up.

In the months that followed I ping-ponged between depression and motivation, confusion and clarity, and never knew what the day would bring emotionally. The grief was so intense that on some days

I just slept all day. When my mom was alive we would talk once or twice a day on the phone. Her absence was sometimes so hard to accept that I would pick up the phone and pretend to call her. I'd have imaginary conversations with her about the impossible reality that she was now gone:

"Hey. I'm not having a good day. I just want to jump out of my life, get away from this pain," I'd say.

"I know. It all feels so impossible. Like it'll never end. It will. I promise. Time does heal," she'd reply.

"I'm sorry we didn't talk more before you died. I was too afraid," I'd say, with tears rolling down my face.

"Me, too. It was too hard. But I'm here now. You can talk to me anytime you need."

"I'm afraid," I would admit.

"It's time to move forward, do what you want to do with *your* life. It's time to live," she would finish.

CHAPTER NINETEEN

True Nature

ABOUT FOUR MONTHS after my mom's death, I found myself in the car driving to the UC campus in Santa Barbara to attend a five-day mindfulness meditation retreat with Thich Nhat Hanh, a Vietnamese Zen master. It was insane of me to do this. I'd never meditated longer than four minutes in my life. But I'd heard his voice on a tape—"Breathing in, you are the mountain; breathing out, you are solid. Breathing in, you are a flower; breathing out, you are fresh . . ." and I knew I just had to go.

For about fifteen years I'd been fascinated with Zen Buddhism, and by "fascinated" I mean confused. I was stumped by the phrase, "Before enlightenment, chop wood carry water; after enlightenment, chop wood and carry water," and wanted to crack the code. I longed to be able to sit still, clear my mind, hush my ego, and learn to become unattached from the roller coaster of life. In my twenties I'd often fantasized about running away to India and giving my life over to a spiritual practice and service to humanity. Of course that might just have been a reaction to my years with Andrew, but it always hung in the back of my mind.

But what I really wanted now from this path was to know how to face death.

Death was the scariest thing I knew, and I wanted to be able to learn to sit with it in a more conscious way. Zen and Buddhist practitioners had been facing death with great wit and aplomb for millennia. I was appalled at how mentally and emotionally checked-out I'd been with my mother during the five weeks between her diagnosis and death. I wanted to do better when it came to my dad's death. And I hoped to do better when it came to my own.

I was terrified of "coming out of the closet" about my spiritual longing to both Bob and my dad. They'd both endured the Catholic Church as children and teens, and were vociferous in their disdain for it, and I feared that disdain would spread onto my choice. And yet, at the same time, they both had a relationship with the sacred in their own ways. But, disdain or not, I was going. I wasn't fucking around anymore. Seeing how fast cancer took my mom, I now understood that on any day I could be hit by a bus, and that I needed to get on with things. There was a rod of strength in me now that said: Do what you need to do for yourself. No one else will do it for you. So off to Santa Barbara I went.

Enlightenment, here I come.

When I got in the car, I realized that I had not driven by myself outside the city since I drove to Lake Elsinore to see Bob during our first week together, five years earlier. I thought, If I make it to Santa Barbara without a panic attack, that'll be my win for the week. Everything else is icing on the cake.

When I triumphantly arrived with nary a hint of panic, I made my way up to the dorms of UCSB to find out that there were about eleven hundred other registered participants. My cult-warning alarms immediately went off. Not only did I hate group anythings, I especially hated the can't-you-tell-by-what-I'm-wearing-that-my-relationship-to-spirituality-is-better-than-yours? type of group things. I took a deep breath and reminded myself, *This is not about them, I am here for me.* When I checked in the news got even grimmer: I had to share a room with a stranger, mindfully walk and eat in silence (whatever the fuck that meant), and do sitting meditation for forty-five minutes at a time, three times a day. I breathed in and I breathed out. I felt like neither a mountain nor a flower.

Every morning at dawn we were invited down to the beach for walking meditation. I'm one of those unhappy morning people. I don't do mornings. But I really wanted to get all I could from this thing, and so I went down to the beach half asleep and joined about four hundred strangers. Damn, I thought, other people slept in? Clearly they didn't want this enlightenment stuff as much as I did. I hadn't been there twelve hours, and I was already getting a spiritual chip on my shoulder. I was well on my way to donning hemp clothing and bowing at every little thing (bowing seemed to be a big thing for these people).

We began walking down the beach mindfully, which meant I was walking so slowly that I might as well have been walking backward. At first I was driven crazy by the snail-like pace, and my mind raced. *How long is this going to take? At this rate I won't have to worry about facing death because I'll be dead before we ever reach the end of this walk. Am I doing it right?* (If my almost falling over during every step was any example, I was not.) *What is the fucking point of this?* Walking had always been about getting somewhere. This was not about that. I recited the mantra *Thay* (Vietnamese for "teacher," which is what everyone calls Thich Nhat Hanh) had given us, to calm my agitation and focus my mind: As I put my right foot down, I said, "I am the earth," and then I put my left foot down: "The earth is me."

As we headed down the beach with *Thay* leading us, I looked out at the Pacific. The blue-on-blue horizon and the salt air in my face gave me permission to relax a bit. The walking meditation became more natural, my mind shut off for a few minutes, and I was just there.

We took a turn inland to the nature-reserve trail and walked single file on two parallel narrow paths up a hill and around a lake.

Four hundred of us mindfully took step after step, with silence filling the space between us. As I emerged onto a plateau, I looked over to my left and saw a red fox about forty feet away. I was completely taken aback. I'd never seen a fox in nature before. It stared intently at a hole in the ground, hunting whatever lived there. It leaped up and pounced in that cute little way foxes do. It was completely unaware that just forty feet away, hundreds of people were walking by. Because we were all mindfully walking, we'd become part of its landscape. I watched it for as long as I could, took a breath, another step, and thought, *I am the earth. . . . Wow, this shit really works. . . . The earth is me. . . . Fuck yeah.*

By the end of the five days, I was still not ready to face death, but at least I'd become a beginner Buddha. I was able to meditate for ten minutes without wanting to run out of the room screaming. I also, much to my chagrin, felt great joy singing along with *Thay*, all the nuns and monks, and the eleven hundred others, "I have arrived. I am home, in the here and in the now," in their singsongy camp-song style. And I realized that one could learn more about enlightenment by watching a Zen master pour a glass of tea and sip it than from all the books in China.

After the retreat the holiday season came barreling toward me. I have no memory of Thanksgiving. I'm pretty sure we ate food somewhere. I didn't care. I wanted my life with my mother back. Not this one without her.

I knew that I could not face Christmas in Los Angeles. My mother, you see, was Christmas. She'd buy too much of exactly what I wanted, and I'd walk away from Christmas morning feeling abundant, loved, and well taken care of. Christmas without my mother was impossible. My father, also grappling with his grief and depression, agreed that we needed to get the fuck out of Dodge, and so he rented a house on the Big Island of Hawaii—a place of beauty and light to hold us in our darkness, in our winter.

The house was on the side of the island that looked like the moon. It was fitting. It looked like how I felt inside—barren. Bob, Dad, Dennis (my cousin now living with my dad at the house in Brentwood), and I settled in. Bob's sister, Liza, who lived on Oahu, joined us for a few days. Mostly we did touristy things like seeing where the Hawaiians had eaten Captain Cook, riding horses on a cattle ranch, and even visiting the volcano where the fiery and volcanic goddess Pele lives. We brought Pele the gifts she loves most—gin and flowers. As I threw the flowers and sprinkled the gin over the rim of a dormant crater, I asked her to heal me and guide me through this liminal space, this time of transition in which I found myself.

For Christmas, Dad booked a helicopter ride to go see Pele and her volcano, Kilauea, from above. As we flew toward that side of the island, we encountered a circular rainbow. It was the most magical thing. The pilot flew right through the center of it. Once at the live volcano, we flew slowly over a very large hole in the ground where we could see the most primal, elementary aspect of life on this planet—liquid rock. Its energy was like nothing I had ever encountered—a raw, unflinching creation happening right before my eyes. My body and mind felt entered by a force beyond anything I'd ever imagined. I knew I was looking at the ultimate unknown/known otherness of life itself.

As the pilot made another pass, I looked over at my dad, and saw that he was holding a small picture of my mom, angled so that she could see Pele, too. In that moment I knew that human love—raw, aching, cut-you-in-half human love—was part of the same creation that was inside that volcano; that both these forces were equal in their ability to build something up, and to cut us in two. My heart burst open with a love so huge, and a small part of me was healed.

CHAPTER TWENTY

When a Triangle Becomes a Square

I'D REACHED A NEW STAGE of my life: I was the perfect jumble of a human being stuck between who I'd been and what I might become. I was in that gooey stage somewhere between caterpillar and butterfly. I had days when strength and clarity filled every inch of me—ready to claim my creative voice and so certain of my place in the world. Then, out of nowhere, a hidden cache of grief and anxiety would surface, and I'd collapse into a heap, a broken-hearted five-year-old aching for her mommy and clinging to her daddy. I had no idea that such contradictions could live inside one mind and body.

I was death and rebirth's bitch.

A few months before our Christmas trip to Hawaii, Bob and I escorted my dad to the Primetime Emmy Awards show. He was nominated for Outstanding Variety, Music or Comedy Special for HBO's *George Carlin: 40 Years of Comedy*. In the limo on the way to the Pasadena Civic Auditorium, my inner five-year-old surfaced, and I began to imagine us walking down the red carpet together, the media asking my dad, And who is this beautiful young woman with you?

This is my beautiful, talented daughter Kelly, he'd reply, and then I'd answer their questions in some witty and charming way, winning over the host of *Entertainment Tonight*.

When we all got out of the limo, some red-carpet wrangler quickly separated us, like curds from the whey, and we were told to stand about fifteen feet behind my dad. Awkwardly we loitered behind him, quickly becoming the unfamiliar faces you often see in the background behind the stars on those fancy red carpets. I felt stupid for my earlier fantasy.

In the auditorium, Bob went to sit with Jerry and his wife, and I got to sit with Dad close to the stage. During commercial breaks everyone stood up and talked to each other. Lots of people came up to my dad to say hello and tell him how sorry they were about my mom. When Garry Shandling came up to us, I nearly died. I was a huge fan of everything he'd ever done. He was very nice and funny, but in the end I felt invisible. My dad had earned his rightful place in the business, but I had not yet earned mine. I clearly saw how my inner five-year-old still needed to borrow my dad's shininess to fit in. I, the thirty-four-year-old, felt like the outsider that I was.

Ultimately Dad was an outsider, too, at least at the Emmys. Although he was nominated five times for a Primetime Emmy over the years, he never won. Admittedly Dad never thought much about award shows, but at least on that day, his old friend from Greenwich Village beat him out: Bette Midler.

As I made my way through that mucky goo between death and rebirth, I started to get a hint at what form my creative wings wanted to spread into once I emerged from the chrysalis. In the early 1990s, before I'd left Andrew, I'd seen Karen Finley, the performance artist, and Spalding Gray the storyteller do their seminal works at UCLA. They sparked a revolution inside me. Although their styles and approaches were quite different from each other, their ability to be raw, funny, and vulnerable on a stage stirred me creatively. I saw the power of a one-person show.

In the fall of 1997, a few months after Mom's death, I began writing a list of stories and events from my life in chronological order, searching for the narrative. I wasn't sure what it'd be about, but I felt in my bones that it could be as powerful as what I'd seen watching those other shows. In my bones I also felt something else— terror. The thought of going onstage and allowing myself to be raw, vulnerable, maybe even funny, struck me as an act of insanity. But I knew I must.

I wasn't quite sure how to start, but I knew I needed to start small, get my feet wet. I loved a local Los Angeles commentator, Sandra Tsing Loh, who was funny and talked about her own personal challenges in her weekly four-minute commentary, called *The Loh Life*, on KCRW. I'd also become enamored with Beth Littleford's work on *The Daily Show*. Playing a character or a slightly exaggerated version of myself while commenting on the world or my life straight to camera felt safer than jumping onstage. Maybe I could produce these segments myself, but where to show them? What my heart really ached to do was a little live show at Luna Park called "UnCabaret." It was a storytelling show where comedians like Janeane Garofalo, Sandra Bernhard, and Taylor Negron got up and shared funny, poignant personal stories instead of doing regular stand-up routines. But that was too scary even to think about. You see, it was in a room with a bunch of stand-ups, and— well—that was a bit complicated for me.

One day when I was hanging out with my dad and sharing some of these thoughts about what I wanted to do next, he asked me, "You're not planning on doing stand-up, are you?"

"Uh, no, why?" I replied.

"It's so different from when I was coming up," he continued.

"Much more competitive now. And the clubs are really tough. The audiences, the owners—" He took a beat. "I'd really discourage you from going that direction."

My dad had never told me not to do anything, except that one time he told me never to smoke cocaine. This wasn't quite as adamant as the cocaine warning, but I thought I got the message loud and clear: You are not good enough to compete with real comedians. Looking back on it now, I'm pretty sure I *hadn't* gotten the message loud and clear. He was probably trying to protect me from the harsh realities of a life in comedy. I could see him imagining some heckler shouting out, Hey, get this cunt off the stage, and bring out the funny Carlin!

But that's not how I took it. I took it as rejection. And not just rejection from my dad, but rejection from George Carlin. Never mind that I'd never even entertained the thought of going into a club and doing stand-up. Never mind all the times he'd praised my writing and talents, or the thousands of times I'd made him laugh. Never mind all that. I now knew the rules—no stand-up. I swept my ego, pride, and hurt under my emotional rug and allowed myself to move toward where I knew I was going—commentary, short films, and storytelling—some real moneymakers. Yeah, right.

Pursuing my craft while finding my voice was not going to pay. I knew that. That's why they call it paying your dues, right? Luckily, due to the overwhelming success of *Brain Droppings*, Dad's career was exploding. The book had climbed onto the *New York Times* bestseller list the first week it was out, in May 1997, and stayed there for eighteen straight weeks. He was very proud of being on that list. In the archives of his stuff that I inherited, I have every single one of those lists that Dad ripped from the paper. Because the book gave him a new wave of momentum for his career, Dad was ready to reach out to more fans and have some fun on this new thing we were all trying to figure out: the World Wide Web. Dad wanted a Web site, and so he hired me to guide its development. He knew he could trust my taste to make it what he wanted. I was back on the Carlin payroll and able to pay some bills while spreading my creative wings.

Wanting to be inspired by the cream of the crop of the comedy world, in February 1998 I went to the Aspen Comedy Festival, produced by HBO. It was an insider festival for the industry to showcase new comedy talent, further the careers of the cool kids of comedy, and rub elbows with VIPs. There were tons of solo shows, sketch comedy, and short films to see, and people to get my schmooze on with.

The first night I was there I went to the opening-night cocktail party. I was not a drinker, but I grabbed a beer at the bar to relax into the atmosphere, and didn't think much about the altitude adding to the alcohol's strength. I saw a man standing by himself at the side of the bar, and I struck up a conversation. He introduced himself as Jim Burrows. My mind quickly woke up. Jim Burrows! Jesus Christ, Jim Burrows was a legend in the world of sitcoms. He was the creator of *Cheers*, and wrote and directed a few others—*Taxi* and *Frasier*. Before I knew it we were doing the cocktail party chit-chat about Aspen, LA, and so on. He seemed genuinely engaged in our conversation, and I was relaxed and felt funny and charming. I told him what I was doing there, and we talked a bit about my dad (the Carlin last name always begged the question: Are you related?).

I could tell the conversation was winding down, so I leaned in and said, "I absolutely loved *As Good as It Gets*." He smiled and said, "That's the other JB—James Brooks." James Brooks—the creator of *Taxi* and *The Mary Tyler Moore Show*, and director of *As Good as It Gets*. My face went sheet white. He put his hand on my shoulder. "We get that all the time. Don't worry." And he walked away. I stood there flooded with shame. Great job, Kelly. Dear foot, please meet mouth. Shit. All I could hear in my head was, *Kid, you'll never work in this town again.*

To this day I blame it on the altitude.

For the rest of the trip I stayed under the radar, introducing myself only to stand-ups that I knew my dad knew, until I saw Ben Stiller and Janeane Garofalo hanging out together at another party. I'd been a huge fan of *The Ben Stiller Show*, and knowing that I'd met him briefly while he was doing a TV movie with my dad—*Working Trash*—I felt comfortable approaching him.

"Ben, Kelly Carlin. We met when my dad did *Working Trash* with you," I said, putting my hand out for a handshake.

"Hey, nice to see you," he said, and smiled at me. "This is Janeane."

"I'm a big fan," I said to her. Not sure where to go next, I said to Ben, "I really loved your show on Fox. I think my favorite sketch was 'Amish Cops.'"

"Oh, thank you. That was all Bob Odenkirk. He wrote that one," Ben said. Awkward silence filled the space between us.

"Oh, well. It was nice to see you," I said, ready to not do any more damage.

"Yeah, same here," he said as someone else grabbed him for a conversation. I backed away once again feeling awkward, and convinced that I should stop striking up conversations with people I didn't know.

The next day, while in line for a sketch show, Bob Odenkirk was standing right behind me. Don't do it, Kelly. Just shut up. I turned around anyway.

"Hey Bob, loved your work on Ben's show. Loved 'Amish Cops.'"

"Oh, thank you so much. I really appreciate that."

Yes. Victory. Redemption.

I did have one piece of actual business to do in Aspen. An old family friend, my former math teacher from Montessori, Sandi Padnos, had worked in cable TV for a decade and had set up a meeting for me. She connected me with a woman who was going to Aspen specifically to find content providers for this new thing that was brewing—Internet television. She worked for a Web site called

ComedyNet that featured stand-up, a talk show, and short films. The screen they played these shows on was maybe a little bigger than two by three inches. It was ridiculous, but it was all we had back then. It was the future, and I wanted to be part of it. I met with Victorria Johnson and told her of my desire to do commentary and short films. She loved the idea and hired me on the spot. It was 1998, the Internet was barely a thing, and a company was actually going to pay me to make short films! I was going to get paid while paying my dues.

Over the next nine months I made short films for them: *The Manual of Life*—my quest for the instruction manual for life I never got; *Who Fucking Cares?*—a string of short clips from tabloid TV followed by a shot of a celebrity looking directly into the camera and saying, "Who fucking cares?"; *Lost in La La Land*—a series of my Beth Littleford–esqe reports from life in Los Angeles; and *Adela*—a black-and-white character piece about a Muslim woman who becomes enamored of butterfly hair clips even though she can't wear them in her hair.

As always, Dad was also busy with his work that year, despite battling depression. He never talked about it directly with me, but I knew he was struggling emotionally. He looked tired and didn't seem to have the vigor he usually had about his work. He was supposed to have done another HBO show in 1998, but he didn't have the motivation to do it. I was worried that he might say, "Fuck it," give up on life, have another heart attack, and join Mom. Luckily, a nice distraction came along when he got a call from Kevin Smith to play Cardinal Ignatius Glick, an arrogant attention whore, in a little movie about religion called *Dogma*. I was so excited for him. Back in 1995, when Bob and I thought we'd become low-budget filmmakers, I met Kevin at the Mill Valley Film Festival at a No-Budget Filmmaking panel. He was a really nice guy, and he was an inspiration to me. Seeing his success with the film *Clerks* let me know that anything is possible. I was so happy that my dad got to go play with Kevin, and Ben Affleck, Matt Damon, Chris Rock, and Linda Fiorentino.

About five weeks before the first anniversary of my mom's death, right around the date that she was diagnosed, I fell into another darkness. The cellular memory of shock, sadness, and fear took over my life, and I was once again a zombie of grief. I realized, due to the timing of her death, that for the rest of my life, I'd now be getting the double anguish of her death anniversary with Mother's Day. Dad also got a double whammy—his birthday, May 12, would always fall on the day after her death for the rest of his life.

The only thing that we both had to distract us from the impending anniversary was that I had demanded that we do a big celebration for Dad's birthday. Because he didn't get to have a sixtieth birthday party the year before, Jerry and I threw him a huge bash with a live big band that played the music that spanned his life—everything from boogie-woogie to disco. We invited family, friends from every era of his life, and people he'd worked with over the years. We decorated the tent with poster-size pictures of Dad from age five to fifty-five.

In addition to organizing the party, I wanted to give my dad a special gift. He was impossible to shop for since he could buy anything he wanted, so I was usually making him collages, or handmade books of quotes and poems, or even painting funny pictures. Mom had usually bought him clothes or books about language or New York. I decided that this year I'd sing him a song. To assuage my stage fright I gathered some allies—my ex-boyfriend Mark Lennon, Dennis Blair (a comic who had opened for my dad for years who used a lot of music in his act), and my cousin Dennis, who was a singer and a drummer, to rehearse a few songs with me. I'm not a professional by any stretch, but like my dad, I have a nice tone and can carry a tune. And although I was very nervous and sang a little sharp in a few places, I managed to sing Joni Mitchell's "Circle Game" to my dad. I don't think there was a dry eye in the place.

The evening was perfect. I wished Mom had been there. But like so many things and events that were occurring then, I realized that they were happening only because she wasn't.

A few months later, in July, while Dad and I were at lunch, somewhere between the bruschetta and the pasta course, he casually announced, "I want you to know that I've met someone, and I went to lunch with her, and I really like her."

Shocked and confused, my body tightened with terror. My mind scrambled around words like: *Excuse me, pardon me, what the fuck did you just say?* But nothing came out of my mouth. Instead I thought, *Be calm. Stay calm. Look cool.*

He continued, "Her name is Sally Wade, and last year she sent me a funny letter addressed to Moe from her dog, Spot. It was really clever and cute. I let her know at the time that I was grieving Mom's death and that I needed a full year to do it properly."

Thank God for that, I thought.

Still, he would not shut up. "After my birthday party, I looked her up and asked her out."

"What does she do?" I asked, trying to stop the buzzing in my ears. I thought I might pass out.

"She's a TV writer. We'd met at Dutton's bookstore briefly last year."

By now he could tell I wasn't coping well with this information, and ended with, "So it was nice. She's really smart and funny."

I'd never imagined my dad with anyone except my mother. Never. We were the Three Musketeers for Christ's sake! I knew in the 1970s he'd probably slept around, because they argued often about it then, but I never let it be a thing that really existed in the world. Our little family had not fallen apart like so many others had that decade. We were indelible. The Carlins would never change. This news about this woman felt impossible.

I somehow managed to form the sentence, "That's great, I'm glad you're getting out and doing stuff."

I calmed myself by imagining that he'd be going out with all sorts of ladies, maybe a string of interesting types that we'd learn to laugh about—nothing too serious. He would become the typical aging man trying to find some company. It would almost make him human in some ways. It would certainly be nothing so serious that it would usurp my mother, or me, or the family that was my inner GPS.

Although shaken, I put the whole thing out of my mind, hoping it would go away.

A few weeks later he informed me, "I'm in love—goofy, silly fantastic love."

My heart exploded into a billion pieces. The little slice of my dad that I'd just gotten back since my mom had died, the slice I thought I now had to myself forever, was going to disappear again. My very existence felt threatened. For my entire life, all my psyche had ever known was our little family system triangle—George, Brenda, Kelly. Now it was—George, Brenda, Kelly, and Sally. This was not a triangle; this was a square. I did not know how to do a square.

I hated this square. And I hated that I wanted my triangle back. I felt as if the whole world were the wrong shape. But, I also knew how lonely and depressed he'd been, and I wanted him to thrive and live another twenty years. Looking into his lovesick eyes, I saw a spark that I'd rarely seen. He was in pure bliss. I couldn't deny it. I just wished this bliss had come in the form of "I've taken up finger painting and mah-jjong, and it's saved my life!"

I couldn't—wouldn't—express any of this to my father. I knew that I had no say in what he was doing. Logically I completely understood that he needed to find a way to have a life after Mom. I know that was what I was doing, too. My reaction was my business.

Plus I already felt as if I'd burdened him with my grief over the last year. I didn't need to burden him with my insecurity, too.

A few months after my mom's passing, he and I had driven out to Palm Desert for a gig he had. I wanted to share with him the music that had been helping me grieve. I played Van Morrison's *Back on Top*. It had been on constant rotation in my CD player, helping to fill the void in my chest.

About five songs in he said, "Can we play something else? This is depressing me." I quickly turned it off, and felt ashamed and weak for letting myself wallow in all this grief.

Now, with this new turn of events, I knew I wouldn't risk sharing any of my feelings about what I was going through because of his relationship with Sally. I was terrified that if I did, I'd lose him forever. I didn't want to be that daughter that makes the new woman's life impossible, and ostracizes herself from her father. I wanted to be the enlightened daughter, the one on the high road. Even though really I just wanted my mommy and my triangle back.

But I also knew that turning my triangle into a square would eventually create something solid to stand on. It would give me the opportunity to learn how to be an autonomous adult and leave behind this family system that had kept me small, silent, and ineffectual in the world.

After getting used to the idea that Sally was here to stay, it was decided that I'd meet her after Dad's show at the Comedy Store in August. He was beginning to work on new material for his next HBO special. Dad was very excited for us to meet and finally connect. I was nervous. I talked to many of Mom's friends about Sally, trying to find some equanimity about the whole thing. But being in the middle of grief isn't necessarily the time for equanimity. I knew I had to feel it.

One thing that helped move the grief through me was giving my mom's things to her friends. Months earlier, after my dad gave me all of my mom's jewelry and clothing, I decided I'd share them

Brenda at the Racquet Club, Dayton, Ohio, around 1961

George and Brenda at their wedding,
June 3, 1961, in Dayton, Ohio

George and Brenda
living the party life,
around 1966

George, Brenda, and Kelly at a cocktail party, around 1965

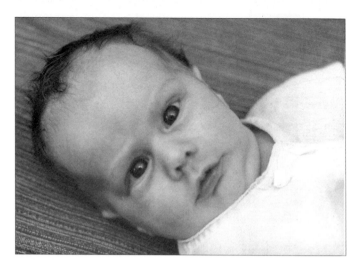

Kelly on the day she was born, 1963

George and Kelly in a
photo booth, New York
City, 1964

The Carlins in Dayton, Ohio, visiting relatives,
around 1966

One of daddy's teaching moments in his office on Beverwil, around 1967

Working a car show,
around 1967

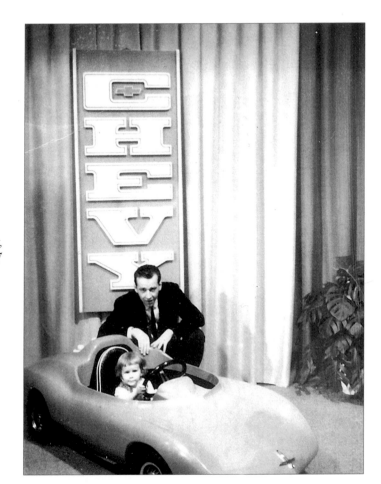

Kelly learning well,
around 1966

New arrivals to LA at the apartment on Beverly Glen, 1966

Kelly clutching daddy's leg at party in 1967

George teaching Kelly
how to properly ride
a tricycle at the apart-
ment on Beverly Glen,
around 1966

George and Kelly
with Gunderilla in
Dayton, 1970

Kelly and Bogie,
Venice Beach, 1971

George and Kelly on the road, 1972

Kelly and Tippy at Tellem Drive house, 1973

Dad illustrating how to play basketball on Tellem Drive, 1974

George and Brenda circa 1974, Tellem Drive

Kelly and Snickers at a horseshow, 1976

Kelly in high school, 1979

Brenda and Kelly at the *Apt-2C* taping in 1984

Kelly, George, and Brenda on the way to the Grammys, 1983

Kelly and Andrew in
St. Maarten, 1985

Kelly on her wedding
day to Andrew, 1985

Brenda and Kelly at the Park Stage Theater, 1987

Bob, Kelly, George, and Brenda at Kelly's thirtieth birthday, 1993

Bob and Kelly's wedding, 1995

The Carlins at Kelly
and Bob's wedding,
1995

Bob and Kelly camping, 1995

George and Kelly cooking
dinner, around 1999

The Carlins at Kelly's UCLA graduation, 1993

George and Kelly at her
fortieth birthday, 2003

with my mom's closest girlfriends. These were women whom my mother had nurtured, remothered, and in some cases, saved their lives. They were mourning her as deeply I was. As I distributed bracelets and rings and cashmere sweaters, I felt my mom's love spread out throughout this group of women.

The big "meet Sally" night came. My stomach was doing triple flips. As I walked through the club, many of my mom's friends came up to me, hugged me, and whispered in my ear how they were wearing my mom's ring or sweater or bracelet tonight, in solidarity. I felt my mother and the love that she represented carry me through the impossible.

After the show the dressing room was packed with comics and friends. The dressing room at the Comedy Store is very dark. It has black walls, black furniture, and a mirror table. I looked down at the mirror and wondered how much cocaine had been done on that table in the last twenty years. I looked across the dimly lit room and saw a woman with blond hair and prominent cheekbones. My heart leaped. It was my mother. I'd been seeing her everywhere those days out of the corner of my eye. Any flash of blond hair on a woman walking down a street would make my heart skip.

I took a beat and let my eyes land on this blond woman again. That's when I realized—it's Sally. *It's Sally, and she looks like my mother. There's the ash-blond hair. There are the cheekbones.* Then it hit me: My dad has a "type." And something relaxed in me. The sting of this whole debacle lessened because I realized that my dad had a type. Why? I don't know. It made him more human? It made the whole thing less about my mom and Sally, and more about what his needs were? Probably.

As I approached her, it was clear she was way more nervous about meeting me than I was about meeting her. She was nice, and funny, and I could see she was not some wicked stepmother type. We laughed about how awkward this was for both of us.

Eventually, after a few months, I saw that she was a woman ten years older than me, interested in writing, performing, and spiritual seeking just like me. She, too, was attempting to find her place in the world. She even had stage fright.

And even though my inner five-year-old was still miserable about Mom and Dad breaking up, my thirty-five-year-old self was genuinely happy for my dad.

CHAPTER TWENTY-ONE

Unspoken Words

"WE TALK ABOUT EVERYTHING," Dad said, describing his new relationship with Sally. "There's no barrier between us. Even when we're having sex, I can tell her what feels good—"

"Dad"—I quickly stopped him—"really. I don't need to hear that."

Sometime during the first few months after Daddy met Sally, he'd turned into a thirteen-year-old boy with no filter. He was over the moon with his new gal Sal and couldn't talk about anything else. If I hadn't been so thrilled by the fact that he was no longer depressed and looking on the edge of death, I might just have slapped him.

I understood, though. New love sets off a gooey gushing of love so big that nothing can contain it. I had felt the same way after meeting Bob. Plus, I knew that my mom and dad's relationship had been far from perfect. They had more baggage than the lost and found at Continental Airlines. When Mom died, they'd loved each other for a long time. They just weren't *in* love with each other. Dad and Sally were in love.

After Dad and Sally had been together almost a year, Dad and I rented a house just outside Yosemite Valley in the foothills of the Sierra Nevada Mountains for the two-year anniversary of Mom's death. I was ready for some family time. After the last year of adjusting to my new world order, spending three full days alone with my dad felt like a hundred Christmases times a thousand birthdays.

Dad had never been to Yosemite before, and I was excited to share it with him. Every morning we went down to the valley floor, and I showed him the magnificent waterfalls and rock formations. And every night we went outside onto the deck, and Dad showed me the stars. Dad loved astronomy. He'd brought up his star charts and astronomy books and excitedly shared with me the constellations, galaxies, and planets.

"Right there, that's Gemini—Castor and Pollux," he said, pointing to two stars low in the western sky. "Soon you won't see them at all until winter." Dad always tried to find Gemini for me, since it was both my and my mom's Zodiac sign.

"And there's Mars. You can always find Mars because it's red. You can't see Jupiter right now," he said, scanning the sky for other familiar objects. "Sally and I are Jupiterians."

"What's that?" I asked, craning my neck up searching for Orion, the only constellation I could recognize on my own.

"We just feel like we don't belong here on Earth, so we decided we're from Jupiter."

I was glad it was dark and he couldn't see me roll my eyes. But then I wondered, *Does Dad think I'm a Jupiterian, too?*

When we weren't out exploring nature, we just occupied the space in the house separately but together—he read while I wrote; he wrote while I read. It was the same space we'd occupied decades ago when I was a young child and he'd be working in his office while I played quietly on the floor. And as usual, music was always playing. Instead of the Stones and the Beatles, it was now Van Dyke Parks and Tom Waits.

The last two nights we were there, we took our time and laughed and cried our way through a huge box of family photos. It was a cav-alcade of dogs and cats—Beanie, Bogie, Tippy, Lil', Abbey, Mur-phy, Annie, Vern, Jeremy, and Moe—and Mom's hairstyles—updos, shags, Twiggy boy cuts, big hair, blond, red, and tawny. Dad put aside about a dozen or so photos of Mom and me for his collection. I pulled out about a hundred for mine.

The last morning we were ready to spread Mom's ashes. We deci-ded we'd let her go into the Merced River and inside a redwood grove next to the valley. As we pulled away from the house, Dad turned on the stereo, and Debussy's "Clair de Lune" began to play. Dad stopped the car. We turned to each other and just stared. During the darkest drug days in the 1970s, my mother would often sit at the piano for hours and play "Clair de Lune" to soothe her haunted soul. This was the only song I ever remember her playing. Dad showed me his arm covered in goose bumps, and I showed him mine.

Dad and I were always such suckers for a perfect moment of syn-chronicity. Since I was a small girl, my dad taught me how to look for signs that the universe was on our side. Whether it was finding coins on the sidewalk or the number three (our family's lucky num-ber) showing up in hotel room numbers or flight times, Dad was al-ways pointing them out and commenting, "Hey, look, 393. Excellent number. A good sign indeed." "Clair de Lune" spontaneously play-ing as we drove down to the valley floor was like a gigantic neon finger pointing right down on us and the universe saying, I see you and hear you.

Brenda was in the house.

Dad and I found a perfect spot along the Merced River and headed down to the bank with a large Ziploc bag filled with Mom's ashes. The river rushed by filled with spring runoff, but there was a quiet little pool near us. We climbed out onto a few flat rocks and both knelt down while each grabbing a handful of the ashes. I held my hand under the water and watched as Mom and the Merced slowly mixed. Dad mentioned that it was this time of day when they got married in Ohio. I looked up and noticed behind him the waterfall across the valley floor. I pointed to it and said, "That's Bridal Veil Falls right there."

"It sure is," Dad said wistfully.

After we'd released about half the ashes, we made our way up and out of the valley, stopping one last time to look at the stunning vista that allows you to see North Dome, El Capitan, and Yosemite Falls in one grand view. In the Mariposa Grove of redwoods, we walked slowly among the giants. Because it was mid-May, we were pretty much the only people there. In a month tourists would be crawling on every square inch of these trails. The dappling light made the grove look like a church. Dad sat down on a rock, and I took the rest of the ashes and circumambulated counterclockwise around one of the redwoods while slowly releasing the ashes from my hand. After I made it once around the tree, I knew I felt complete. Well, almost complete. There were still ashes left in the bag. But, I knew I'd keep them to scatter in Big Sur or maybe even Dayton at some point in the future.

As we drove away from the redwoods, Dad said, "I'm done. No more rituals or ashes spreading for me. I need this grief to be over now, Kel. I'm done."

Tears filled my eyes. I felt so alone.

I was not done. I had just begun.

Before my mom's death, I'd begun to feel an anger simmering in me for myself, my mother, and all women who'd stifled their creative voices in the service of safety and love. After leaving Andrew I carried the heavy truth that I'd wasted a whole decade of my life trailing after him and his needs. Now, with my mom's life cut short, I wasn't going to let another year go by without honoring my creative life. I would not be quiet anymore. Because she'd never allowed herself to nurture and fully claim her own creative and expressive self, I was on a mission—I needed her life and her death to have some meaning. I needed to carry the creative torch forward for her and all women.

I'd never been a feminist with a capital F. I'd gone to prochoice rallies and written a few things for the feminist paper at UCLA, but I'd never really felt called to the front lines to fight the female fight. I think this was mostly due to my complicated childhood relationship with my mother, which left me untrusting of women in general. This ultimately translated into me not knowing how to trust myself, especially when it came to my creativity. I didn't trust my talent or ideas. I never learned to nurture my own creative process.

Yes, I'd grown up with one of the greatest role models of how to be a creative right under my nose—he was my dad—but it just didn't translate for me. I needed some female role models, so I found Frida Kahlo and Georgia O'Keeffe. I immersed myself in their paintings and their life stories. I relished their courage to radically follow the call of the image, their imagination, even if that meant not being the women society wanted them to be. Neither of them let their voices be stifled. I breathed in their fierceness and allowed it to give me just enough courage to go forward with my idea for a work I felt destined to create—a one-woman show.

About three months before the trip to Yosemite with my dad, in February 1999, Bob and I had gone to New York to watch him tape his eleventh HBO special, *You Are All Diseased*. Cheery title. Dad was in a mood. When people talk about my dad during this period, they often call it the "angry George Carlin" period. Was this a reflection of the depression and grief he'd just dealt with? Or was it some unleashing of a side of him that he'd repressed while Mom was alive? I did not know. But in this show he took no prisoners. He went after big institutions—big business and religion. But no one was safe from his disdain—angel worshippers, Harley-Davidson riders, and white guys who played the blues were all fair game. Dad and I often joked during this period that Bob and I had been given personal dispensations for some of our trespasses—golf and cowboy-boot wearing.

Even with this dispensation, a little part of me feared that I'd

end up on his increasingly long list of "People I Can Do Without."
I was terrified that he harbored some of this disdain for me and my
life choices. I had no proof of it, but it lived deep inside me.

Dad always taped two shows over two nights so that they could
cut them together if they needed. Whenever I watched my dad shoot
his HBO shows, it was as if I were on the stage with him. This night
was no different. When he first walked out, I felt an enormous flood
of pride when the crowd went ape-shit upon seeing him. He was
such a rock star up there. Then, as the first show progressed, I could
feel every part of my body tighten in an effort to carry him through
it. He was uncharacteristically unfocused, and fumbled some. My
heart went out to him as I watched him struggle a bit with some timing and memorization stuff.

The second night of taping there was none of that. He came out
and killed it.

The after party of one of Dad's HBO shows was usually a mel-
low affair—the staff, crew, and family having a few drinks and a nice
meal at an Italian restaurant around the corner from the Beacon
Theater, but the party that night felt more like a real celebration. I
think everyone was happy that Dad was back. I think Dad was
happy that he was back.

There were a few comics there (Bob and I had a nice conversation with David Cross), and I had some friends there too. I had
gotten tickets to the show for my ComedyNet colleagues, Mark
Graff and Victorria Johnson. Before becoming part of ComedyNet,
I didn't have my own New York friends. I'd never mixed my work
with my dad's world, and having them there made me feel like I
had finally arrived in the business myself. I felt like a goddamn-
real-live grown-up.

As the party was winding down, Rocco Urbisci, the director of
Dad's show, insisted that Bob and I join him and his managers at
the *Saturday Night Live* party in the Village. Gee, twist my arm!
As we all jumped into a cab, Rocco said to his managers, "Kelly's

been doing some great work with these short films for ComedyNet. You should check them out. She's quite a talent."

I was taken aback and deeply touched.

"What are you working on now?" asked Jane, one of the managers.

"Actually, I've started to work on a one-woman show about growing up with all my parents' craziness. I have a bunch of funny, wild stories from my childhood," I replied.

"You know, HBO has a space in LA that they use to develop one-person shows. We should talk about getting you in there," the other manager, Frank, said.

I wanted to stop the cab and run around and do the happy dance. Real managers were talking to me about wanting to help me develop my one-person show with HBO. HBO and Carlin. This was not happening. I felt higher than if I'd just snorted an eight ball of coke.

"That sounds great. Let's talk when we get back home," I replied as nonchalantly as I could. I didn't want to look like a total rube.

By the time we'd made our way in to the party, spent way too much on a few vodka drinks, and been ignored by the majority of the partygoers, I felt like I'd truly arrived—I was kind of, sort of, maybe represented by Rocco's managers.

When I got back to LA, the managers weren't ready to sign me officially since I was still an unknown quantity, but they took me under their wing. I went with them to the taping of the three one-person shows that HBO had just developed in the last year. They were okay. They were funny and lightweight fare, but nothing wowed me. They were basically stand-up comedians doing longer versions of some of their premises. If this was what was being seen as the best of the work there, I knew I could do this.

As I began to develop my show, I got excited. I'd come up with a great premise and title: *Driven to Distraction*. I wanted to examine how I'd been surrounded by things that distracted me from my true, authentic self for most of my life—messages from the culture's media, my parents' addictions and chaos, my privileged-Hollywood teen years, my poor choices within my relationship with Andrew—and how my mother's sudden death had woken me up to what was real—love. I wanted to share the funny stories from my crazy life, talk about the pain and confusion of watching her die, but really the whole show led up to that moment at my mom's memorial, when the space that only death can crack open appeared before me and transformed my world. I knew I could talk about funny things and deep scary things onstage within the same show. I knew I could be clever, silly, serious, and real.

In the fall of 1999, after I'd turned in a rough draft to the managers, they told me, "We think you need to scrap the death stuff. It's just too morbid. Stay with the funny." I was offended. I didn't *want* to just "stay with the funny."

"Also, HBO has shut down their one-person show program," they added. "They're no longer looking to develop shows."

Fuck it, I thought. I'll do it my way. I'll do it myself. I walked away from the managers.

About a month later Dad informed me that he'd sold the house on Old Oak Road. Another blow. That house was the last thing that connected me to my mother, and I'd always imagined that the house would be mine someday. I'd dreamed about growing old within those adobe walls. But Dad and Sally were now basically cohabitating, and every square inch of that house in Brentwood was my mom. Every color choice, piece of furniture, and Indian rug said Brenda. There was no way Sally was moving in there. I couldn't blame her. If I were her, I wouldn't have either.

Dad said we had five months to clear things out. Every time I went over to the house during that time, there'd be another pile of boxes to go through. It was like constantly ripping open a just-healed-over scab. Nothing within me could fully move on. As I stepped through the decades of our life as a family, I was ultimately confronted with the question: What will life be like when Dad's gone, and I have no one left to share these memories with?

The Three Musketeers were fading away.

To move forward with my one-woman show, I gathered a new team around me. I asked my friend, the actress and director Amy Wieczorek, to be my director and collaborator. I sat her down and read my rough draft out loud to her. She laughed and wept throughout the reading. This was a good sign. She said she'd be honored to help me bring this into the world. My friend Meredith Flynn came onboard as a producer. We met with the woman who ran the Hudson Theater in Hollywood, and planned a five-week run sometime in late summer of 2000.

I gathered a group of people I trusted with my creative life—my therapist, acting coaches, other writers and actors, and some friends—to come to a series of readings while I developed the script. I wanted to make sure that what I'd written was not self-indulgent but a universal story of a woman in search of herself. The readings went well. For the first time in my life, I felt like I was on the right track in my creative life. Before I committed to the next step of rehearsals, there was just one more thing that I needed to do: send the script to my dad.

I was excited to know what he thought because not only had he always encouraged my writing, but some of the stories I shared in the show had been part of our Carlin folklore for years. I knew he'd get a kick out of me telling the "Sun Exploded" story from my perspective.

After three weeks I hadn't heard anything from him, but wasn't too worried because he was always so busy. When five weeks had passed with no reaction, I got a stomachache. I gathered myself and called him up.

"Hey Dad, how's it going?" I asked, trying to sound casual.

"Good," he replied with a bit of tension in his voice.

I took a deep breath and asked, "So I was wondering. Have you gotten a chance to look at my script yet?"

"Yeah, I have." He continued, "We need to talk—at your therapist's office."

Fuck.

Dad and I showed up at the appointment at Berenice's office. After a few pleasantries she said, "Well, George, you've called us together. What do you need to say?"

Dad turned to me and said, "Kelly, you know I love you, but—"

But. But. Oh dear.

"But I need you to know that I feel deeply betrayed by this," he continued.

The room began to spin. I thought I might lose my mind. I began to sob and sob and sob. The kind of sobbing you do at age three, and you can't quite get enough air because your body is in a panic, so you take big gulps of air. I could not stop gulping and sobbing. I had betrayed my daddy—the very thing I'd been desperate to avoid my entire life. Without my dad, I was dead. I believed that. With my mom drinking, and falling, and driving up neighbors' lawns, I had believed that if I were to push my dad away in any way, I would be dead. And now that she was gone, I had gone and pushed him away. Now there'd be no one to keep me safe.

He continued, "But I am an artist, and you are an artist, and I would never ask you to change a single word of it." Some air came back into the room. "But I can't be there to watch it. It would just be too hard for me. I just can't sit there and be in the audience."

My breathing slowed a little more. He didn't hate me. He hadn't stopped loving me. My inner three-year-old realized that I hadn't died because Daddy was disappointed with me. The walls had not fallen in, nor had the earth opened up and swallowed me. Somehow my daddy was still here. But I also saw that he was genuinely worried about the audience judging him as much as he judged himself for those dark drug days in the seventies. He still carried an enormous amount of guilt for those times, and he didn't want to be reminded of them.

Then he said, "But I do have to ask, why didn't you tell me directly how upset you were when I left to go on the book tour when Mom was sick?"

A clarity came over me, and the words poured out of me. "I don't know. Maybe I thought I needed to be on your stage for you to finally see and hear me" came tumbling out of my mouth.

Dad looked visibly taken aback, but then he smiled slightly and said, "Touché, Kiddo. Touché."

All those years of our family's mutual denial sat in the space between us. All the times he had asked, "Hi, how are you?" and I had answered, "Fine" when I hadn't been, finally came to roost. I was more comfortable speaking openly to a roomful of strangers about what had gone on deep inside me during the darkest days of our life together than I was speaking directly to my own dad.

I canceled my theatrical run. Even with the insights of that session, I was afraid that if I went ahead and had success with my show, I would lose my father forever. That I'd end up permanently on his "People I Can Do Without" list. My inner three-year-old still needed time to trust the new reality.

I performed my show only three times. My dad never attended. It's a shame, because by the end of each performance the audience loved him even more than they had before.

CHAPTER TWENTY-TWO

The Clown and the Guru

AFTER MY THREE PERFORMANCES of *Driven to Distraction*, I once again found myself at a crossroads in my professional life. I should have been looking forward to writing and performing another solo show that would fulfill me creatively and might get me some attention from Hollywood. But instead something was gnawing at me, giving me pause.

In the past decade I'd found plenty of reasons to stall the progress of my career: fear of failure, disdain for the corporate interests of the industry, and just feeling ill suited for the overall task. But with the confidence I'd gained doing my show, those reasons no longer applied.

No worries. I had a new one up my sleeve—was the entertainment industry itself even the proper path for me?

One thing I knew I wanted for sure was to be on a stage talking about my circuitous and humbling human journey, like Spalding Gray did, while also using humor to wake up audiences from their American Dream slumber, like my dad did. However, a whole new set of doubts about being an entertainer was bubbling up inside me.

After a few years on the Buddhist path, I felt called to be of greater service to the world more directly. I wanted to make a real dent in the world; help real people find their strength to create real change in their lives. I'd caught a glimpse of what that felt like while doing my shows. The people who saw them were genuinely touched by my work. A few had told me that my work had shifted something for them. This was huge. I saw how I might weave together the two main forces that were always wrestling within me: the Clown and the Guru. I wanted to be irreverently reverent, while being reverently irreverent. I wanted to bring humor to the deep suffering of human life, while bringing depth and soul to entertainment. Or as Joseph Campbell had said, "Participate joyfully in the suffering of the world."

I wasn't sure that a life in showbiz, which tended to be mostly a shallow, ego-driven pursuit, would help me do any of that. Of course the people I admired most in the business had done it. They had a much wider impact in the world than just puffing up their own egos. But they were superstars. I wasn't on their level, and didn't know if I'd ever be successful enough to make that kind of impact.

That thinking then brought me to the next big doubt: Would I ever be successful? Now that I was thirty-eight, I accepted that it was probably too late for me in this youth-obsessed business. I was afraid that I'd have to do the kind of work that did not feed my soul but paid the bills. And after my mom's death, and especially after writing and performing my own solo show, I just couldn't go backward. I wanted to feed my soul, make a living, *and* change the world.

But underneath all that thinking lay another reason, maybe even the real reason, to walk away from a life in showbiz—my dear old dad.

I was afraid that if I went ahead with another solo show, I'd lose him forever, so I found a way to please us both—Pacifica Graduate Institute.

Pacifica is a small grad school nestled in the bosom of the hills of Santa Barbara, filled with adults in search of the sacred through psychology—more specifically, Jungian psychology. Their motto is *Anima Mundi Collende Gratia*—"Tending the Soul of and in the World." That all sounds rather fluffy, full of bullshit, and way too "woo-woo." But it was music to my ears. And soul. Not only was it a place where I could finally discover what makes humans tick, but it would also allow me to study the importance of storytelling as an integral feature of the human experience. Pacifica was a graduate program built on the shoulders of Carl Jung, one of the founders of modern psychology; and my old buddy, the mythologist Joseph Campbell. These two men had introduced terms like "archetype," "myth," "the hero," and "collective unconscious" into our modern-day vernacular. They both believed that the path of the human was a spiritual one to be found through one's individual foibles, fears, and longings. I knew in my heart that the teachings and legacy of these men would help me to interweave my inner clown and guru. And I knew in my bones that I could use what I learned there to create art and entertainment that just might help to heal and trans-form the world.

And of course the other good part about going to grad school was that it would make my dad happy.

First of all I'd no longer be spilling my personal guts on a stage. Instead I'd be spilling them in the confines of the walls of a grad school. Also, I'd be off in some institution of higher learning, some-thing I knew my dad loved from my days at UCLA. Dad took such pride in my academic achievements. Last, I'd be pursuing something more tangible and solid than a precarious career in showbiz. At the end of three years Pacifica would give me a solid plan B for life—a Master's in Counseling Psychology that would allow me to become a therapist if I chose to.

Win-win.

With all that, there was one thing in particular that tipped the scales for me. A few years earlier I'd read *Fathers' Daughters: Break-ing the Ties That Bind*, by Maureen Murdock, a Jungian psycholo-gist and lecturer at Pacifica. In it she focused on her struggle to claim her personal power and unique voice while climbing out from under the shadow of her father. The back jacket states: "In order to sustain his approval, protection, and love, she often distances herself from her mother and rejects her own feminine nature. By identifying solely with her father, her development as a woman is arrested in daughterhood."

I could have written those very same words myself.

I knew that Maureen had much to teach me.

When I went up to Santa Barbara for my interview, I was nervous. This was such a huge leap in a new direction that I wasn't sure I could do it. As I waited in the room with about a dozen other applicants for the orientation to begin, I looked around and thought, I'm making a huge mistake. These people all look like therapists. What am I doing here? And then a woman said, "Sorry, I'm late. I hit some traffic." And I looked up, and walking in was Maureen Murdock. She was our host for the day.

Hello sign from the universe.

My interview later that day confirmed my growing enthusiasm. Kathee Miller, a full-time therapist, and photographer and dancer, interviewed me. As we sat down in her office she said, "Your writing is beautiful."

"Oh, thank you," I replied. "It was an amazing experience for me. Very healing in some ways."

I'd used the script of *Driven to Distraction* as the essay requirement in my application. Because I hadn't been in school for almost a decade, and had zero background in psychology, I'd hoped it would tip the scales in my favor. Plus I wanted to communicate to the powers that be there that I saw myself as an artist first, and a pursuer of healing second.

"It's so honest and raw—really great work," she added.

I was filled with an intense warmth and hope. I felt seen and loved. I saw that this school could be more than just a place of learning and understanding about the human psyche. I saw that it could be a place of deep healing for me, too. These women of Pacifica—Maureen and Kathee—would see me, could acknowledge me, and thus really support me—all things that my own mother, due to her alcoholism, had found difficult to do until later in life. If I could be seen and heard in this unconditional way by these role models, these women, maybe I'd finally learn to trust myself fully and not be "arrested in daughterhood" as Maureen mentions on the back of her book.

My "father issues" may have led me to Pacifica, but it would be my mother issues that would be healed by this place.

Kathee and I continued to talk a bit about why I wanted to attend Pacifica.

"I'm so curious about the human psyche. Why are we the way we are? Why do we take certain paths? Being a solo show artist, I want to be able to take all that information and weave it into future works," I told her.

"What about the therapy part?" she asked.

"Well, I feel like I've been a therapist since I was three years old, and that I'd have a particularly good leg up in that department. But in the end I'm not sure that's what I want to do the rest of my life. But I *am* interested in helping people heal. I'm hoping to be able to use that knowledge in some way other than one-on-one therapy."

"Not everyone who comes here goes on to be licensed. There are many modalities that this stuff can be used for. And as far as the creative aspect," she continued, "many of the classes allow you to do an art project as your final assignment."

I felt as if I'd just been given the key to the Emerald City.

She closed my folder and said, "It looks like everything is in order. You should be getting a letter in the mail next week telling you that you've been accepted. I can't see any reason why not."

As I drove down the coast back to Los Angeles, I felt exhilarated and terrified. It was now hitting me what a huge commitment I was making. Not only was I saying yes to a great undertaking—a forty-thousand-dollar student loan, a two-year program, writing a thesis, and at least two years interning as a therapist—but also the possibility of a whole new direction in my life. I didn't know who I'd be or where I'd be going when I was done. There was a very good chance I'd be leaving showbiz—the only life I'd ever imagined up until this point. Everything was now wide open for me. That was both the exhilaration and the terror of it. That and the fact I'd be walking away from the world that held my father in the highest regard. I'd no longer be in his domain. I'd no longer be in the solar system that revolved around my personal sun—my father.

I needed some advice. So, I reached out to my dad.

After the therapy session the two of us had about my solo show, Dad and I realized that we didn't really know how to talk to each other, and so we deliberately set out to communicate more frequently and more honestly with each other. No longer did our exchanges resemble those from my childhood and adolescence, which consisted of nothing more than Dad asking, "Hey, how are you?" and me replying, "Fine." We were now *actually* communicating.

Here's the actual e-mail I sent my dad that day after my visit to Pacifica, with his responses in parentheses (which *he* embedded in the e-mail):

> Hey there,
> I went to Pacifica Grad Institute today and it was really great. It's a beautiful campus—two exits before San Ysidro— and has an interesting program for the MA in counseling psychology. I found out that a lot of people with an artistic orientation go there, and that the school supports and encourages that aspect of people. In fact, you can do an art project as your thesis. I think it could be a real home for me.
> The other side is that I feel overwhelmed and completely unprepared for this adventure.

(Just like that other adventure I felt overwhelmed by and completely unprepared for: that adventure of doing a live stage show about you and Mom and all my pain.)

I'm so used to hiding from my power, gifts, and the world that it seems like an act of insanity to go outside of all the safety I have created for myself.

(Therefore I took it for granted that I could never do a show like that, and I stayed in that nice safe spot I had created for myself, and never answered the call of my soul.)

Is it possible to have the life one imagines?

(I know my Dad sat in the movies when he was ten and imagined he could be a famous comedian, but I'm nothing like my Dad. We have no traits in common.)

I know it is for others, but I have always doubted it for myself. It looks so simple from the audience.

(Kelly—In life, one is never in the audience. One is always on the stage.)

Hope I can stay awake for the Letterman. Hope all is well.

(Hope you can stay awake for your next great adventure.)

Later,

(Now!)

Love,

(Power!)

Kel

(Dad)

Hey Squirt!

You know your direction; there's no down side. There is only the wonderful, scary sensation of succeeding . . . and the joy. The great joy of being completely alive. Oddly, joy takes courage.

You walked away from Andrew and into the light. That took courage.

You went back to a school that had once overwhelmed you, and for which you had been completely unprepared . . .

and you thrived. Magna cum laude. You walked into the light.
That took courage.

Look to your courage; walk to your light.

Here's my advice about your above message: Every time
you start reciting your second paragraph in your head, shout
the first paragraph out loud; especially the last line.

Love and all that stuff,

The father of KELLY

PS—The Letterman was great. I'll lend you the tape when it
comes in.

As I read those words, I wept. My father saw me, acknowledged
me, and supported me. He always had—I'd just had a hard time
seeing it and receiving it. I'd always thought I needed to be perfect
in his presence, and had therefore hidden my anxieties about my
life's path from him. Of course this had kept me feeling alone and
scared for so long. But the moment I risked being open with him,
he was instantly present, perceptive, and full of unconditional love.
What took me so long?

I drank it all up like water at an oasis, and took the leap toward
my master's degree.

I began the program in September 2001, two weeks after 9/11. The
world had gone mad. But in the womb of that campus, curriculum,
and those thoughtful teachers/psychologists, I felt safe, and in a privileged position to make sense of the world and maybe even humanity. But first I had to unearth a few things from my own psyche.

In my first winter quarter at Pacifica, January 2002, I got to work
with Maureen Murdock. I was beyond excited. Because of the seren-
dipity of my encounters with her—the book and the orientation—I
felt an odd attraction to her. I desperately needed her to see me, acknowledge me, and love me (my mother issues clearly present). At
the beginning of the first class, I was only semiconscious of the fact

that I was projecting all of my own mother shit all over her. I'm sure that as a seasoned psychologist, she could feel me flinging all of this toward her. But even after I realized that my reaction to her was heightened and unconscious, I still couldn't control myself. I had some work to do in this department.

Maureen's class was called Myth and Memoir. She was developing material for her next book, *Unreliable Truth: On Memory and Memoir.* I was very excited to be focusing on memoir stuff. I felt like a bit of an expert after doing my solo show. *I wonder if I'll get brownie points from her for this?* I was also intrigued by the subject because I thought it might help me with my thesis and any other projects I did in the future.

As psychology students, what we were to take away from the course was how our clients construct narratives from the events of their lives, and how these then filter what they think about the world, and thus shape the choices they make. In order to write our final paper, she asked us to think about a myth or a narrative, and to explore the mythology that we had lived out within our own lives. *Alice in Wonderland* immediately popped into my head. I'd certainly felt like I'd fallen down the rabbit hole a number of times in my life. After class, I approached her.

"Hi, Maureen. We met on orientation day?"

"Yes. Welcome again," she offered.

"I didn't get a chance to tell you then, but your book *Fathers' Daughters* really affected me. It's why I wanted to come to Pacifica. You see, my dad is George Carlin and, well, there's a lot of stuff there—and now this memoir stuff. I did a one-woman show last year about it, and this stuff is so intriguing to me." Ugh. I felt like a fan talking to a rock star.

"I can only imagine what that must've been like, growing up with him, in his shadow," she said, with not quite the enthusiasm I wanted from her.

But her clinical distance did nothing to dissuade my admiration for her. In fact it just fed my need to please her even more.

"Anyway, I was thinking about the story of Alice in Wonderland as my myth," I said. "It really seems to hold so much of my story. I feel like most of my life was lived in a world that was upside down."

She looked at me sternly and said, "I really think you should wait until the next class, when we explore the myth of Demeter and Persephone through a reenactment."

I had no idea what this Demeter/Persephone myth was all about, and felt like a kid who was just told to eat her vegetables. I continued, "Or maybe Psyche and Eros," hoping to continue our conversation and connection.

"I think you'll really resonate with Demeter and Persephone. It's the mother/daughter myth," she said. "Just wait until after the reenactment, then decide."

I felt gutted, just like I had every time my own mother had not supported me the way I wanted. I didn't want to do the "mother/daughter myth," I thought as I walked away.

But something wiser and deeper than the petulant and needy child within me told me to trust Maureen. She'd led me here to Pacifica, and I was here, ultimately, to trust something else besides my old story line, and so I acquiesced and waited.

During the monthlong break between classes (Pacifica was a monthly three-day program), Maureen had e-mailed us all with her casting. I saw that I'd been cast as Metaneira, and the actor in me immediately went to the script to see how big my part was. I was only in one scene, and had only a few lines. I'd hoped that she'd seen my potential and given me a leading part like Demeter or Persephone. No such luck.

On the day of the reenactment, people brought costumes and props with them to enhance their roles and the overall production. I was underwhelmed by the thought of it all until Maureen walked up to me, smiling, and said, "I've brought you something special—my own baby doll to play the part of your son, De-mophoon. Please take care of it. It means a lot to me." I was filled with a warmth throughout my whole body, privileged to be the keeper of her precious baby. Maybe there was a chance for her and me to connect after all.

We did the reenactment, and nothing exciting happened for me. It felt like a bad run-through at some community theater. It was fun to see certain people really get into their parts—my friend Taylor, normally the class clown, was transformed by playing Zeus. As he spoke Zeus' lines, and sat on a throne, he suddenly looked as if he truly did have the power to smite any and all who crossed him. I was impressed by how speaking as an archetype—in his case the great father god—could transform somebody. But other than that I didn't feel anything toward this mother/daughter myth. I had no idea what Maureen had been alluding to when she'd told me to wait for this day. I was thoroughly disappointed.

Then, after the reenactment, Maureen had the main characters—Demeter, Persephone, Zeus, and Hades—stay on the stage. She turned to the rest of us and asked, "Does anyone have any questions for these archetypes?"

A few asked some questions to Zeus (the father of Persephone and husband to Demeter), Hades (Zeus' brother and the one who abducts Persephone into the underworld), and Demeter (Perse-phone's mother). Then, suddenly, I felt a heat in my chest. I knew that I must ask Persephone (played by Lisa, our youngest classmate at age twenty-four, who genuinely looked the part of the naive waif), a question. I stood up with my heart beating firmly in my chest. "Persephone, now that you have been to the underworld, separated from your mother, how does it feel to have found a place in the world and in your life that she cannot share? Something that is all yours?"

Lisa/Persephone replied perkily, "Well I'm so happy to be back with my mother, and I feel deeply connected to her."

I waited for more, but nothing else came. What? No sense of freedom? No great surge of empowerment? I needed more. I needed some clues on how to find my own place within my psyche that was separate and individuated from my own mother. I didn't need this warm and fuzzy shit that Lisa had given me. Knowing my long history with my mother issues, and then seeing my own struggle with Maureen this last month, I wanted more. I sat down, frustrated. A few more people asked questions of the archetypes, but I was no longer listening. I was stewing.

Maureen then asked the group, "Does anyone wish to come on-stage and speak through the archetypes present here?" My hand rose before I knew what was happening, and suddenly I found myself standing and walking onto the stage. Something had taken over my body and walked me onto that stage. I noticed that no one else was getting up, and I thought, *Here you go again, Kelly, always the one who needs attention on a stage.*

Maureen instructed me to stand behind the archetype that called to me. I walked behind Persephone. Maureen walked behind Demeter. There we were—me as Persephone, the daughter, and Maureen as Demeter, the mother. My mother complex now fully activated and personified for all the world to see.

"What was your question for Persephone?" Maureen asked me. I repeated what I'd said before: "Now that you have been to the underworld, separated from your mother, and found a place in the world and in your life that she cannot share, how do you feel?" Maureen then said, "Feel free to answer it as Persephone."

Looking directly into Maureen/Demeter/my mother's eyes, I/Persephone/Kelly said, "Now that I have been to the underworld, I have a place, a realm, that is just mine. One that I'll never be able to share with you. And while I love you, and I am happy to be back for now, this new place—the underworld—is my place, not yours. And, in the end, it is okay that I will return to it, and not be with you."

Maureen/Demeter/my mother, with deep pain in her face, then said to me, "I hear what you are saying, but it is still a betrayal. And my heart is broken."

I was floored. There was that word "betrayal" again. The very word my dad had used to describe what he'd felt about my show. I thought for sure that Maureen/Demeter/my mother was going to say that me being separate and having my own realm was a great thing. Wasn't it the parents' job to hide their disappointment in service of the child's evolution? I was not expecting this.

My heart beat heavily, and a surge of energy filled my limbs. I apprehended for the first time in my life that there was nothing I could do about Maureen/my mother/my father's feelings of betrayal and disappointment. I took a deep breath and said, with tears in my eyes, "Well, I guess that's just the way it has to be."

Maureen nodded, acknowledging the truth of my statement: This is just the way it is. As we grow up and find our own space separate from our parents, they feel betrayed, and we feel empowered. And life goes on.

I nodded back at Maureen, communicating to her that our connection was now different. Moments ago we were a child and a mother, and now we were equals. And although separated, I felt more deeply connected to her than I could ever have imagined. I no longer needed her love to exist.

I turned around, walked off the stage, sat down and wondered, *What the fuck just happened?*

I felt the intense sting of reality in my whole being. I was facing the fact that if I were finally to claim my place in the world, I'd have to "betray" my internal, unconscious pact with my mother (and my father, eventually). Since her death I'd been immersed in my grief about losing her, and hadn't really begun the difficult work of dismantling the baggage that had accumulated between us from her alcoholism. I finally understood that disappointing and betraying my parents was inevitable and necessary if I was ever to fully grow up. I knew I had some work to do.

I ended up doing my master's thesis on the Persephone/Demeter myth and theme after all.

Just as Maureen predicted.

CHAPTER TWENTY-THREE

Plan B

IN JUNE 2004 I was ready to graduate from Pacifica.

That's a lie. I did have all my work done, but I wasn't ready to leave. For the last three years, I was the happiest I'd ever been. I got to spend my days doing what I loved most—reading, writing, and contemplating the meaning of life. All the while doing something most of the world deemed productive—getting a postgraduate degree. I was in my bliss and an upstanding citizen of the world at the same time. It was heaven.

Of course not all had gone perfectly.

During my second year at Pacifica, my classmates and I were required to do traineeships as counselors in our respective communities. Still on the fence about becoming a full-time licensed therapist, I was unsure about this part. I didn't mind the idea of dealing with crazy people. I just didn't want to be dealing with *crazy* people. I'd heard nightmare stories from some of my peers, one of whom had had to jump into the fray at a home for schizophrenics and lead group therapy sessions her first week. I didn't want to deal with schizophrenics, psychotics, or anyone not grounded in reality. I couldn't imagine that. I wanted some run-of-the-mill West

LA neurotics—anxious yuppies, blocked writers, or a confused twenty-something or two. I was determined to get a cushy placement, and I got lucky. I ended up at an elementary school, counseling kids in a community that was known for its artists and freethinkers. My people.

After the first day at my new traineeship, I was relieved. I realized that I'd be able to handle the crazy of "my people." They were no different from my parents or me. I knew what kind of kids would be coming my way: kids who came from families that had dealt or were dealing with addiction; kids who were left to their own devices because their parents were workaholics in "the business"; and kids who just hadn't found their sea legs yet. I knew between my training and the work I'd done on my own issues that I could do this. I was excited.

What I didn't see coming was the little girl I'll call Rebecca.

On my second day at the school, the principal called me into his office. "Kelly, we've just gotten a phone call. One of our fifth graders, Rebecca—well, her grandmother just called to say that her mom died in a car crash today. Seems after she dropped her off at school, the mom was rushing down the canyon to work and drove off the road and into a tree."

My stomach dropped twelve stories. *Jesus Christ. What the fuck!*

He continued, "Anyway, she's on her way here, and—well, we were wondering if you could be there when she told Rebecca the news."

Trying to collect my thoughts, I said, "Where's her dad?"

"He's not in the picture. It's just her mom and grandma," he answered.

My head began to get fuzzy, like a panic attack might come on. I said, "Um, yeah. Um, let me call my supervisor. She'll know what to do."

I called my supervisor, Gwen, and told her what was going on.

"Jesus Christ," she said.

"Right? What the fuck do I do?" I asked, hoping she'd drive up and deal with it all herself.

Gwen was actually an old friend of mine from Crossroads, and she'd been a licensed marriage and family therapist for quite a while. I was thrilled she was at my traineeship. She knew me, got me, and was very cool.

She calmly laid it all out. "Well, first of all. You don't have to do this if you don't feel ready. This is a lot for one's first week on the job."

"Yeah, okay," I said, relieved that I had some wiggle room.

"And second," she continued. "There's nothing you can do. All you can do is hold the space for this little girl and her grandmother. It's just one of those things about this job. Sometimes all we can do is just be present and a witness for others."

A wave of calm came over me. I said, "Well, I know I can do that," suddenly knowing that I must do this for this girl.

"And they'll probably need some grief counseling for her. Thank God you'll be there all year," Gwen concluded.

"Yeah," I said. I was already readying myself for the task. "Well, I'm going to go down there, and tell them that I'll be there. I'll call you when I'm done."

Once the grandmother arrived, we waited in the nurse's office while someone fetched Rebecca. The grandmother was very nervous, and I assured her that there was no right or wrong way to do this. She'd be fine.

When Rebecca walked into the room, my heart shattered. She was a stringbean of a thing. Big brown eyes and a presence that said, Save me. She looked at the three of us with confusion. She asked, "What are you doing here? Where's Mommy?"

"Hey, Sweetie," her grandma said as she stood up and hugged her. "We need to talk."

Rebecca looked at me, wondering who I was.

"So Rebecca," the grandmother continued as she sat them down on the cot. "I have to tell you something. Today after your mom dropped you off here—well, she got in a car accident—" She hesitated.

"Is she okay?" Rebecca asked as tears welled up in her eyes.

"Well . . . she . . . uh. Well, she . . . no, Darling. She isn't okay," said the grandmother.

My heart ached as I sat there watching all this as if it were a movie. I said to myself, Oh my god! This is the part where she tells her that her mother is dead. This is really happening.

The grandmother plowed ahead. "Rebecca, your mom is not coming back. She died in the accident."

Rebecca began to cry for real now, and fell right into her grandma's bosom. They both cried. I looked over them at the principal. We both had tears in our eyes.

"What happened?" Rebecca asked after a few minutes.

"We don't know everything yet," the grandma answered.

Rebecca, wide-eyed, looked at me again. The principal said, "This is Kelly. She's the new counselor here."

I smiled a subtle smile, wanting to communicate that I respected what she was going through but also that I was here for her. "I'm so sorry about your mom, Rebecca," I said.

Tears rolled down her now pink and swollen face.

The principal continued, "Kelly will be here all year. You can talk to her if and whenever you want."

"Whenever and whatever you want, Rebecca," I added, wishing I could offer this poor lost child something more than that, but that was all I had.

After about ten more minutes of crying and a few questions, Grandma took Rebecca by the hand, and they both walked out the door and into her life without a mother. Even though I'd lost my mom only a few years earlier, I could not imagine what it must be like to be ten years old with no father, and now no mother. My heart ached for her.

I would indeed see Rebecca every week that year, and a few months into the next year, even after I'd moved on to my next internship. Getting to sit with Rebecca on that day was one of the most profound and privileged experiences of my life. I did nothing. I was just a human heart witnessing the breaking of another human heart. But sometimes that's all we have. I hoped it was enough.

I think of her often.

Fortunately most of my days at my traineeship were not so eventful. I helped a handful of families deal with crises, quite a few students cope with some ongoing behavioral issues, and referred a few other families to other therapists for family therapy. Luckily my job was rather easy. Because my clients were kids, all they really needed was a safe place to play or talk or draw. I had one client who did nothing but play hangman with me all year long. But by the end of the term, his angry outbursts and defiant attitude had dissolved. Go figure.

But in other ways my job was not so easy because my clients were kids. Like Rebecca, some of these kids were facing challenges beyond their power to change. They were in families that had deep systemic problems that a bit of play therapy would not resolve. Those kids had parents who were in denial about their own issues, and it deeply affected the whole family. I could do little for them. It was those kids who weighed on me. I saw myself in them, and hoped the little attention and space I gave them would help carry them through. Others that faced even tougher challenges were harder to have hope for. Seeing the suffering of such innocence was a burden I hadn't expected to carry, and one that kept me awake more than a few nights. After a year I was glad to move on.

Once my third year at Pacifica began, classroom time was over. It was time to focus on my thesis. Starting in the fall of 2003, I began to work on *Music for the Mourning: A Film of Song and Rebirth*. Just as Maureen Murdock had predicted, I became enchanted with the Demeter/Persephone myth. I needed to continue my exploration of my relationship with my mother and her death, and my thesis gave me a chance to do just that. And just as I'd hoped from the beginning, I did an art project for my thesis—I wrote a screenplay. I wrote a musical using the lyrics of modern songs (à la Baz Luhrmann) while weaving together the stories of Demeter/Persephone with the story of my losing my mother to cancer. I bet no one has ever pitched *that* to Warner Bros.!

Although the academic aspect of the thesis could be a bit dry, I loved doing the research into the myth and its psychological underpinnings, and studying what others had written about the mother/daughter relationship and the process of mourning. In my thesis I was able to examine the process of grief, and reveal that, although it is filled with feelings of loss and pain, endings do eventually lead to new beginnings, if you are conscious enough to allow it. If you can weather the storm, rebirth can come from death.

But the best part of the process was writing the musical. I let the music of Johnny Cash, Blue Oyster Cult, U2, Paul Simon, and a host of others weave a tapestry of image and story. The academic piece took me five months to research and write. The screenplay took me ten days. It shot out of me like an arrow of love. It was a great feeling of accomplishment. And a huge relief.

I was fulfilled creatively, spiritually, and intellectually. And the bonus—I was no longer obsessed about my career in showbiz. I no longer lived under the shadow of my dad's fame and accomplishments. I had my own now. I was finally busy with my own life.

Dad, as usual, was busy, too. In 2001, the year I'd started school, he'd published his second book, *Napalm and Silly Putty*, and taped his twelfth HBO special, *Complaints and Grievances*. None of which I paid much attention to due to the fact that I was now in school. That year Dad also shot another film with Kevin Smith, *Jay and Silent Bob Strike Back*, in which he played a hitchhiker willing to give a blow job for a ride. Dad loved that Kevin had written that for him.

Then, in 2002, Dad started to have some new symptoms with his heart. Twice he was hospitalized while on the road because he was getting rapid heartbeats and some arrhythmia. Nothing was worse than getting a call from him that started, "Hey, Kiddo. I'm at the emergency room." My stomach would tighten, and then I would breathe half a sigh of relief knowing that at least he was at a hospital, and no one was rushing him into an operating room yet. Still, there was always the reality in the back of my mind, knowing that his heart, after three heart attacks and multiple angioplasties, wasn't shipshape.

The arrhythmia eventually got so bad that Dad's cardiologist, Dr. Buchbinder, decided that he'd be a good candidate for an ablation—a procedure that is used to fix heart rhythm issues, so he sent him to a specialist—Dr. Swerdlow.

In May 2003, Bob, Sally, and I sat in the waiting room at Cedars-Sinai waiting for the doctor to come out to tell us that Dad was done and all was good. This scene felt both familiar and yet new. Too many times I'd sat in this hospital's or St. John's waiting rooms anxious to see a doctor walk out with a smile on his face after some procedure, and tell us how great Dad was doing. But what was different this time was that Mom wasn't here. It had always been Mom and me waiting for the doctor. Even though it'd be nerve racking, I'd feel okay because in those situations, my mom was a rock. No matter what might have happened during the procedure, she'd be strong and ready to ask the doctors all the right questions. She held the space so firmly and calmly.

But now I had to be the rock not only for me but for Sally, too. Sally was a nervous wreck. She hadn't yet had to deal with Dad's heart stuff. Because Dad always underplayed it so well, I'm not sure how deeply she understood the extent of his heart disease. But today the reality was in her face. And in mine. We were all on pins and needles because the ablation was only supposed to take about an hour and a half, and we were now in hour number three.

Finally, after four hours, the doctor came out. His face was sheet-white. My heart dropped. *Oh shit. Oh fuck.*

"Is everything okay?" I asked anxiously.

"Oh yes. He's fine. He's fine," he quickly answered. "Can we sit a minute?"

Fuck. "Yeah, sure," I said as my heart pounded out of my chest.

"Everything went well, for the most part. Sorry it took so much time. It's just that we had to go really slow. You see, his heart is being held together with scaffolding—with all the stents and scar tissue." He drew a little picture of the heart and what he'd done to Dad. Then he took a beat and said, "You do know that it's a miracle he's alive every day?" he added.

I knew his heart was not in great shape. I knew that he had a few stents in his heart that kept the arteries from closing or collapsing. And I knew he took a handful of heart pills a few times a day that kept his blood thin, blood pressure even, and heart rhythm consistent. For twenty-five years I had been dreading that phone call in the middle of the night from my mom or Jerry telling me that Dad had died onstage in bum-fuck Iowa. But I never let the idea that he might die any day take hold in my mind. For decades I had managed to put *that* reality in a box and hide it high on a shelf inside my psyche. Now, with this doctor's words rattling inside of me, I knew that I had to take that box down and open it.

Dad's days were numbered.

On May 29, 2004, I graduated from Pacifica. Dad had cleared his schedule months beforehand so he would be certain that he could come to the commencement, and I was beyond thrilled. He was giddy, too. As we drove up to the campus he said, "This is a great little car."

"We just got it a few months ago," I said. Bob and I had bought our first car together—a Mercedes wagon—a German tank for safety, with a roof rack for camping.

"I want to get it for you," his mood expansive. "Let me pay it off for you. As a gift, for all your hard work."

Bob stiffened. He was never comfortable with my dad paying for anything. I ignored this and said to my dad, "Are you sure?" It's not that I didn't respect Bob's stance. I did, and had weaned myself off of the daddy dole the last few years. It's just that I could hear in my dad's voice how much he wanted to do this for me.

"Yes, of course. I'd really like to do this for you," Dad answered.

I reached forward from the backseat and touched Dad's arm on the armrest. "That would be very nice, Dad. Thank you," I said. He patted my hand with a strong hand, like he did when he wanted to communicate that he loved me more than he could say.

The commencement ceremony was on Pacifica's main campus, an estate on the border between Carpinteria and Montecito near Santa Barbara. It was gorgeous. As I sat among my peers on a beautiful June day looking out from the stage, I could see my dad in the crowd, beaming with pride. He sat with Bob, our dear friend Theresa, and her sister Sue. Every few minutes I could see that he was also taking notes. Turns out he was scribbling down all the New Age vernacular people were using to describe their "journeys, through the labyrinth of the sacred and collective space that Pacifica" provided. He was taking notes for a future bit on language.

A few months later Dad was on *Leno*. While he sat on the panel, he mentioned to Jay that I'd just gotten my master's in psychology. I nearly fell out of bed. My dad never talked about our family or personal life onstage or on TV. Never. I welled up. I couldn't believe he was talking about his real life. That's when I knew for sure that he was so proud of me—because he said it on TV. Dad was proud because not only was I the first Carlin to graduate college, but now the first to get a master's degree. This really meant something to him. Because he'd dropped out of school in ninth grade, he'd even admitted that he'd spent his entire life trying to prove how clever he was to the very things he hated—institutions. He'd wanted their acceptance, and through me I think he finally got it. He felt

empowered by my accomplishments, just like I had, well—since forever.

After graduation I continued at my second internship, which had
started in the fall of 2003. I planned on staying until I figured out
if this life as a therapist was for me. I was now at a nonprofit run by
one of my favorite teachers at Pacifica, Pat Katsky. I wanted to be
her when I grew up. She'd been one of the women at Pacifica who
had remothered me. If I was going to be doing this therapist thing,
I at least wanted to be surrounded by other Jungians, both interns
and supervisors, who understood my schooling and orientation. Plus
being at Pat's place kept me connected to my bliss and my new life
that I'd created outside the business.

The center did sliding-scale counseling, and I got a wide array
of clients to begin with—thankfully a general group of mostly
neurotic, anxious people just like me. But soon I got clients who
were even *more* like me. As they say in the therapy business, you
eventually get the clients you really need—the ones who will stretch
you and make you face your own unconscious issues. My schedule
became filled with stand-up comedians, comedy writers, and actors.

It started with one stand-up, then another, and then pretty soon,
my whole practice was filled with a bunch of people in the biz. I
even had the child of a famous comedian as a client. Talk about
getting the clients you need. *Wow!* It was like I was looking in a
mirror every day.

For the first year it was fun and very fulfilling. I knew I was making a difference in my clients' lives. I was helping them get over
stage fright, tackling the roller coaster ride of going on auditions and
living the life of a freelancer in Hollywood. Together we were shift-
ing their perspectives to handle the vicissitudes of being a creative
soul in a soulless business. I was deeply honored to be a handrail
along their circuitous path of life. To witness them as they went from

feeling powerless and lost to taking bold steps toward their dreams filled me with feelings of purpose and love.

But soon, while driving home on the 405 from the office, I'd find myself fantasizing about being on a stage again. The longings I'd put aside when I walked off the stage after my solo show were bubbling up. I had more to say to the world. I had more stories to tell. I wanted to be seen and heard again.

Was this just my ego? Was I just afraid to live a life out of the limelight? I was irritated by these longings. I had felt so free while in grad school, not having to deal with my showbiz ambitions, and now here they were again, trying to ruin everything.

Why can't I just be happy as a therapist?

Plus I was *good* at being a therapist. My clients were thriving, and my practice was expanding. I liked the work. Well, more specifically, I liked the work while I was doing it, actually sitting in the room with my clients. And I liked the idea of the work. I loved having a solid answer to the question, What do you do? I'm a therapist. It sounded so damn official, grown-up, and normal.

But when I thought about spending the next four years in the small, poorly lit, horribly decorated office in Van Nuys accumulating hours for my licensing while I supported other writers, comedians, and actors in reaching their creative dreams, I became depressed and filled with despair. I knew there was only one thing I could do.

I had to write and perform again.

CHAPTER TWENTY-FOUR

Long and Winding Road

JUST AFTER THANKSGIVING 2005, I got a shocking phone call from my dad:

"Hey, Kiddo. I wanted to let you know. I'm going up to Promises in Malibu tomorrow for a thirty-day rehab stay."

"Uh, okay." Perplexed, I asked, "You okay?" He'd quit cocaine decades ago. I was confused.

"Yeah, I've just been binge-drinking red wine while on the road, and taking a few more Vicodin than I know is good for me. I just want to take care of this once and for all."

At age sixty-eight, I guess my dad was finally ready to go from sober-ish to sober.

I didn't think to ask him, Why this week? But looking back, I wonder if a little incident during his show the month before at the MGM Grand in Las Vegas played a role.

While onstage doing a new bit about suicide bombings and be-headings, Dad had started complaining, to himself mostly, that he couldn't wait to get out of "this fucking hotel" and Las Vegas. He stated that he wanted to go back east, "where the real people are."

This wasn't a new theme for him. Dad hated Vegas. More

specifically he hated Vegas audiences. They just weren't "his" audiences. Maybe about a quarter of the people in the audience each night were hard-core Carlin fans, but the rest either couldn't get into that night's Cirque du Soleil show or thought it might be fun to see that guy who used to do the "Hippie-Dippie Weatherman."

He continued his rant. "People who go to Las Vegas, you've got to question their fucking intellect to start with. Traveling hundreds and thousands of miles to essentially give your money to a large corporation is kind of fucking moronic. That's what I'm always getting here is these kind of fucking people with very limited intellects."

An audience member shouted, "Stop degrading us!"

Dad, unable to hear what they'd said, responded with, "Thank you very much, whatever that was. I hope it was positive; if not, well, blow me."

Whenever I saw him perform in Vegas, I always had mixed emotions. When about a third of the audience would clear out during his more shocking material, I'd cringe. No one wants to see that. But at the same time another part of me was emboldened. I agreed with Dad—fuck 'em if they can't deal with it. Comics who came by to see his set would stand in the back, trying to guess how many people would leave on any given night. They got a real kick out of it. He was their hero.

The only reason Dad put up with Vegas was because it was a solution for him. It kept him off the road and out of airports for about twelve weeks a year, and it was a great place for him to write during the day in his condo, and develop new material at night. But just like in 1969, when he was fired from the Frontier Hotel, he'd once again crossed a line, according to the powers that be. He was fired again. This time it wasn't for saying "ass" or "shit"—it was for talking about autoerotic asphyxiation. The times, oh how they've changed!

After a few days in rehab, Dad called me.

"Hey there. I was wondering if you could come up. I wanna talk to you about something."

Oh, fuck. I couldn't imagine what he wanted.

As we sat outside a mansion at the top of a hill in Malibu, Dad leaned toward me and said, "I need some help with this idea of a 'higher power' that AA talks about."

I was taken aback. And yet deeply touched. My dad had come to me for spiritual advice.

I shared the bare scratchings of my own understanding on the topic. "Well, as you probably know, having read Alan Watts and others, in Zen practice there's no personal God, there's just the experience of transcendence. It is 'that which is beyond words . . . that which holds everything.' And from what I've learned from Jung, he saw that transcendent state as something he called the Higher Self, an archetype within the collective unconscious. So it's a part of who we are, and we all have access to it. But really, it's about acknowledging that there is something bigger than your personal ego. That's what AA is really focused on. The part of you that is bigger than you, bigger than the part of you that needs to get high."

Dad jumped in, "You know what I really love? I love the way the Native Americans use Mother Earth and Father Sky to hold all of that."

I smiled at him. "Well, Dad, you just gotta go with what's in your heart. What works for *you*."

He smiled back at me and said, "You know, Kiddo, I've always seen you as the shaman of the family."

My heart soared. I was thrilled by this title.

Although Dad saw me as some wise sage, I was still wrestling with my conflict about being a therapist versus a performer. I wanted to continue to help people find their voices and paths in life, but I also wanted the freedom to be an artist and get on a stage and yell, Fuck you, America! if I felt like it.

I was pretty sure the American Psychological Association would not smile upon me doing both. To be a therapist—a good, ethical therapist—my job was to be a blank slate for my clients, so they could project their issues onto me, and thus solve deep-seated patterns. If I, the therapist, overtly allowed my own needs, wishes, and personality to show up in the office, it could easily undermine the therapeutic relationship. If I pursued a public persona through my art, I feared that my "me-ness" would leak into the therapeutic container. I knew that if for now I was to be a therapist and a performer, I'd have to stay under the radar a bit.

By the summer of 2005, I began to write personal essays and perform them at small storytelling venues around LA. Despite my anxieties, it felt great to be writing something other than academic papers, and to be in front of live audiences again. There really is nothing like getting a laugh. As the months went by, I found a confidence I'd never had. I was finding my voice, my perspective, and I was not afraid of it anymore. I saw that the more I wrote, the better I got; the more I performed, the more comfortable I became onstage.

One night at Tasty Words, a salon run by my friend and mentor Wendy Kamenoff, my dad came to watch me perform. Finally! I was so excited to show him what I could do on "his" stage. It was a story about fame and how it seizes the human psyche. More specifically, I told the story of how, when I was backstage at Carnegie Hall when I was eight years old, I took the buzz of my dad's fame into my young being like a drug. I was nervous to perform in front of him, but I knew the piece was solid. And it was. I killed that night. I got laughs in all the right places, and I could feel the depth of silence in the places where people were drinking it all in. Afterward he hugged me and said, "You definitely know what you're doing up there."

Phew! Not bad. I wanted more words from him, and maybe some gushing, but he was there, and more important, he didn't tell me to shut the fuck up. I took in his encouragement and let it be enough. I let it be a green light to carry on writing and performing. But a few months later, the father of one of my clients performed on the same show I did, and my client and I saw each other there. It was okay in the moment, but I knew that because most of my clients were in the biz, and the work I wanted to do was also in that biz, my two worlds were now crossing boundaries. This was not good.

By the fall I knew I would not be happy spending the next twenty years of my life as a therapist in a darkened room, handing my clients Kleenex. Being a licensed therapist was not my path. I obviously deeply admired and respected those who did that work, but I knew it was not for me. I gave my three-month notice to my clients, giving us enough time to end our relationships in a conscious way.

I was nervous about telling my dad that I was moving on, especially knowing how proud he was of my new path. But he understood. Plus it helped that I wasn't leaving it *all* behind. I was going to employ plan C: becoming a life coach. Working with high-functioning, nontherapy clients would give me far more freedom to balance my two paths.

In November 2005, Bob and I flew to New York to see my dad shoot his thirteenth HBO special, *Life Is Worth Losing.* I was excited— my dad rarely let me glimpse his new material before he shot it for HBO. He liked having me experience the material in its full and polished form. It was always a thrill for me to sit in the audience, not knowing what was coming. This year I was especially looking forward to seeing him. We'd both been really busy, and hadn't seen each other in about three months.

After walking up the stairs backstage at the Beacon Theater, I caught my breath and walked into his dressing room. I saw a short, white-haired man with his back to me. When he turned around, it was my dad. I was stunned. *Who took my father and left this elderly man in his place?* My dad's face was puffy, he was two inches shorter, and he looked like he was fighting to breathe. What the fuck?

I'd noticed the last few times I'd talked with him on the phone that he'd been a bit scatterbrained—very unlike my dad. He'd forgotten the name of his assistant once, and one day he didn't show up at a breakfast we'd planned. I thought at the time it must be age, but seeing him now backstage, I knew something was really wrong: People don't age this quickly.

I didn't say anything to him, not wanting to distract him from the task ahead that night. But as I walked to my seat in the audience, I worried if he'd be able to make it through the show. I steeled myself for the worst. Would he be okay? How would the audience respond to how he looked? Might he even collapse?

But when he took the stage he came alive.

It was like a superhuman force of energy moved through him and propelled him into his first bit, "A Modern Man." His verbal gymnastics, leaps of logic, and rap-star pacing blew every person in that audience away. He gave the tour-de-force performance of his life during those three and a half minutes. And as I watched this, all I could think was: If he could just stay on that stage, he just might live forever.

A month later he *really* couldn't breathe.

Christmas Eve morning, Sally called. "Kelly, we're at Cedar's. George's in the emergency room." Bob and I raced north on La Cienega Boulevard, and found Sally in the waiting room, shaken up. "They've stabilized him. He's doing better."

About twenty minutes later the ER doctor came out.

"He's doing much better than when he came in. We gave him some medicine, Lasix, to help remove some of the fluid from his lungs and stabilize the heart failure."

The *what*?

Heart failure. That's what had been going on with him in New York. Heart failure. It is a condition they could stabilize with medicine for a few years, but eventually only a heart transplant would fix it permanently.

After a while they let me see him. As I sat alone with him in the emergency room, he admitted to me that he'd had symptoms for months and months, and had ignored them so he could do his HBO special. I wanted to kill him. But on the other hand, I got it: It was a great show.

As he lay there dozing, I sat at the foot of his bed with my hands on his feet meditating and sending him as much life force as I could. I was doing my best to uphold my shaman duties. I'd never felt so peaceful in his presence before. There was a sweetness to it.

A week later they released him from the hospital, but now he had a device implanted in his chest—a combination pacemaker, heart pump, and defibrillator. Dad was oddly proud of it. He even bragged, "It's the same device they implanted in the chest of Dick Cheney!"

During 2006 I became certified as a life coach, built up my practice, and continued performing. Being a life coach allowed me to use my skills as a therapist and my knowledge of Jungian psychology and Zen Buddhism in the service of working with clients who were looking to create a concrete change in their lives. Although many of my new clients had similar issues as my therapy clients (and some were from my old therapy practice), the approach of coaching is to not dwell on the story of your past, but to see it, own it, and move beyond it. I liked that. This philosophy fit where I was now in my own life—I had healed so much of my past and was ready to move beyond it all.

Dad and I met for coffee once every six weeks or so, mostly at the Cow's End in Venice, to catch up. Over coffee I'd share with him about the writing and the readings I'd been doing around town, and how my new coaching practice was evolving. On the outside I looked like a person who was doing all she could to have a good and successful adult life, but I still could never quite let myself feel that way. Between my crazy twenties with Andrew and the creative schizophrenia of my thirties, I didn't want my dad to think that my forties would be plagued by more confusion. Hell, even more than he, *I* didn't want that for myself. So, since I'd walked away from pursuing the legitimate path of getting my marriage-family therapist license, I felt I needed to impress my dad with all my efforts. Most of our coffee time I'd spend yammering on and on about my plans, and how busy I was. One day he stopped me in midsentence, leaned over to me, and said, "You're doing great, Kid," as he lightly patted my cheek. "Relax."

But I just couldn't. Nothing felt like enough. I had to keep pushing forward. I wanted to write a book. I wanted something tangible I could hold up and say, I did that. I took my old solo show, and personal essays I'd written, and began to write a spiritual memoir— my own *Eat, Pray, Love.* I told him about the memoir during one of our lunches. His face got all squinted up and he said, "Didn't you get that out of your system with your solo show?"

I felt a sharp pain in my chest. I was unable to reply. He went on, "You know, Kel, real artists—well, they do their autobiographical work at the beginning of their careers. You know, like me when I did *Class Clown.* But then they move on, and talk about other stuff."

I still didn't know what to say, so I didn't say anything. I just listened incredulously. My mind spun, trying to find a way to challenge his thinking, but I was so filled with anxiety that nothing came to me. *He must be right. Why don't I have this out of my system? What's wrong with me?* I took the invisible knife out of my chest, smiled, and went home.

Later that night I thought of what I should have said: Gee, Dad, I don't think Richard Pryor ever moved on. But I knew I could never have said it to his face, even if it had come to me in that moment. I put the memoir on a shelf for someday in the future when it could no longer scare the shit out of my dad.

Or me.

CHAPTER TWENTY-FIVE

Out on a Limb

"FUCK YOU!" IS WHAT I *wanted* to shout down to the retreat leader, Patrick Ryan, but I knew it wasn't his fault that I was now forty feet up a redwood tree, hugging it for dear life. No, the fault was definitely all mine.

Still, I was shocked to be up there.

Only minutes earlier while still on the ground I'd deployed my inner four-year-old to cry my way out of having to climb the tree—a tactic that had worked for most of my childhood whenever I wanted to get out of something. But Patrick, intuiting all that, ignored my ploy, smiled at me, and asked, "What's up?"

Talking through my tears, I said, "Well, I'm tired—and I've already done the other two tree climbs today, which is *way* more than I ever thought I could—and I just can't do another—"

With a calm smile on his face that I wanted to smack right off, he then asked, "So, if you don't go all the way up, how far up *are* you willing to go?"

I looked up the tree to the small platform that had a plank sticking out of it. Once I reached that plank, I was supposed to walk off the end of it and jump. Even though I was attached by a rope and harness to a belay team for safety, I couldn't fathom how I would ever do that. It was impossible. I knew I had signed up for this, but fuck it. I wasn't doing it.

The year before, on the first day of my life-coach training, my instructor had told me I should go to "Leadership." Leadership was a program that trained you to be a front-of-the-room leader for workshops and the like, but was also an intense empowerment program, like Landmark or the Forum. I saw this as the ultimate up-sell moment you get in these kinds of classes: Hey, you're doing great, but if you want a real breakthrough, you should do the advanced course. Yeah, right.

But, by the end of my six-month training, I'd met enough instructors who'd done the leadership course, which was a requirement for them, that I knew I wanted what they had—a graceful command of themselves and the space around them. They all were down-to-earth and yet able to inspire, challenge, and keep a roomful of diverse people on track.

They all told me that doing the leadership course had changed their lives. Many said, "It changed my DNA." Although I loved most of my DNA, there were a few parts I could do without. Like the part that could never accept that I was good enough, and believed that if I ever accepted that, I would probably die, or the planet would implode, or something else just as unlikely. Yeah, that part could definitely use a change, and so I wanted in.

Plus I just knew that completing this course would help me figure out how to implement my big life plan. It wasn't a "Danny Kaye plan," but it was a vision I had for my future—leading workshops, public speaking, maybe a documentary or theater piece, while upholding the Carlin way. Basically, if I could stand on a stage, use the word "cocksucker," and change the world, I'd be a happy woman. I knew the leadership course could give me the courage, a plan, and support to do all that.

To complete Leadership there was a required high-ropes course component. I was deathly afraid of heights, so I figured that if I could climb up a tree, I'd finally conquer that last little something in me that held me back. And if I could do that, then just maybe I could change the world. But first I had to change myself, and that is how I found myself crying like a baby at the bottom of this tree, not giving a flying fuck about changing anything except Patrick's resolve to get me up that tree.

As my fellow Leadership tribe members (we were the "Wolves") patiently waited while I worked out my issues, I once again looked all the way up that tree, and knew that if I didn't at least try to climb it, I'd hate myself forever. Patrick patiently asked again, "How far up?"

"Um . . . to . . . um . . . to touch the platform?"

"Great! And when you touch the platform," he asked patiently, "may I then ask you if you are willing to go further?"

"Sure," I answered, knowing full well what he was up to, and not liking it at all. "I mean that's what I pay you the big bucks for, right?" Everyone laughed. I looked over at the four people holding the ropes attached to the harness around my body and said, "Belay team, are you ready?"

In unison they smiled and said, "Ready!"

I grabbed the first peg, and before I knew it, I'd climbed up thirty-five feet to the bottom of the platform. I was shocked at how easy it had been. My body clearly knew what to do even though my mind had screamed in protest.

Once up there, I realized that I'd definitely not be happy if I just stopped there.

"You okay?" Patrick shouted up.

"Yes," I answered, understanding what had stopped me from starting the climb—I couldn't see a clear path of pegs to the platform. I shouted down to Patrick, "How do I get onto the platform?"

"There's a peg to your left," he said. "Grab that, and then climb up, and you'll be level with it." All of a sudden I was standing on the platform. Wow! Amazing. There was just one problem. I was now facing the tree, my arms in a death grip around it. I was in a panic because this platform was not a luxurious space to spend a sunny afternoon picnicking on. It was practically nonexistent. It was barely bigger than my pair of hiking boots now standing on it. Terrified, I was sure I was going to die. This is why I wanted to yell, "FUCK YOU!" down to Patrick. But I had more pressing issues, like turning around. I had no idea how to do that. This simple action that I'd been doing perfectly well for almost forty-four years, now completely eluded me. My mind was blank.

"Patrick, how do I turn around?"

"Turn both your feet to the right," he said.

Aha! Yes. And so I did. I was now looking out into the most beautiful redwood forest. I was *in* the forest. I *was* the forest. If it hadn't been for the terror-induced adrenaline racing through my veins, I might even have described it as magical.

"What's your name?" Patrick asked next. It was part of the exercise—to claim "who you were" to the trees. Yeah, we were in California.

Without missing a beat, I said, "My name is Inigo Montoya. You killed my father. Prepare to die." The whole group cracked up. I smiled and relaxed.

"My name is Kelly Marie Carlin McCall!" For a moment I felt as big as the forest around me.

But then came the next moment of truth. I had to walk the plank that was in front of me and jump off it. Once again my mind was blank, and my feet wouldn't move. I began to wonder how I might get down without having to jump off the end of that plank. Maybe they could just lower me?

I looked down at Patrick, and my new friends holding the rope and cheering me on, and said, "Patrick?"

"Yes, Kelly?"

"My fear, right in this moment—my fear, it's just an illusion, right? I mean, it just isn't real, is it?"

"Yes, Kelly, right in this moment, your fear is just an illusion. You are perfectly safe."

I am perfectly safe even though my mind is having a shit fit. My mind is full of shit, I thought.

And so I inched my right foot forward and spontaneously began to sing, "Oh Lord won't you buy me a Mercedes Benz? My friends all drive—" I have no idea why I sang that. But as long as I focused on singing the song, my fear couldn't paralyze me. And so I let Janis Joplin sing me out to the end of that plank inch by inch. And when I got to the end, I leaped into the empty space with everything I had. It felt like the most elegant swan dive ever done. When I saw video of it later, I laughed. I looked more like a sack of potatoes falling off the end. But I had done it. I had conquered my fears. I felt transformed.

I did indeed feel like my DNA had changed.

By the fall of 2007 I was at the end of my leadership course and was excited by what lay ahead of me. Three master coaches had asked me to learn their models of coaching, and invited me to co-lead workshops with them. I'd be making some money, traveling, and doing the transformational work I wanted to do.

On top of that I had decided on my next creative project—a documentary called *Waking from the American Dream*. The title of the project had been inspired by my father's quote, "It's called the American Dream because you have to be asleep to believe in it." I'd heard him say it during the taping of *Life Is Worth Losing* a few years back, and the title had just popped into my mind. I hoped to travel around America with Bob, filming ordinary people talking about their American Dreams. We'd also discuss the evolution of business, education, and financial institutions with thought leaders and innovators. I wanted to find out if there was a way to wake from the myth so that my generation and future generations had something we could believe in, going forward. My dad may have given up on the planet, but I was only forty-four, and still needed something to live toward.

Leadership had allowed me to feel like there was more of me present in the world. I now had access to an infinite amount of inner knowing, strength, and love to move forward.

I didn't know it, but boy, was I going to need it!

Sometime in the fall of 2007, Dad and Sally went to New York City to consult with some heart specialists about his heart failure. It was getting more complicated to manage, and his blood pressure oscillated dangerously. He now carried a machine to measure it while he was on the road.

While there, Sally secretly called me to say that she was really worried about him. He was refusing to get out of bed, having trouble breathing, and sleeping a lot. She wasn't sure if these New York doctors were helping him. She thought it might be depression, or a side effect of the medication, but she wasn't sure. I called him to check in, and could tell right away that something was up.

Trying to sound casual, I asked, "Hey Dad, how are things? You feeling any better?"

"I'm okay," he replied curtly.

I continued cautiously. "I was talking to Sally earlier, and she said—well, she's a little worried about you."

"I'm fine," he said, sounding like he had no interest in talking to me.

The conversation continued this way for another few minutes. I'd never heard him so cold and distant. He was usually a little brusque on the phone because he hated talking on it, but this was bordering on rude. Confused, I wondered if he was mad at me, but I couldn't figure out why.

And then I thought, *Maybe this is it.*

Maybe this is what the end looks like. He's dying. He's giving up.

I gathered some courage and said, "I want to come see you, make sure everything is okay." I was beginning to cry, but tried not to show it.

"No. I don't want you here. Do not come. I forbid you from coming," he replied with a vehemence that knocked the breath out of me.

My heart shattered into a million thousand pieces.

My dad and I had certainly had moments of tension in the last few years, but he'd never spoken to me this way. Ever. I felt at sea, completely rejected. My throat and eyes stung, trying to hold back a tidal wave of tears.

"Well, okay. If that's what you want." Not wanting to upset him any more, I signed off and hung up.

I'd never felt more alone in my life. Confused and panicked by this strange turn of events, I cried deeply for about an hour.

And then I got pissed.

How dare *he! He might be dying, and he won't let me come and see him?* It wasn't like I was going to go to New York and fucking sit and stare at him lying in his bed all day. I just wanted to be in the city in case anything went wrong, and see with my own eyes what the hell was going on.

As the fire of rage flickered in my chest, something shifted inside me. A clarity surfaced. I saw that I could no longer accept his version of reality as the only version. His perspective about things was not infallible. Just because he was my dad, just because he was George Carlin, didn't make him god. I was not going to make myself wrong for caring about him and his condition, and for wanting to be with him. I allowed for the possibility that he might be wrong for not wanting that care. But still I did not get on a plane.

He came back to Los Angeles a few weeks later, seemingly recovered. His mood had lifted, life went on, and nothing was ever said about it again.

But from that day forward, I knew that every minute I got to spend with my dad would be taken from borrowed time—and I didn't know how much more time that was. All I wanted was to be with him and take in his essence. I wanted to implant in my mind and body what it was like to be in his presence so I could never forget what that felt like. It was such a powerful presence, I hoped it would linger in me forever. When I was with him, no matter what was going on between us, I felt whole. He was my DNA. He was my father. He was part of me.

We continued to see each other every six weeks or so over a breakfast, but it never felt like enough. Sally would encourage me to drop by whenever I wanted to, but that never worked. I tried it once, but Dad was tense and distracted the whole time I was there. Dad did not do spontaneous moments. He had his days mapped out, controlled.

I often thought, *I know we're running out of time; why doesn't he?* It was killing me. I began to consciously grieve his absence. I didn't want to be left emotionally unprepared like I had been with my mom. The only solace I could evoke to assuage the pain of not getting that time was thinking that maybe, unconsciously, he was preparing me for his permanent absence by pulling away. I began to see his lack of urgency to spend time with me as an act of love. Any other interpretation just hurt too much.

In March 2008, I went up to Santa Rosa to watch my dad tape his fourteenth HBO show, *It's Bad for Ya*. I thought it was one of his best shows in more than a decade. He let the "goofy George Carlin" show up again. He just seemed lighter and freer. Even the huge hunks he did on the dark topics of getting old and death were done without the anger and frustration he'd been expressing in the last few shows. I laughed with everyone else while he dismantled our culture's assumptions and euphemisms on the subject:

> So, you know what I've been doing? Goin' through my address book, and crossing out the dead people. You do that? That's a lotta fun. . . . Gives you a feeling of superiority—to have outlasted another old friend. But you can't do it too soon. You know, you can't come running home from the funeral *and get the book out [LEAFING THROUGH, MUMBLING]. You can't do that. A little time has to pass. . . . I have a rule of thumb: Six weeks. If you're a friend of mine and you're in my book, and you die, I leave you alone for an ex-*

*tra six weeks. Six extra weeks in the book, on the house, it's
on me. But after that, Hey, facts are facts, fuck you, you're
dead, PFTTT, FTT, FTT! Out ya fuckin' go! We need the
space! You have to have standards: My standard, six weeks.*

And another one:

> *This one happens after the funeral . . . Sooner or later,
> someone is bound to say this. Especially if he's had a couple
> of drinks: "You know, I think he's up there now, smiling down
> at us. And I think he's pleased."*
>
> *Now. First of all, there is no . . . "up there" . . . for people
> to be smiling . . . "down from." It's quaint. It's poetic. And I
> imagine for superstitious people, it's vaguely comforting. But
> it doesn't exist. But . . . if it did. If it did. And if someone did,
> somehow, survive death in a nonphysical form, I, personally,
> think he'd be far too busy with other activities than to be
> standing around Paradise, smiling down . . . on live people.
> What kind of a fuckin' eternity is that?*

Once again I was so in awe of his ability to humorously strip us
of all our illusions. And then something else hit me—it felt like he
was talking to me. Like this was an indirect communication from
Dad to me about death. I felt alone with him in the theater. No one
else was in on it. It sounds crazy, but maybe he was preparing himself, and me, and the audience for the inevitability of it. We Carlins
had never spoken to each other directly about death in the past, so
why start now? I laughed at the thought that the closest we'd ever
come to addressing this delicate subject was through a comedy routine in front of thousands of people.

When I went backstage to see him, I couldn't help but notice he
was officially looking elderly now. Although he'd been brilliant that
night, he was no longer laser sharp on stage. And even though he
was genuinely happy to see me and all our Northern California

friends, he was now permanently puffy and stooped. It was hard to take in.

Two months later, Dad, Sally, Bob, and I went to lunch at Ford's Filling Station in Culver City for dad's seventy-first birthday celebration. Dad looked really good, and seemed sharper than ever. It was like having my old dad back. I relaxed a bit, letting my fear of his imminent demise fall away. As the lunch unfolded, I realized that the last few times I'd been with him, I could really relax in his presence and more easily plug into my own personal power. I'd consciously use his higher vibration to help jump-start mine—like how a tennis player becomes a better player when they play with someone of a higher caliber—but I knew I was no longer borrowing his buzz as I had so many decades ago at Carnegie Hall. I was buzzing at my own higher vibration now. As I walked back to my car after lunch, a voice came into my head. It nearly stopped me in my tracks. It said, Kelly, you can no longer depend on your father to take you to that higher vibration. You now must, and can, do this for yourself. I had no idea what this voice was talking about. Well, maybe I did, but who wants to hear that.

I put that voice aside because I had an exciting and crazy month ahead of me. It was a whirlwind of travel. In late May, Bob and I went to Toronto for our friend Alexandra's fortieth birthday party. Then we all were off to Scotland for ten days to stay with Alexandra and her husband at their estate in Perthshire, where we would stare all day at the most beautiful countryside and eat way too much clotted cream. After that Bob flew home alone while I went on to Oslo, Norway. This was for a three-day training in how to lead a workshop called "The Act of Leadership." This was one of the workshops I hoped to be teaching throughout Europe in the year to come.

But I wasn't done there. In mid-June, after my return from Oslo, I officiated at the wedding of my dear friend Wendy Kamenoff, now Wendy Hammer (at Elayne Boosler's house). And finally, to top it all off, five days later, June nineteenth, I was off to Maui to officiate at another stand-up comedian's wedding—Craig Shoemaker. *Whew!*

Before I left for Hawaii, Dad and I laughed on the phone about how I was officiating at so many comics' weddings.

"You know, Dad, I may not be a stand-up comic, but, strangely, I have followed in your footsteps," I said. We were both ministers in the Church of Universal Life. In the 1970s my dad had cut out an ad in the back of *Rolling Stone* magazine and become ordained as a minister. He'd even officiated at a wedding.

I continued, "Of course, all I needed to do was go to their website and press a button that said, 'Ordain Me Now!' " We both chuckled. "I've finally found a way to merge my inner Lucille Ball with my Marianne Williamson—I'm the official comedian officiant."

The weirdest part was that I'd never really hung out with comics or spent much time at comedy clubs. I didn't know many comics except for my dad, and the few I did were clients from when I was a therapist. That's how I met Craig. I had helped him navigate his separation and divorce from his ex-wife. I guess he thought, *Who better to help me start my new life than the woman who helped me end my old one?*

I felt great talking to my dad. I was building an international coaching business, getting to travel to amazing places, creating sacred and loving space for friends' weddings, and working on *Waking from the American Dream.* He was feeling better and starting a new book. Plus he'd just found out he was getting the Kennedy Center Mark Twain Prize for Humor. I was so thrilled for him. I always thought he'd deserved it years before. I mean, I like Billy Crystal, but really? Before my dad? It was going to be a great rest of the year.

I got to Maui a few days before the wedding. I had some time to kill, so I decided to visit the Napili Kai Resort, that place where thirty-five years earlier I had tried to contain the chaos of the Carlins by writing out that UN-style peace treaty. I was so curious to see if there were any lingering effects of those dark days left on my soul.

I first stopped in Lahaina to see if I could find the bar where my mom, dad, and I had spent the day trying to score coke. I found it.

It was now a tourist-trap daiquiri bar. I had a virgin strawberry daiquiri and stared out at the ocean. I got back in the car, headed north following the signs to Napili Bay. I had no idea if the resort would even be there. And then I came around a corner, and there it was: the Napili Kai.

My stomach tightened. I took a deep breath, pulled in, and parked. I made my way through the resort toward the water, and there was Napili Bay—curved and calm. And then, there to my left was the infamous bar that had served my mom too much of the Mateus rosé, and to the right was the bungalow where I had written the treaty. It's so weird visiting places that have an iconic place in your psyche. It was like visiting a set of a famous movie I'd seen over and over. I couldn't believe I was actually there.

As I walked down the beach, I felt at peace. All the pain, the terror, and the confusion from those dark days were remarkably gone. They'd been dropped off, released, and transformed. A door shut, an era was over, a wounded self had been healed. I was astounded, relieved, and thrilled.

I don't normally believe in miracles, but I did in that moment.

The Carlins were whole again.

As I drove back down the coast to my condo, I was so excited about what had happened that I had to call my dad. There was no one else on the planet whom I could share this with. He rarely picked up his phone, and I was expecting to leave a voice mail when he said, "Hey, Kiddo, what's up?"

Excitedly I jumped right in, "Dad, guess where I just was?" I took a dramatic pause, "The Napili Kai."

"Wow!"

"I know. I know! And I have to tell you that there was this space there inside of me with no pain, or confusion or anything." Tears began to fill my eyes. "It's done. I'm done. We're done."

There was a slight pause and quiet in his voice. "That's great. That's *really*, really great."

And then out of nowhere these words tumbled out of my mouth: "And Dad, I want you to know that the parts of ourselves, of you, and me, and Mom, the parts of our souls that we left there thirty-five years ago—I just reclaimed them for us. It really *is* done."

There was silence on the other end of the phone. Tears now streamed down my face.

I could tell Dad was crying, too. All he could manage was, "Yes."

A deep and silent calm held between us for a few moments, nothing more needing to be said. I looked out at the bluest ocean I'd ever seen and knew that we'd just connected in a way that I'd always longed for—deeply, from our hearts, not hiding one single square inch of ourselves from the other. I felt like all of me was present with him. I was his equal, his daughter, his teacher, his soul companion.

I wanted this feeling to last forever.

That was the last conversation I ever had with my dad.

CHAPTER TWENTY-SIX

Sunday Will Definitely Never Be the Same

My last day in Hawaii, Sunday, June 22, 2008, was absolutely perfect—the wedding was behind me, my phone was unplugged, I had lain on the beach and swum with the turtles in the morning, to finish the day with a fabulous lomilomi massage, and the all-important afternoon nap. Between the crazy month I'd just had and the heap of work waiting for me when I got home, I reveled in my day of complete peace and quiet.

I'd barely woken up from my long nap when Craig Shoemaker frantically knocked on my condo door. When I opened it, all I could see was the look of panic on his face.

"Is your phone off? Bob's been trying to reach you for hours," he said nervously.

My heart sank so quickly and deeply I almost couldn't breathe.

"Um, yeah, I had a massage and then a nap," I said as I went to turn on my phone.

Craig stood there for a moment and then said, "If you need anything, we're in 605," and left.

When I saw that I had five missed calls from Bob and Theresa, I knew that whatever was going on was bad. Fuck.

As the phone rang in my ear, I was already crying. When Bob picked up, I said, "What's going on?"

Bob's voice was soft, like he knew the words would land hard, and he didn't want to add to their blow. "Kelly, your dad . . . died."

Time stopped. The space swirled around me. I looked for something to make sense. I stumbled toward the door leading out to the lanai and shouted, "No, no, not today!" to no one in particular. As I spoke I realized that those were the exact words I had uttered at the moment of my mom's death, eleven years earlier. I found it strange that I was noticing this very moment as I was saying it.

"What happened?" I asked.

"We don't know exactly, but he couldn't breathe, and Sally took him to the hospital, and they tried to stabilize him, but it was too much. They couldn't save him."

I said nothing for a few moments, just trying to wrap my head around what he had said.

"I'm coming home right now. I'll go to the airport and switch my ticket."

I frantically found my way up to Craig and Mika's condo. They both embraced me. I cried a bit, but mostly I just stood there in shock. "I need someone to take me and my car to the airport," I said to Craig.

Craig's youngest son, five-year-old Jared, asked me why I was crying. I didn't have the wherewithal to lie. "My daddy died," I answered matter-of-factly. Craig told me later that for the rest of the trip, every time someone came to the door, Jared would ask the person, "Did your daddy die?" Jesus, not only did my former client have to see his former therapist fall apart, but I also somehow managed to scar his youngest child. Way to go, therapist Kelly.

On the way to the airport Craig and I said very little to each other. There isn't much one can say in that moment. There really are no words. Plus I was in shock. Language had left me, for the most part.

Once Craig dropped me at the airport and I was alone, I felt that wave of familiar strangeness that only death can bring—the thin veil between the "here and now" and the "beyond" falling away. It felt like everything around me was a movie.

I walked up to the United Airlines counter to try to get upgraded to first class. I was sure that they'd allow me this dignity because of the horror I was living through. I mean, it's suffering enough to have to fly home alone to a dead father, but quite another thing altogether to have to do it in economy.

I put on my most charming self for the man behind the counter, "Hi there, I was wondering—well, my dad just died—today. I need to change my flight, and—well, is there a way to upgrade me to first class? Is there a bereavement thing?"

"Do you have a first-class ticket?" the perfectly lovely Hawaiian man said to me.

"No. I have a regular ticket for tomorrow, but I just found out my dad died." I leaned forward and lowered my voice, "You see my dad is George Carlin, and—well, I wondered if there was any way for you to upgrade me." Throwing down my "I'm special" card.

"I'm sorry, who is your father?"

Oh, thank God, I thought. "George Carlin," I said.

He looked at me like I'd just said my father was Joe Blow. "I don't know who that is," he said with a hint of snideness in his voice.

"You know, the comedian. 'Hippie-Dippie Weatherman'? 'Seven Dirty Words'?" I added desperately.

Blank stare from him. "Sorry," he said.

You've got to be kidding me. How do I manage to get the one human over the age of forty in the United States who has no idea who my dad is? Fucking Hawaiians.

"There are a few seats available both in economy and first class for the next flight. Would you like to upgrade your ticket?"

I fought back rage and tears. "Yes." I handed him my American

Express card. *Fuck it, I'll work it out later.* "How much?" I asked, wanting to know how much damage it would do.

"One thousand and twenty," he said.

"Great," I said. He printed my ticket, handed it to me, and I walked toward the gates feeling more alone and a bit poorer than I ever had.

I had more than an hour to kill before my flight. My body hurt all over as the shock began to wear off and the grief began to set in. I called Bob. He told me, "So, I guess your dad had an appointment with the doctor last Friday because he was having some symptoms. The doctor was worried and wanted to admit him right there and then. But your dad said he had a few things to take care of over the weekend, and wanted to know if he could go in Monday for the tests. The doctor didn't like it, but he agreed."

Jesus. Dad. What the fuck?

I hung up. I thought of going to the bar to get a drink. I really needed a drink, or ten, but I feared that I'd look up at the TV and see CNN's news scroll saying, George Carlin dead, blah, blah, blah . . . and then I'd—well, I wasn't sure what I'd do, and I didn't want to find out, so I decided against the bar. I wandered around the terminal diligently avoiding the ubiquitous TVs. I finally just sat down. I felt like a wraith as I observed the humans pulling luggage and bustling to their gates. I wanted to yell at them, What's the point? In the end it all just goes away!

My phone rang, startling me out of my trance. It was my friend Jon. He was part of my tribe, the Wolves, from Leadership.

"Kel, I heard. I'm so sorry."

Crying again, I said, "Yeah, I'm in the airport on my way home from Maui. It's so fucking weird. I'm avoiding all the TVs because I'm not sure I'm ready to let it be real." I laughed.

"I can't even imagine. It must be so weird," he said. "Speaking of weird . . . Um, I wanted to know if it would be okay for my partner, Janet, and I to help your dad to the other side?" Jon had trained with a number of South American shamans, and practiced the art of soul retrieval. I wasn't sure exactly what he was asking or what he wanted to do, but I didn't care. I felt so far away from the ones I loved and my dad, and I kept picturing my dad terrified as he was dying. If I could comfort him in any way, I wanted to try.

"Sure," I said.

Jon continued, "I have the feeling that he's needing a bit of guidance right now."

"Do what you feel is right," I said.

"Okay, I'll call you back when we know more."

It helped me to feel a bit less alone. People were here for me. People were here for my dad. God, I hoped he hadn't suffered.

As I waited for Jon to call back, I gathered some courage and went in search of a public Internet terminal. I didn't really want to see the news sprawled across the Internet, but I also felt compelled to get the moment over with. I knew I could only delay the inevitability of my new life for so long. Eventually I was going to have to see what it felt like to experience the reality that this was not a private event but a public one. I was curious to see what it would feel like, and yet terrified that it would begin some snowball effect in my life—that my life would no longer be mine. I would become the grieving daughter of the famous comedian.

I sat down at the terminal, swiped my credit card, and Googled "George Carlin." And *boom*! the first item that appeared was from *Entertainment Tonight*: "George Carlin, age 71, dies of heart failure at St. John's Hospital in Santa Monica, CA at 5PM PST today."

It was official. My dad was dead. It was real.

It was real because *Entertainment Tonight* said so. The surreality notched up another click.

About thirty minutes later Jon called back. "So, we found him and connected with him. He was disoriented because of all of the medications and drugs from the procedures they put him through. I really don't think he thought he was going to die today. We said some prayers and did a ritual to usher him along. After a few minutes I heard him say, 'Oh, shit. Oh, fuck.'"

I laughed through the tears falling down my face. "Well, that certainly sounds like my dad."

I had no idea if the afterlife was real or if my dad was lost in the ethers. In the past, when my dad and I had talked about this stuff, we'd both felt that we'd only know what really happens once we'd gone. So, at this moment just after his death, I was willing to err on the side that he was "up there" somewhere. And if Dad was a bit confused, it didn't surprise me, because everyone, including him, thought he'd live forever. He'd just always be here.

I boarded the plane and took my very expensive window seat in first class. This was going to be the longest flight of my life, and I was happy not only for the extra legroom, but also for the extra emotional room around me. As I stared out the window, I couldn't contain my grief, and I let myself cry as I watched the ground crew load the luggage. A flight attendant offered me some champagne, and I took it. I didn't want to seem crazy for crying, so I told her that my dad had just died. And then I added, "My dad was George Carlin." Name-dropping my father's name may seem obnoxious, but I was alone on that plane and didn't want to bear the loss by myself. I was hoping she was a fan and would share a piece of the burden with me. She smiled. "Oh, I'm so, so sorry. I hadn't heard. If there's anything else you need, please let me know."

I knew exactly what I needed, but she couldn't bring it to me. I needed my mom. I needed Bob. I needed some comfort and strength. I needed all this to go away.

A woman sat down in the seat next to me. Oh good, I thought, at least it's some feminine energy. She also accepted a glass of champagne while she arranged her bags. After we took off, we exchanged a few pleasantries. I could see from her reading material that she was some kind of a minister. *Oh good*, I thought, *she's a compassionate soul*. I said to her, "I, um—well, my dad just died, and so I'm a bit of a mess right now. I just heard a few hours ago."

"I'm so sorry to hear that," she said.

"Yeah, it's so strange. My mom is gone too. And well, my dad was George Carlin. . . ."

All the warmth disappeared from her face. "Hmm. Well, I'm so sorry for your loss," she said as she grabbed a pile of folders and began to read.

Really? Oh yeah, that's right. She's one of those professional Christians my dad talked about. The kind that can manage to extend compassion only to people they approve of. I turned my back on her for the rest of the flight and spent my time looking out the window for some comfort. When I saw Jupiter in the sky, I smiled.

I wondered if Dad had made it there yet.

I landed back in Los Angeles around four in the morning. Bob gathered me up. I was numb, in shock, barely present. Once home, I lay on the bed on top of the covers fully clothed, unable to sleep, fearing the reality that I would face when I awoke—a world without my dad. Bob lay down beside me and held me until I slept.

Hours later I was awakened by the phone ringing. Bob answered it in the kitchen. Once I realized where I was, and what was happening, I thought, *It has begun.*

"No, she's not available right now. Can I take a message? Sure. Yes. I'll let her know."

Bob came down the hall and leaned on the doorjamb. Still lying on the bed, I whispered, "Who was it?"

"Larry King," he answered.

"Larry King, Larry King?" I said, confused, as I sat up in bed. *My God, it really has begun.*

"Yeah. Larry King, Larry King. He wants to send a car for you so that you can come on his show today to talk about your dad," he said.

I sat there barely able to fathom the notion of making it to the bathroom to pee let alone the idea of cars and lights and cameras and microphones. And yet it was my dad. *I must rally*, I told myself. *I need to make sure I'm doing the right things.*

Bob interrupted my inner monologue. "You know, you don't have to do it."

"I don't?" I asked innocently.

"No," he said.

Relieved, "Yeah. Okay. Yeah. Good. I don't think I can."

As Bob turned and walked up the hallway, I said loudly, "Maybe I can call in?" I would call in.

Larry King was just the beginning. The phone rang, e-mails dinged, and the doorbell dinged and donged. All day long flowers and telegrams began to arrive, and they didn't stop. White flowers in every shape and form—orchids, roses, daisies, lilies—flowed into our home and took up nearly every square inch of horizontal space we had. By the end of the week I walked into the living room and blurted out, "Jesus Christ, it looks like a fucking funeral parlor in here. It's so fucking depressing," and then laughed, realizing the irony of what I'd just said.

Larry King fortunately indeed allowed me to call in later that day. As I sat on hold, waiting to be connected to him live on the air, I did a little dance. This "dance" was one I'd created at the leadership program the year before in order to be able to recover my sense of self. It helped me to get out of my head and back into my body. It worked wonders in any situation when anxiety took over, when I could no longer think straight. As I listened to Larry throwing it to commercial—"We'll be right back with George's daughter, Kelly"—I'm sure I looked insane swinging my hips and shooting my arms around like a disco queen. But, by the time he said, "We have George's daughter, Kelly, on the line," I was relatively calm and felt reconnected to myself—or at least as much of myself as there was to be connected with, considering the state I was in.

Before I called in, I'd been watching parts of the show. It was tough. I could barely watch the videos of my dad. It physically hurt. I managed to watch a few minutes of Jerry Seinfeld, and then Bill Maher, and a bit of Lewis Black, and Roseanne Barr. It was so surreal to see these superstars talking about my dad in such a reverential way. It was heartbreaking, too. They all looked like they couldn't quite believe it had happened. I could see the grief on Lewis's face, and it made the loss even more real to me.

The first time Larry went to commercial and I saw the big graphic behind him that said, "Remembering George Carlin, 1937–2008," I thought, Dad would get a kick out of that. Even though he'd dismissed the industry and awards and such, that little boy who lived within him, the one who'd dreamed of being Danny Kaye, reveled in and got excited about that kind of stuff. I could hear myself saying to Dad, "See, Dad, you were loved. People were paying attention."

But it was surreal. Here he was, *my* dad, *my* papa, and yet, he was *the legend, the icon* now. He was the dead famous guy that people talk about on TV now. And I was the daughter of the dead famous guy about to talk about him on TV now.

We went live. "Kelly, thank you for being here . . . ," said Larry King. And I have no memory of what happened after that. He asked questions, and I answered them. I do remember thinking, *Wow, he's a good interviewer!* After it was over, I was unsure if I'd done the right thing by even being on the show. I felt awkward and vulnerable. I thought, *Maybe I just need to lie low.*

Later that night I walked into my bedroom alone, and a vision came to me: I am backstage at a theater standing in the wings looking out at the stage—a very familiar vantage point from my entire life watching my dad perform. But during this vision there was no one on the stage. It was empty except for a single microphone stand lit by a spot-light. My heart began to ache, and then my father's voice came into my head and said, "It's all lined up for ya, Kiddo. Go for it."

And I knew that from that moment forward, my life would never be the same.

CHAPTER TWENTY-SEVEN

Episode Number 268 of Kelly's Surreal Life, Or The Sun and the Buddha (I Can't Decide)

ON TUESDAY MORNING someone brought me a copy of Monday's *New York Times*. I saw that Dad had made the front page. Fuck, yeah. I could feel my dad smiling from the great beyond. The article talked mostly about his career, but at the end it said he was survived by his daughter, Kelly, and wife, Sally Wade. Hmm. I knew he called her "his spouse" and even "his wife" in public because he felt that "girlfriend" or "significant other" was just silly for a man in his sixties. For a second I was set into a tailspin. Would he have married her without me knowing? No, I knew he hadn't. Get it together, *New York Times*.

I gathered myself together as much as I could because today was plan-the-memorial day. While fully immersed in that surreal is-this-really-happening-in-my-life? mode, I was also filled with an intense inner knowing about what was needed to honor my dad. I could feel his presence right next to me. He was my inner GPS telling me what was needed, what was not; what to go for and what to ignore. It was as if I were seeing the world through his eyes. It was a very weird feeling, because I was so used to him being the absent father. But now that he was gone, he was more present than ever.

Bob and I went to Jerry's house to talk about the memorial we would have there on Saturday. If I had any doubt at all about what we should do for Dad, it was alleviated because Dad had left instructions:

> *Upon my death, I wish to be cremated. The disposition of my ashes (dispersal at sea, on land, or in the air) shall be determined by my surviving family (wife and daughter) in accordance with their knowledge of my prejudices and philosophies regarding geography and spirituality. Under no circumstances are my ashes to be retained by anyone or buried in a particular location. The eventual dispersal can be delayed for any reasonable length of time required to reach a decision, but not to exceed one month following my death.*
>
> *I wish no public service of any kind.*
>
> *I wish no religious service of any kind.*
>
> *I prefer a private gathering at my house, attended by friends and family members who shall be determined by my immediate surviving family.*
>
> *The exact nature of this gathering shall be determined by my surviving family. It should be extremely informal, they should play rhythm and blues music, and they should laugh a lot. Vague references to spirituality (secular) will be permitted.*
>
> *George Carlin*
> *5/1/90*

I was shocked by two things when Jerry showed me the typed-out document: (1) that he'd written these instructions at all; and (2) that he hadn't amended them since 1990. I wondered if he even remembered that he'd written them. I imagined he'd smoked a joint and gotten into some kind of existential fugue when he wrote them. I was happy he had. It gave me direction. I envisioned the memorial immediately. We would play some videos of Dad, inter-spersing them throughout so we would all remember to laugh. We would have Spanky McFarlane sing the blues, and I knew I had to have Kenny Rankin sing "Here's That Rainy Day." We would have the people whom he'd known and loved be able to share their memories—Jerry Hamza, Sally Wade, Pat Carlin, Dennis Carlin, Jon Reigrod, Theresa McKeown, Jack Burns, Rocco Urbisci, and me—and maybe a few comics, too. This memorial would rock.

After the meeting, Bob and I went to visit Sally to check up on her and to grab Dad's address book. I needed to call our extended family, and also wanted to reach out to some comics to invite them to the memorial.

Sally was inconsolable. I was very worried about her. She was in deep shock and could barely function. I understood. Even though I'd never lost my soul mate, I knew what she was feeling. When my mom died, it felt like a limb had been ripped from my body. She was part of the very fabric of my being. Dad and Sally had been attached at the hip for ten years. While he was on the road, he texted her constantly and called her numerous times a day. They were deeply enmeshed, just like my mom and I had been. I'm sure his absence and the silence was excruciating and terrifying for her.

I knew there was little I could say or do to ease her pain. Only time would do that. There was no bringing him back. There was only being with, and moving through, what was. I was doing my best to do that myself. I felt lucky I'd had some practice with all this from losing my mom. And although I may have looked from the outside like I was functioning, I, too, was gutted, of course, and had my own bucket of grief to shoulder. I knew I couldn't be the one to take care of her. I was grateful her family had come in from out of state to do just that.

Once I got back to my house, the adventures of my new surreal life continued. Garry Shandling called. Before my dad's death I'd known one or two comics, and that was only because they'd been my therapy clients. This daughter of comedy did not hang out at comedy clubs or even really follow comics' careers. I wasn't a comedy nerd. Now they were reaching out to me to ease my pain.

As I sat on my bathroom floor crying on the phone with Garry, it was clear he was as torn up about my dad's death as I was. We talked for more than thirty minutes, and it turned out that we had much in common. He too had been studying Buddhist philosophy for quite a while. Talking to him made me feel less alone. He was a wise soul, and his humor and insight steadied me. I invited him to the memorial.

Buoyed by my conversation with Garry, I called Lewis Black. He was a wreck, too. He was kind and gracious, and I instantly felt like I was talking to a long-lost friend. I thanked him for being on Larry King, and also invited him to the memorial.

We were all wrecks on the phone that day.

Then Richard Belzer called. He said he couldn't make it out to the memorial, but let me know that David Letterman wanted to do a tribute to my dad on the show, and had asked Richard to come on to talk about my dad and his work. I was so touched. And then he said to me, "Kelly, you are family. Your father meant the world to me, and you are now a part of my family. If there is anything I can do for you, call me. I am here."

My father was gone, but I was not alone. I didn't have to fear falling down a rabbit hole of grief because these men were stretching out their hearts and declaring, We are here for you. I realized that these men were, in some ways, my father's other children. He had inspired, shaped, and determined their lives as much as he had shaped mine. They, too, were his heirs. I felt an instant kinship with them. They were my brothers and uncles. I felt a net of love and light catch me and carry me forward.

I had lost my father, but gained a family—a comedy family.

As I perused my dad's phone book trying to figure out whom else I needed to call for the memorial, I saw a number for Jon Stewart. Before I knew it, I was dialing the number. I expected an assistant.

A man's voice that sounded just like Jon Stewart answered. "Hello?"

"Jon?" I cautiously asked, realizing I'd gotten his private work number.

He said, "Yes?"

"This is Kelly Carlin, George's daughter."

"Omigod. Kelly."

I began to choke up as I said, "I just wanted to call to thank you for the tribute you did on your show last night." Jon had taken a moment at the end of *The Daily Show* the night before to play a clip of my dad's work.

"Of course. Of course. I am—well, we are all—so torn up about it. It's just so shitty." I could tell there was emotion in his voice.

"Yes, shitty, indeed." Jon had done a brilliant interview with my dad in 1997 at the Aspen Comedy Festival that was part of the special *George Carlin: 40 Years of Comedy*. I knew my dad meant a lot to him. I continued, "We're having a memorial on Saturday. If you want, I want you to know that you are welcome to come."

"I wish I could. I wish I could," he said.

On Wednesday morning Sally called to tell me that a friend of hers was going to bring a trance-channeler over to her house to help her contact George, someone who claimed to be able to access realms beyond our human life. She wanted to know if I wanted to be there.

Now, in the past, my parents and I had done this kind of thing a bunch of times with a gentleman from Canada, Doug Cottrell. Doug is considered to be like Edgar Cayce—a medical intuitive who also tells you about your past lives and helps guide you through current life issues. To do this he goes into a trance and accesses what they call the Akashic records—a collection of knowledge supposedly stored in the astral plane. Mom often invited him to come down to stay with them for a week, and he'd do sessions there. Dad, ever the seeker, was open-minded about such things, and would have sessions with Doug, as would I. Over the years he'd helped me put my life in perspective. My mom had even witnessed him give people un-cannily accurate medical diagnoses. But even though I was no stranger to this kind of thing, I was not up for it that week, and told Sally so. But, I thought, hoped, and prayed it might give Sally some solace, and I told her she should do it.

After the session Sally called me.

She said, "So your grandma Mary was the first person to greet him when he arrived. Your mom was there, too, in the background." I laughed. I could see my mom, ever the producer, hovering in the background with a clipboard and a list of things for my dad to do. Sally continued, "And the first thing that George said was, 'Oh, shit. Oh, fuck.'"

I nearly dropped the phone.

I told Sally what Jon had said to me on Sunday when he had con-tacted my dad, and how I'd laughed about it, but how it had also made me worry about him.

Sally continued, "Oh, but the channeler said that his, 'Oh, shit. Oh, fuck,' weren't cries of pain or despair, but a comment on how amazing it all was. He couldn't believe how beautiful it was."

I cried tears of joy. I sure hoped it was. I was comforted by the image.

After being busy and preoccupied all week with planning the memorial, Friday came sooner than I wanted. I was dreading it because it was the day we'd set aside to see Dad's body and say good-bye to him. Jerry, Patrick, Dennis, Sally, Theresa, and Bob and I all gathered at the funeral home. It was the same one we'd used for Mom. I thought, *Does this mean we now have a family mortuary?* Sitting in the waiting area, I was again reminded what a strange ritual this is. We were there to look at the dead body of a person we loved. As I looked at everyone's faces in the waiting room, I really understood the term "grief-stricken." It was such a hell.

Each of us went into the room where we would have our personal good-byes with Dad. Patrick put a nice fat joint in Dad's pocket—a little something to ease his way. As I sat waiting for my turn, I was very worried about Sally. She looked completely unraveled. I wasn't sure if she'd slept or eaten in days. She said that she wasn't sure she could go in and say good-bye. Looking at her, I wasn't sure if she could either, but still I encouraged her to do so. I knew it would be the hardest thing she'd ever do in her life, but if she didn't do it, she'd regret it. That much I was sure of.

Because I had grieved my mother's death already, I knew how important it was to say our good-byes at these times. It begins the healing process.

When Sally finally went in, I was startled by the wail of grief that came out of her. It was unnerving. I immediately regretted encouraging her, afraid it was too much, but told myself that she was stronger than even she knew. Sally would survive this. It would take her some time to find her way through all of this, but she would survive.

Then it was my turn to say good-bye. Bob and I went in together. Thank God for Bob. He, like he is every day, had been my rock that week. He'd been my arms, and eyes, and brain. He'd fed me, hugged me, and helped guide me through every moment. I was so grateful for his steady love.

We walked up to the coffin and looked at my dad. He looked pretty good, but his skin was waxy and fake looking. It was just so weird. Death is so fucking weird. Bob tearfully said his good-byes, hugged me, and then left me alone with my dad. I sat on the couch at the other side of the room, not sure what to do. I took one of the mints from a bowl on the table in front of me. I put it in my mouth, and then took another one, walked over to the casket and placed it on my dad's chest.

"Here's that rainy day they told me about . . ." I began to sing. I sang the whole song to him while I cried, and then I began to laugh.

"Dad, this is just so fucking weird. Here we are. A day that I knew would come, but that I never thought would come. I thought for sure you'd live forever. So did you. Wow!" I began to cry again. "I love you so much."

Then I took a postcard with a picture of the Buddha on it out of my purse. I read aloud what I'd written on the back. "Dear Dad, This is just a finger pointing at the moon. You now know the Real Deal. Congratulations! Love, Your Baby Doll." I put the postcard on his chest. The "finger pointing at the moon" was a picture of the Buddha on the front of the postcard. This saying was an old Buddhist adage that meant that any depiction of enlightenment was only a symbol of the idea; it was not the experience itself. Which was what I meant by the next line: "You now know the Real Deal." Dad was now on the other side. Whatever that was like, he was there. I'd felt he'd quietly struggled with finding peace his whole life, and no matter what, he had it now. I was truly happy for him. His struggle with his body, and the planet, and humanity was over.

Then I took off my necklace. It was silver and had a painting of an orange sun on it. As I laid it on his chest, I cried as I told him, "Dad, you've been the sun in my solar system forever. It's been a great ride. I wouldn't have changed a thing. But now I must be the sun in my life. My life must be for me. I love you. I will forever. Thank you for everything you have given me. I will do well with it all. I promise. You will live in my heart forever." I took one last long look at him and touched his face.

I walked out of the room knowing that for today, he and I were complete.

CHAPTER TWENTY-EIGHT

He Was Here Just a Minute Ago

Is IT OKAY to "kill" at your father's memorial?

I sure hope so.

No, I didn't want to *kill* anyone. I wanted to crush, shine, knock it out of the park. You know, kill.

As people gathered in Jerry's backyard, R & B music from the fifties and sixties played. Just like Dad had requested, his memorial was a small and private affair. There were less than seventy people gathered, but all of them had been deeply influenced in some way by Dad's life—extended family from both the Bearey and Carlin sides, a few friends from Dad's old neighborhood in Manhattan, many people who over the years had worked closely with him, close family friends of my parents, my own close friends, a few comics, and of course, me, Bob, Jerry, Sally, Dad's brother, Patrick, and my cousin Dennis.

We had everything we needed—a dais and a big TV monitor for videos; food and drink; and one another. I decided earlier in the week that I would emcee the event so I could set the tone and provide context for each of the speakers. Before I went on, I went into the bathroom to do my "move." It instantly grounded me in the present moment, and I thought, *Thank God I went to Leadership.* It felt like all the work I'd done on myself the last eight years—Pacifica, Life Coaching, and Leadership—had been to prepare me for this very moment, and the next era in my life. I was immensely grateful because although I was weary and heartbroken, I was ready for this day. My mind was clear, and my heart was full of love.

Once everyone gathered and sat down in Jerry's backyard, I got up and began.

"Welcome," I said calmly, and then I took a beat, looked out at everyone, and said, "Fuck! I don't know what to say. There are no words, and yet we are all here to say a few of them. Dad knew exactly what he wanted this day to be like. He left us instructions. Jerry will read those to you in a bit, but first to give you an idea of what to expect today: There will be some speakers, some music, if you need to get up to leave or get some food or a drink, do what you need to do. This is family.

"I apologize for what might be called the Carlinesque bit I am about to do, but hey, I'm a Carlin, and so, as my dad would say— FUCK YOU." This got a huge laugh. I breathed, as did everyone else. The tension emptied out of the space.

I continued having fun with what I was saying. "Anyway, here are a few things that hopefully we will not be talking about today: I hope that no one will mention that my dad has 'passed away' or that we 'lost him,' or that he's 'gone to a better place.' He has died. That is all the language we need to use. He would want it that way.

"Also, he is not looking DOWN on us. As he recently told us in his last special—there is no UP THERE up there. And let's please refrain from pondering if Dad has gotten back all the lost keys, pens, lighters, and wallets now that he is heaven. Also, we will never know if he got his two-minute warning, so let's not try to figure out the clever thing that God may have said to him.

"And for all of you who have already said, 'If there is anything

that you need, please ask me'—well, I now have all your phone numbers, and you will be getting a call from us in a few weeks. I'm sure
I can find something for you to do around the house.

"Okay, enough of that shit. Let's start with a little video."

The afternoon was filled with videos of Dad's most epic career
moments, and with people talking about how much he had touched
their lives. Jerry read the instructions Dad had left for the memorial, and talked a bit about their forty years working together on the
road. Theresa got up and told a funny story about accidentally seeing my dad naked one day, and how she'd never seen an ass so white.
Patrick talked about how Dad was always the hippest guy in the
room, and the most generous brother you could have. Bill Maher
talked about how Dad was the rabbit that he'd always chased in his
career—how Dad always was out in front—and how he didn't know
what he'd do without that rabbit now. Dennis Carlin talked about
the things my dad had taught him about life.

Jack Burns stood up in the beautiful sunshine-filled backyard
and started with, "The family would like to thank you all for brav-
ing the brutal weather today," and got a huge laugh. Both Lewis
Black and Garry Shandling shared how their own courage to move
forward in their careers had only happened because of the kind
words my dad had said to them about their work. Kenny Rankin
managed to sing "Here's That Rainy Day" even though he was crying. And Spanky not only sang the blues, but also told a great story
my dad had shared with her decades ago. He had told her about being at Ed Sullivan's apartment for a party in the sixties, and taking
a big shit in the bathroom. He then explained that the shit was so
big it wouldn't flush down the toilet, and Dad, not wanting to leave
it in the bowl, took his eyeglasses off and used them to break the
turd up. I think the audience was a bit shocked by the story, but it
was raw and very funny. My dad would have loved it.

Sally, having pulled herself together beautifully, shared her
charming and funny self—the Sally my dad adored—while telling
a few sweet stories about their life together.

Then I got up to speak. Here are my words from that day:

"I have gotten countless emails this past week from fans—friends and complete strangers around the globe. Many have talked about how my father changed their lives in some way—helped them wake up, made them laugh, and one woman even said that Dad had converted her Catholic mother after only one listening of *Class Clown*.

"There were also some messages that said something like, 'The world has lost a great man, but you have lost your dad. Thank you for sharing him with the whole world.' These took my breath away. I had never really thought of it that way before—I was sharing him with you. This brought me solace and peace. When you grow up in the glow of such an immense force like my father, someone who has made such a huge dent, you start to think that his public impact is the only thing that he was really here to achieve—I know, a fucked-up thought, but it is where the mind can go at times.

"But this week I got a complete reframe of my whole life. I now get what the whole world got to have of him and his impact. I, of course, got that part of him, too. I, too, loved his work, cheered him on when he said the things that I wished I had the balls to say, was shocked by him, scolded by him, and profoundly amused by him.

"But here's the shift for me—that what I got from my dad, no one else could ever get. I was his daughter, I was his only child, I was it, the receiver of something most precious—his fatherly love. And so I thought today I would share some of the gifts that came through his fatherly love. I guess I'm used to sharing him with others, and don't worry, I know that these gifts are for me.

"Here are seven of the seven thousand things he taught me:

"Number one: It's okay to eat pancakes for dinner. When I was really young—four or five—and Mom wasn't around, Dad would make for dinner the only thing he knew how to cook—pancakes. And I remember it impacted me in the same way as if he had just magically turned night into day. He taught me that anything is possible.

"Number two: Music. Some of my most vivid memories from childhood are of Dad teaching me about music; starting at around four years old, hanging with Dad in his office or wherever while he worked, music was always playing—early Stones, Cream, *The White Album*. He traveled on the road in those days with vinyl records and a small turntable. His vinyl collection was huge—hundreds of albums. He always said that it was *my* collection. He made good on that about seven years ago when he gave it to me. It is one of my most treasured possessions.

"He was so passionate about his music if I woke up in the middle of the night and noticed that he was awake, I would join him in the living room. He would take off his headphones, say to me, 'You have to hear this,' and put them on me. One night he sat me down and played the whole album of *Tubular Bells* for me. I had no idea what it was, but it blew my mind.

"Number three: Of course my dad would be remiss if he didn't teach me what I'm sure every comic teaches their child. . . ." I then crossed my eyes, patted my head, rubbed my stomach, and moved my feet crisscross across the stage. And then I did an artificial fart under my arm.

"Number four: Walk down the street like you own it. Coming from the rough streets of New York, this was a lesson of paramount importance to him. I remember being eight years old, and we had just moved to Venice in 1971, and it was a neighborhood filled with nothing but bikers, hippies, and Russian immigrants. So Dad took me out for a walk the first week we lived there and taught me— actually demonstrated—how to walk down the street so, as he put it, 'no one would fuck with you.'"

I continued. "Number five: It is pronounced *prim*-er, not *pry*-mer, and *forte*, not *for*-tay.

"Number six: Treat all people as equal. Another huge lesson, and it showed up in many forms. Two of which are: history lessons about the struggle of black people in America; and him modeling kind-ness and respect to all people, especially those who may be helping or serving you. He physically showed me how to properly tip a person—how to fold up the bill so it is a nice little sliver, and then just let it stick out enough so the person can see it coming and receive it with dignity. If anyone needs more details, see me later.

"Number seven: You can say the word 'fuck,' but not at school or in front of other kids' parents. Yes, he was a man who loved to cross limits, but he didn't want it to ever hurt *my* way in the world.

"I just want to finish here with a few words about legacy. Now, I know that part of my dad didn't think about things like legacies, and yet I also know that a part of him did—I mean, he was only human. And I don't know what he would think about me talking to you about this, but he's not here to make sense of this for me, so I am doing the best I can.

"So here is what I have to say about it:

"First, being my father's daughter, I looked up the etymology of the word 'legacy' the other night. The first thing I found was that it was from the Old French, circa 1375, meaning 'a body of persons sent on a mission.' I really like that. It's not about him. It's about us.

"Each of us knows in our hearts what that mission is that he has sent us on, that he has been such a model of. It may be to speak your truth, or find the line and cross it, or be kind to everyone you meet, or just make someone laugh. You choose.

"And make him proud."

A warm sense of satisfaction filled me up, and I knew that if he'd been there, he'd have been proud of me and of what I'd said. I felt complete. But there was one more piece of business.

I resumed. "As much as I would love to have the last word here, I feel it's only fitting that we let my dad have it today." We then rolled the clip of him doing "Modern Man."

As I watched him perform, it hit me again what a genius he was. His insight, artistry, poetics, and showmanship were unsurpassed. The world was going to miss his unique contribution to the big conversation about what is real and important and funny about life. As the video came to an end, it became clear how poignant the ending of the piece was when he said, "I'm hanging in, there ain't no doubt. And I'm hanging tough, over and out."

And then he took a bow.

Over and out—yes indeed.

It was perfect. I knew that we had sent my dad off in a beautiful way. There'd been a funny story about shitting, Bill Maher had gotten emotional, and there'd been a few mentions of the "Big Electron," but not a single one about God.

Now was the hard part—the rest of my life without him.

Feeling not quite ready for that to start yet, I invited my close friends, family, and Spanky and her band to come down to my house for the after party. I mean, this was a Carlin memorial. There had to be an after party.

We brought the leftover food, and we had some drinks. My uncle rolled some joints, and we all gathered in the studio space in our backyard. Spanky took a chair in the center of the room, and she was flanked by her guitar player, John, and her daughter, DeeCee. She and the band began to play and sing some songs. She sang the blues, some standards, and then some sixties classics. I knew there was magic happening when everyone sang along to "California Dreamin'" in perfect harmony. I was in my bliss.

Then Spanky looked at John and said, "Should we do 'Sunday'?"

I looked at her and said, "You must. It will kill me, but you must."

As she began to sing, "I remember Sunday morning . . ." I sat on my knees at the foot of her chair, and she held my hands. Time spun backward, and I was four years old again singing those words with my daddy in our living room on Beverwil Drive. The space crackled with an aliveness. Spanky and I belted out the chorus, "Sunday will never be the same/I've lost my Sunday-song/He'll not be back again." I wept, she wept, everyone wept. It felt like we were all in a spaceship beyond the space-time continuum. We were love and grace and light.

All the love that flowed out of Spanky wove itself into my heart, and it shattered, and I finally let myself feel the pain and reality—he was gone forever. My daddy, the center of my solar system, the latchkey kid who taught me to walk down the street like a New Yorker, the rebel who taught me the "Seven Dirty Words," the picky eater who never made me eat my vegetables, the protector who shielded me from my mother's alcoholic rage, the artist who stood on a stage and challenged my comfort zone, the cool dad who bought me horses and cars and weed, the dreamer who taught me that anything was possible, the teacher who corrected my grammar, the seeker who saw me as his shaman, the comedian who taught me what was funny, the warrior who taught me what was just, the dad who called me "Kiddo" and asked me if I was his "Stinkpot or Baby Doll," my hero, my father, George Denis Patrick Carlin, was gone.

CHAPTER TWENTY-NINE

Ashes to Ashes

DAD, ALWAYS ONE TO CROSS an item off of a to-do list as soon as possible, gave me thirty days to disperse his ashes. I was a bit irked by the limited timeline. I'd quite enjoyed taking my time with my mom's ashes, spreading a bit here and a bit there, as the whims of life took me to different places. In fact, I still had a small baby food jar full of them left on a shelf that I'd turned into a minishrine to her. I guess I'd been waiting to determine her final resting place.

I did not have the luxury of whims with Dad. I had less than thirty days to figure this out. After the memorial my mind was such a blender of feelings, thoughts, and demands I couldn't imagine that I had enough time to do this right. Dad had once joked that he wanted his final resting place to be determined by throwing his body out of a helicopter and leaving it wherever it landed. I knew that wasn't an option. We'd cremated him. Once I sat quietly with myself, I knew exactly what to do with dad's ashes. They were going to New York City.

But first I had a guru to meet.

A week before I was going to New York, my friend Jon, the one who'd helped Dad move along to the "other side" the day he died, called me to say that one of his teachers, Swamiji, was in town and asked me if I wanted to meet him. I'd never met an Indian swami. My practice of Zen Buddhism had steered me away from the whole yoga/yogi scene. It all seemed a bit creepy to me—bowing to the guru, treating him or her like a living god. Not my cup of tea. But over the decades I'd always admired one proponent of that path— Ram Dass. He was a nice Jewish boy, Richard Alpert, from Boston who during the early sixties while studying at Harvard, dropped acid, went to India, and came back as Ram Dass. Between his book *Be Here Now* and the many lectures I'd heard him give about Eastern philosophy, he'd always held the perfect balance between the guru and the clown. I admired him greatly. So I thought, *What the hell. Let's go see this guru Swamiji. Maybe he'll have some words of wisdom for me.*

I arrived at a house in the hills overlooking the San Fernando Valley. I was glad that this encounter would be an intimate gathering in a private home. My nervous system felt as if its sensitivity dial was stuck at eleven, and I was not up for a horde of worshipping types. I walked in, saw everyone's shoes by the door, and immediately took mine off. The kitchen was filled with people cooking what smelled like delicious Indian food. Many were dressed all in white, and some in more colorful orange saris. The atmosphere felt cushioned by love and acceptance. Although I felt awkward as the outsider, I trusted that if I just relaxed, this evening would at least soothe.

I found Jon, and he introduced me to his friend Jessica, who was a close follower of Swamiji. She was perfectly normal—intelligent, funny, and irreverent. No signs of weird cult worship going on. I relaxed another notch. People were sitting around listening to some live kirtan music when a small man in peach-and-orange robes came out, and everyone stood up. He was radiant. He bowed to everyone, and then smiled. His smile sent a wave of love over me. I'd never seen that much joy in a face before. He sat on a platform in front of the audience, and Jon explained that during the evening people would approach Swamiji and talk about whatever they wanted to with him. There was no protocol. I could just go up when the urge came upon me.

I wasn't sure if I had the courage to speak with him, but I really wanted to. To see what it was all about, I watched as others sat with him. Sometimes he sat quietly with the person, and other times he asked them questions. Always he would smile, and sometimes he would laugh. When the conversation was over he handed the person a piece of fruit. Jon explained that he had blessed the fruit, and that by eating it you were ingesting his blessing.

I roamed around to the back of the yard, where the tea was. I looked over at a row of chairs and saw Drew Carey sitting there. It was a sign. I was definitely in the right place. I went up to him and introduced myself, and we had a lovely conversation. My dad was one of his heroes, and he gushed, and also shared his own grief about his death. One of the "comedy beings" was here. Feeling at home, I was ready to sit with Swamiji.

He smiled at me as I sat down. He stared intensely into my eyes as we sat in silence for about a minute. I felt like he was reading my soul. He then broke the moment with a smile. I leaned forward and explained that I was friends with Jon and Jessica, and that I was here because my father had just died, and my heart was very heavy. I explained that my father was a comedian and a great teacher here in America, who, through his truth telling, had done some enlightening of the people himself. Swamiji did not know of him, so I explained that he was known and loved by millions of people, and that he was very missed by me and many. He acknowledged that he understood, and closed his eyes. I closed mine, too, and let myself be present with him and the moment. After a minute or so I opened my eyes, and he opened his. He leaned forward. I leaned in to meet him.

"Well, there is only one thing we can do in such a circumstance," he began.

I was on pins and needles. Thank God, some wisdom to help me through the heartache and chaos I felt in my body and mind. He then said, with a great burst of energy, "We must laugh!" And he proceeded to break out in the biggest and most joyous belly laugh I had ever heard. Caught up in the surprise of his answer and his joy, I laughed and laughed and laughed with him. We laughed together until tears came to my eyes. I felt the gift of what he was giving me, the gift that my father had given to me and the world: laughter and joy. There was nothing else I or any of us could do. Dad was gone. He had moved on to whatever and wherever one goes after death. All I could do was revel in the life he had lived. Death is real. Grief is real. But so is joy. And life after death. My life.

Silently Swamiji and I acknowledeged all of that through our eye contact, and he smiled. He then closed his eyes, and put his hand on my forehead. I had not seen him do this with anyone else. I did not know why he was doing it, but I closed my eyes and sat quietly. After about thirty seconds, he lifted his hand. I opened my eyes, and he handed me a piece of fruit, but then he also took a flower from the altar and handed it to me. I thanked him as I choked back tears, and bowed deeply and stood up. I found a chair in the very back corner of the yard, and wept for about twenty minutes straight while I ate the apple he had given me. When I was done with the apple, I felt like I weighed ten thousand pounds. I could barely lift my arms. I had never felt so attached to the earth in my life.

After about forty minutes, Jon came and sat with me. "Well?"

"Wow," I said. He smiled. I asked, "He touched my head. What was that about?"

"Oh, he removed your karma," Jon answered.

"Cool."

As Swamiji was walking out, he turned and looked right at me. "Kelly," he said, as he gestured for me to come over to him. He'd remembered my name. I was touched. "If you wish to have your dad's ashes spread into the Ganges River, you can send them to my ashram, and we will do a *puja* ceremony. He will be honored and taken care of."

"I would like that very much. Thank you," I said.

I guess Dad was going to India and New York.

Or so I thought. Here's a tip when shipping something internationally: When asked what's in the box, don't answer, "Human ashes." That makes customs agents nervous. I recommend lying. Otherwise they will be rejected. Two days later the box was on my doorstep, having been returned by U.S. Customs people. I knew there was no way I could resend them and make it under the thirty-day deadline Dad had set.

New York, here we come.

Bob and I arrived at JFK late in the day on July 18. After we checked in to the hotel, we immediately headed downtown to the club Co-mix to see Richard Belzer. Belzer was making a rare appearance that night, and had arranged for us to see the show. As I sat there watching him onstage, I was hit hard with the realization that I would never see my dad on a stage again. While everyone else in the club was laughing, I was crying.

After the show we headed toward the dressing room. Before I could open the backstage door, Taylor Negron came walking out. Taylor and I had met at a spoken-word gig in Los Angeles the year before. I was very fond of him. He was a great human and a fantastic writer/performer. We hugged. I knew I was home, safe and sound, with family. And that feeling grew as I made my way into the dressing room. Belzer was so lovely, and kind.

Then Gilbert Gottfried came out of the bathroom. I was a huge fan, but he also made me nervous. I can't explain it, really. It feels like he's from another planet, and so I'm never sure what he's going to do or say. Richard introduced us, and Gilbert asked, "What are you doing in New York?"

"I'm here to spread my dad's ashes."

"Do you have any on you now?"

I had put a small Ziploc bag of ashes in my purse before leaving the hotel room, knowing we'd be near Greenwich Village that night, and maybe there'd be a chance to spread them at The Bitter End. But I lied to Gilbert and said no. I lied because I really didn't know what he would do if I'd said yes. I feared he might eat them.

Gilbert then asked me, "Whose career is more dead—mine or George's?" Without a beat, my friend Amy said, "Yours, Gilbert." Everyone laughed. These were my people.

Before we left, Taylor invited us to go to a performance of his one-man show in the Village the next day. I told him that we had plans in the late morning, but we'd see if we could make it.

The next day, phase one of "Farewell to Dad: Ashes Spreading Tour" began. After Bob and I ate breakfast at the overpriced-but-oh-so-scrumptious Brooklyn Diner on Fifty-seventh Street, we headed up to Connor's, an Irish bar on Broadway. The Moylen, Dad's neighborhood hangout, was closed, otherwise we would've met there. Eddie Harnby and Uncle Pat had told the old "Irish Harlem" neighborhood gang, the people whom my dad had known since he was a kid and stayed in touch with for six decades, that I was coming to town with my dad's ashes, and that we were gathering at the bar to raise a glass and tell some tales.

Uncle Pat and my cousin Dennis came down to the city from Woodstock to meet us for the day's events. I didn't know many of the faces that showed up, but I knew their names from all the stories Dad had told me. They filled my heart with great stories about my dad as a kid, my parents when they lived in New York, and meeting me as a child. They all were so proud of my dad and what he'd done, and they loved that he had stayed close with all of them over the years. Whenever Dad was in the area, he always got tickets for them to come to his shows, and hung out with them afterward.

At noon I told the group that we were leaving the bar to go up to the "Question Mark." They all knew exactly what I was talking about. The Question Mark was where the wall along Riverside Park ends at 120th Street. The wall, if you were to look at it from above, is shaped like a backward question mark. I knew that this spot would be the first place to receive my dad's ashes because it held the fondest memories for him. It was monumental in the Carlin saga—it's where he and his friends would get loaded when they were teens. It was a legendary site from his life. I knew it must be honored.

Pat, Dennis, my friend Amy, Bob, and I all walked the twelve or so blocks up to the Question Mark from the bar. While we walked in the sunshine along the path of Riverside Park, Uncle Pat lit up a joint, and he, Dennis, and I each took a hit off it in honor of the occasion. Once all had gathered, I stood up on the wall and spoke for a few minutes.

"As you are all from this neighborhood, you all know about this spot. I knew that this was where I wanted to honor my dad in the neighborhood with you today. All of you and this neighborhood meant everything to my dad. It shaped him as a child and a teen, and it defined who he was his entire life. He carried this neighborhood in his heart no matter where he was in the world," I said. I then took a very large bag, the bag his ashes came in from the mortuary, and opened it. I continued, "Dad wished for me to determine how to dispose of his ashes. I knew that this place, and you, his dear friends, had to be a big part of this process. I invite you to come and grab a handful of ashes and throw them over the wall so that Dad may come home one last time."

I grabbed a handful of ashes to lead the way, and flung them over the wall. Some sailed down along the wall, while the rest took to the air like a ghost. Uncle Patrick, Dennis, and Bob all dug in and tossed Dad over the wall. I laughed when I saw some of Dad's old friends, still good Catholics, take part in this impromptu paganesque ceremony. People laughed and cried as we launched the ashy remains of a man we loved onto the landscape that had shaped his soul.

I have no idea what the passersby must have thought, but we were all immersed in that web of light and love that was beginning to be the norm for my life, and that's all that mattered.

Dad's first girlfriend asked if she could take some home, and I explained to her that I couldn't let her do that because Dad had insisted that all his ashes be dispersed. Another friend of Dad's asked if he could take a bit to the park down the street where he and Dad would often sit on a particular bench, "shoot the shit and smoke a jay." He made a small pouch from a piece of paper he had, and I gave him some ashes. He hugged me and scurried off to the park to say a private prayer to Dad.

Pat, Dennis, Bob, and I said our good-byes to everyone and made our way up to 519 West 121st Street—our old apartment building. A few tenants came out. One knew Pat, and they chatted about my dad and the good old days.

We each took some ashes and spread them around the small tree and flowers out in front of the building. I felt my dad close by, and could almost hear him saying, "Hey, Kiddo, you're doing great." I knew I was. I knew these were the spots where he needed to reintegrate into the land.

In the late afternoon, we three Carlins and Bob went down to the Village to meet up with Belzer and his family (his daughter, her boyfriend, and his bandmates) to see Taylor Negron's show, *Satellites*.

After the show we all went to a restaurant and sat outside on a back patio in the Village. It was a perfect late-July evening. As the light faded, I looked down this long table that seated about eighteen people filled with amazing artists—comedians, writers, musicians, painters—and my heart swelled. This was the life I'd always wanted. I'd always wanted to be part of a community of artists, a peer of people seeking, expressing, and living life through a prism of curiosity and wonder. As my heart filled with gratitude, my eyes filled with tears. I knew that this moment would not have happened if Dad were still here. I sat in awe of the complexity of life.

After dinner I gathered Belzer and his gang, Taylor and Logan (his musical partner), and their friend Carey, and my family in front of the restaurant. I said to the group, "Follow me. We are going to spread Dad's ashes in front of The Bitter End." While we walked east on Bleecker Street toward the club, I realized that this particular group of people couldn't have been more perfect for the task ahead. I knew exactly what I'd say when we got to the club.

The Bleecker Street of 2008 was very different from the Bleecker Street of 1963. What we found was a neighborhood full of clubs and restaurants trying to lure folks into their establishments with barkers and lots of neon signs. Long gone was the quiet neighborhood dotted with cafés and folk music clubs. Outside The Bitter End was a "roach coach," with its generator going. Not the most conducive environment for a ritual, but it didn't slow me down a beat, because there was also a sweet little tree surrounded by a small patch of dirt ready to receive Dad. This is where we would spread his ashes.

I began, "I'm so happy that you are all here. Here we are, a group of comics, writers, performers, and musicians all doing our best to live the creative life. Expressing our hearts and souls through all sorts of avenues. This spot, The Bitter End, is the very spot where my dad began his creative life. This club is where he would come to hone his craft, speak his truth, and experiment with his art form at the beginning of his career. This spot is about birthing, creating, and nurturing that which lives in all of us here and now, and wants, needs, must be expressed. So I ask, as you take some ashes and spread them around this tree, that you hold in your heart all that wants to be birthed in you. Ask for it to be blessed by this moment, this place, and the memory of my dad."

I then took a handful of ashes and slowly released them in a circle around the tree, and asked that life honor me with the privilege to be a part of a community of artists where I could express all that wants to be expressed to the world. *Let me be of service to others through my work.*

Then slowly each person—Pat, Taylor, Dennis, Logan, Belzer, Jessica, Carey, Timbo, Bob—all took ashes and communed with the moment. After Belzer spread his, he became emotional and disappeared around the corner. Pat joined him. I stayed present at the tree until everyone had their turn. When I came around the corner, Pat and some of the others were smoking a jay and laughing with tears in their eyes—the perfect ending to a perfect day.

And yet what I had in store for Dad the next day was even better.

The next day Bob and I rented a car and headed up to Lake Spofford, New Hampshire. We were joining Pat and Dennis there to find the site of Camp Notre Dame, the place where my dad had gone to camp as a kid. Camp Notre Dame held a special place in my dad's heart. It was the first place in his life where he was recognized by his peers as an entertainer—every summer he was there he'd won their drama award. One year the award had come in the form of a necklace bearing the comedy-tragedy masks. My dad cherished that necklace and wore it often, including the day he died. I knew, that if Dad was watching from "above," he was knocked out to see that I had figured out that this spot at Lake Spofford should be included in the "Farewell to Dad: Ashes Spreading Tour."

The skies threatened to storm as we circled around the lake looking for some sign of the camp. We stopped some locals, and they told us that the camp was long gone. We found a public beach that had access to the shore, and made our way to the edge of the water. It was quiet. All you could hear was the meditative rhythm of the water lapping up against the shore. After the din and dance of the city the last few days, I felt myself land back in my body. There was no one to host or wrangle, and no audience of loved ones to hold. It was now just family. I took a large handful of ashes and leaned down, letting the water take them from my hand. The pulsing of the water slowly expanded the ashes into a large ghost-shaped swirl.

I finally let myself really cry.

Once we were done Bob and I followed Pat and Dennis back to the house in Woodstock. Dad had bought his brother this house on eleven acres of land right after my mom had died. It would be mine someday. I loved that land. We spent the evening in the easy space that our family always had. I was so lucky to have a family where I could fully relax and be myself, knowing we all love each other unconditionally and could make each other laugh all day long.

In the morning I knew that this land was the last place in New York I needed to put my dad's ashes. I knew that this was his final resting place. And I also knew it was time to let my mom go, too. Before Bob and I had left for this trip, I had spontaneously grabbed the last jar of Mom's ashes and put them in my suitcase. I stood in the dry creek bed that wound itself through the property, with both my mom and dad in my hands. Marlene, my aunt, came bounding out of the house calling, "I have Moe, too!" Moe was my mom and dad's last dog, a Maltese (the one who loved to hump Vern the cat). When he got elderly, Dad sent him to be loved and cared for by Marlene and Pat. I smiled as I looked up at her running toward me with the bag of ashes. It was so perfect—Mom, Dad, and Moe together in the end. All of us took handfuls of ashes and began to spread them around the meadow and small thicket of trees surrounding the house. Patrick spread a bunch around his favorite oak. In the months to come, Pat would tell me that he'd go out to the oak every morning and have a conversation with my dad.

I then went back into the dry creek bed. There was a storm coming later in the day, and I knew that this creek would fill with water and then head toward the Hudson River. I also knew that the water that leaves the Hudson River is picked up by the Gulf Stream and makes its way across the Atlantic Ocean to Ireland. I knew that the ashes of my father that I was leaving in this creek would take him to our ancestral home—the west coast of Ireland.

As we were finishing up, Dennis said, "I know you want to be done here, but can I have this last little bit to take back into the city? Being a musician, and knowing how much your dad was influenced by the jazz players of his youth, can I take them to the original Birdland tonight and leave some there?"

"Yes, of course. I think that is wonderful."

And so that night Bob and Dennis and I headed out to our last stop on the "Farewell to Dad: Ashes Spreading Tour" from our friend's apartment near Columbus Circle. The three of us figured out where the original Birdland had been and made our way down to Fifty-Second Street. We found the address, 1678 Broadway. It was a strip club. I laughed. Being exhausted, and having no desire to pay twenty bucks each to go in, Bob and I decided to let Dennis have his night with my dad and Birdland, and the strippers. As Dennis disappeared down into the bowels of the club, I leaned over to the bouncer, a big Irish-looking guy, and said, "If you would, keep an eye on my cousin who just went in. We're on a bit of a mission, you see. My dad was George Carlin, and this was Birdland, a place that he haunted the backstage door of in the forties and fifties so he could get autographs of all the greats."

The bouncer looked at me with shock in his eyes. "Your dad was George Carlin?"

"Yeah."

"I used to drive a cab, and I had the great privilege to drive him twice. Once seemed enough for a lifetime, but I got to drive him twice. And he was always cheerful, and talkative, and curious what was going on around him. We had two great conversations. Wow. Wow! I'll keep an eye on your cousin."

"Thank you. He's emotional, and I worry about him sometimes."

Bob and I went to sleep around midnight. When Bob got up at 4:00 A.M. to pee, he saw that Dennis wasn't sleeping on the couch.

He woke me, "Kel, Dennis isn't back yet." I sprang out of bed. "Shit."

I checked my phone. No calls. I had texted him the address, but I also knew that he'd been drinking that night, and now I was really worried. I texted him again, but there was no answer. Bob got dressed and made his way to the club, stopping at a few bars along the way just to make sure he wasn't in those. When he reached "Bird-land," Dennis was coming up the stairs, buzzed but happy. He'd spread Dad's ashes everywhere and managed to get the phone number of one of the dancers. Bob immediately texted me that all was well; they were on their way back.

Now we were done. Absolute. Final. Done.

When we got to JFK the next day, we were told that our plane had been struck by lightning when it landed, and that the good people at Virgin America were trying to get us on a Jet Blue flight—tomorrow. After frantically calling some friends to find a place to crash for the night, I was able to settle into my seat on the train back to the city and contemplate this turn of events. I was befuddled. I couldn't believe we were going back to the city. Our time there had felt so complete. I felt like our mission was done. Why weren't we finished? Why were we still in New York? What was missing? This is when Dennis pulled a Baggie out of his pocket and said, "Oh, by the way, I didn't spread all of the ashes last night. Here's the rest."

The rest!?! There are ashes left?!? We weren't done with this tour, after all.

The minute we walked into the hotel room in the Trump Tower on Columbus Circle (my friends had come through, big-time), the sky cracked open with the most violent and spectacular thunderstorm I had ever witnessed. Bob, Dennis, and I sat and watched Central Park light up, and listened to the echoes of the thunder god Thor reverberate off every building around us.

I laughed inside and thought, "Okay, Dad. I get it. I can hear you. We'll get it done." But even so, I was not sure where.

I woke up just after dawn. Bob and Dennis were still sleeping. I looked out the window and noticed the rain had lightened up. And then it hit me—Central Park! How could I have forgotten? It was the very place that marked most of my childhood memories of this city with my dad—the zoo, the elephant rides, the horse-drawn carriages, the Plaza Hotel, Carnegie Hall, Rumpelmayer's, climbing the outcroppings of schist in the park.

I walked into the park and wandered around. I saw an outcropping of schist rock, took the ashes out, and had my private goodbye with my dad—just him and me, alone in a space of love and sadness. Dad was home.

He was done. I was done. We were done.

Well, almost.

I lied.

I saved a small amount of ashes so that Sally and I could take Dad down to the Pacific Ocean under the Venice Pier, and let him go forever.

It seemed more than fitting. Although Dad's life began in New York, the majority of it unfolded here in Los Angeles. It was where Dad found fame, Mom lost herself, and the Three Musketeers were born. It was where Dad discovered his true north, Mom got a second and a third chance at life, and I got to be one of the luckiest kids in the world. It was where a family—my family—got a front-row seat to the freak show, and survived it by loving each other no matter what.

Like a trail of bread crumbs, there are only traces of my family left in this city. Wispy memories as I drive through Brentwood, Venice, the Palisades, and Beverly Hills, slowly being eaten up by progress and the present. I smile softly as they pass by, and I see in it all that our love endured through this City of Angels.

And there may be hundreds of images and thousands of words created by my dad floating for eternity in the ethers of cyberspace, but there was only one of him, my dad. And he is gone, except for the etchings he left on my heart.

Epilogue

SINCE MY DAD DIED, strangely, he has become more of a presence in my life than he had ever been when he was alive. From that first day I was on *Larry King*, I was catapulted into a world where I was now the face and voice of my dad's legacy. And his heart, too.

What immediately became clear was that there were tens of thousands of people who mourned his death as deeply as I did. I had lost my dad, but they had lost their uncle George. He had extraordinary talent, but he was everyman on that stage. He was the man who was capable of allowing every person who saw or heard him to feel less alone, or not so crazy in their family growing up. He had awakened people to new ways of seeing, much like a Zen master does for his acolytes. He was a god you could sit down and smoke a joint with.

My dad talked often about how his family was small, but that his extended family was thousands strong. He knew he could go to any city or town in America and there would be someone there whom he'd be able to connect with because of his work. But until he died, I had never felt a part of *that* family.

All of that has changed. Since his death, whenever I meet his fans, *my* new family, I know what my role is now: to be a receptacle for the love people have for my dad. I no longer need to live in my father's shadow, or try to catch up with him, or latch on to the buzz of his fame. All I need to do is listen and receive. One day I was talking to a fan and it hit me: Just by being present, and graciously accepting what was being said, I could be a physical link between this world and the magical other—in this case, George Carlin.

I guess Dad was right—I am the family shaman after all.

The fans, and the dozens of comedians I have met during this time, have given me so much. They are no doubt my family. The amount of love and support *I* have received has been immeasurable. And, after losing the last wing of the Three Musketeers, essential. I am strong. I have survived much. But without my new family's love and light, I'm not sure how well I would have fared. Without them my world would not only be lonelier, but more boring, too.

My father gave me so much—a sense of humor and justice, a passion for language, financial support, a love of peanut-butter fold-overs and the music of The Band—but the two biggest things he gave me were curiosity and trust in oneself. I use both daily to help me find my way to a larger and deeper sense of myself. Balancing being "George's daughter" with being me, a separate person, has always been my path to walk, but even more so now. And it has been a dance, for sure. But I move forward. I am filled with curiosity about what life presents me, and I have been emboldened by a deep trust that all that I have seen, lived through, overcome, and received from my life with my father has prepared me for whatever comes next.

Knowing what I know now, my seat belt is buckled, and I'm ready for anything.

Postscript

SIX YEARS LATER, my dad is still in my phone book. Sorry, Dad. Just can't do it yet.

This Air Marshal Carlin says, "Go fuck yourself!"

Acknowledgments

BECAUSE THIS IS MY FIRST book, I feel like I could thank everyone I've ever come across—friend, enemy, ally, and bystander. I trust in some way, our interaction has led me to this unique moment in my life. But due to the constraints of the space-time continuum, I will keep the list to those who were instrumental in the writing of this book.

I am forever grateful for my editor, Hannah Braaten. There would be no book without her. She has been my champion, taskmaster, cheerleader, and teacher. In the future, I will never write another sentence that is not shaped in some way by her guidance.

Eddie Pietzak, my literary agent—thank you for e-mailing me out of the blue and asking me if I had an agent or a book deal. Your chutzpah changed my life

Jerry Hamza, my friend, father-figure, manager, business partner—thank you for taking care of my parents for over thirty years, and now teaching me how to take care of myself.

My comedy uncles and brothers—Lewis Black, for inviting me to tell a few stories while on a cruise ship with him, which ultimately led to my solo show that led to this book; Paul Provenza, who has been my Yoda, shepherd, mentor, shrink, and fellow traveler and director of said solo show; Garry Shandling, for always seeing me so clearly and sharing his wise soul. Rick Overton—you are my brother.

My friends who read through my pages and cheered me on— your enduring love and confidence in my voice emboldens me daily. And to all my comrades in art and life that dance, laugh, and gather around the fire pit with me—you're the net that holds me up.

And lastly, my parents, for everything. Really. Everything.